PORTRAITS OF THE INSANE

PORTRAITS OF THE INSANE
Théodore Géricault and the
Subject of Psychotherapy

Robert Snell

KARNAC

First published in 2017 by
Karnac Books Ltd
118 Finchley Road
London NW3 5HT

British Library Cataloguing in Publication Data

A C.I.P. for this book is available from the British Library

ISBN-13: 978-1-78220-247-9

Typeset by Medlar Publishing Solutions Pvt Ltd, India

Printed in Great Britain by TJ International Ltd, Padstow, Cornwall

www.karnacbooks.com

For Kim, with love

… since when has it been permissible to reject a fact for want of an explanation for it? Doubt first, then examination, that is how a wise mind proceeds, indeed any man who is not thrown off balance by prejudice and believes nature still holds secrets for him.

—*Etienne Georget, in his contribution to an enquiry into animal magnetism in 1826, cited in Postel, 1972, p. 21, translated for this edition*

CONTENTS

ACKNOWLEDGEMENTS

With warm thanks to Dennis Creffield, Therese Dolan, Frank Gray, Del Loewenthal, Richard Morgan-Jones, Michael Parsons, and Sarah Soutar, for encouragement and conversations, some recent, others going back over years. Special thanks too, for their tremendous care and patience, to Rod Tweedy, Kate Pearce, and Cecily Blench at Karnac.

ABOUT THE AUTHOR

Robert Snell is an analytic psychotherapist, a member of the British Psychoanalytic Council and the British Psychotherapy Foundation, and an honorary senior research fellow in the Centre for Therapeutic Education at Roehampton University. He has a doctorate in the history of art from the Courtauld Institute, and is the author of *Théophile Gautier: A Romantic Critic of the Visual Arts* (Oxford University Press, 1982), co-author with Del Loewenthal of *Postmodernism for Psychotherapists. A Critical Reader* (Routledge, 2003), and author of *Uncertainties, Mysteries, Doubts. Romanticism and the Analytic Attitude* (Routledge, 2012).

INTRODUCTION

Some time in the early 1820s, not long before his death, the French painter Théodore Géricault made a group of portraits of anonymous inmates of an asylum or a clinic for the insane. They are powerful, startling works—but they are far from voyeuristic or prurient. They show ordinary, recognisably individual, idiosyncratic people. At the same time, these people seem distracted, estranged from us. With a directness shared by few other portraits in the history of Western art, the paintings point us straight to the most profound, human questions. Who is this other person? What does she or he want of me? How do I respond to the call that her mere presence seems to make on me? What does he stir in me? How do I see and hear her? What if there are more like him? Under what conditions might I be open to our common humanity?

When I am not too anxious or terrified myself, might be one answer. Precisely because they are merely paintings (but what paintings), Géricault's five portraits offer us safe and hospitable enough conditions for an imaginative exploration of such questions and their attendant terrors. These questions could hardly be more urgent. For in the political and emotional climate of the first decades of the twenty-first century, they speak to widely held fears: about being taken over, taken from, overrun by nameless others. The portraits, I wish to argue, offer us help.

Remarkably little is known for certain about the circumstances in which they were made, except that they were painted in an asylum or clinic, in some sort of partnership with a doctor. Although plausible accounts of their genesis can be put forward, none is absolutely incontrovertible or definitive. They remind and oblige us to keep open minds.

In this respect they are like other works from the late eighteenth and early nineteenth centuries, from the Romantic era: they require us to respect their mystery, to bring our "free-floating attention" to them, the kind of attention Freud recommended psychoanalysts bring to their patients. This was the theme explored in my previous book, *Uncertainties, Mysteries, Doubts. Romanticism and the Analytic Attitude* (Snell, 2012), which argued that the work of Romantic art, with its constitutive ambiguities and refusals of easy elucidation, invites in the spectator, reader, or listener a kind of receptive, waking dreaming, or reverie: a proto-"analytic attitude". But these particular paintings, because their subject matter is madness, present their own, additional challenges, and have their own historical fascination.

The present book contains two parallel stories, both with powerful sequels: the life of a revolutionary and foundational figure in the history of modern art; and the story of the beginnings of modern attitudes to insanity. Both stories start in the early years of perhaps the most momentous decade in modern history, the decade of the French Revolution. Géricault was born in 1791; in the same year the new National Assembly was addressing the plight of the nation's mad, with unprecedented urgency. Géricault died in 1824; at the same time a new branch of medicine, known in France as *aliénisme*, was approaching the autumn of a brief "Golden Age" (the word *psychiatrie* only found favour towards the end of the century). The two stories intersect around 1820, and crystallise in the portraits.

The nineteenth century regarded Géricault as the prototypical painter of French Romanticism. Modern scholarship tends to see him as a transitional figure, between revolutionary neo-classicism and later nineteenth-century naturalism, who found himself living in a transitional moment, during the very birth pangs of modernity. The medical alienists who were his contemporaries and near-contemporaries—Philippe Pinel, Jean-Etienne Esquirol, Etienne Georget—occupy a similar place in the history of the treatment of the mad. They are no longer just celebrated, as they were in the nineteenth century, as liberators and the founding heroes of modern psychiatry, striking off the chains of the insane and releasing them from their dungeons. They are now generally seen to occupy a more ambiguous position, and a fairly narrow historical window. On one side of this window were indeed the insane as bestial, possessed, haunting the civilised imagination, either hidden away or exhibited, for purposes of exorcism or entertainment, as spectacle. As inheritors of Enlightenment philanthropy and philosophical method, the French alienists put the humane therapeutic treatment of the insane on a sound professional footing. The portraits, which have no forebears in the Western iconography of madness, reflect this, and like the alienists themselves sit at one of the points of origin of modern psychotherapy. But the early nineteenth-century alienists' endeavours also led, partly directly, partly as reaction, to the great Europe- and America-wide asylum-building programmes of the mid- and later nineteenth century. On the other side of their historical window lie the "total institution" and the concomitant triumph of organicist, medical psychiatry, with its theories of degeneracy and maladaptation.

But it is precisely because painter and alienists dwelt in such in-between positions that they offer themselves to us as fertile resources. They open up possibilities for critical reflection for our own uneasy times, and in particular for those of us involved in the practice of psychoanalysis and psychotherapy, occupying as this practice does its own uncertain and ambiguous place. History can inform and help us reflect on our current values and practices, as well as revealing some of their foundations. At the same time, the way we see history is inflected by what concerns us today—politically, socially, economically, culturally, ethically, unconsciously. How are we to see the paintings? In viewing them through a range of art-historical lenses, this book aims to raise questions and thoughts for the analytic practitioner—but not only for the analytic practitioner—as to where she is positioned in making her own responses and interpretations. For interpretations, in art history as in psychoanalysis as in daily life, of course always imply a position on the interpreter's part. As she reads, in the chapters that follow, about different approaches to Géricault's portraits, the reader is invited to reflect on ways in which each of these approaches might echo an interpretative position vis-à-vis the other person, how each might evoke or approximate to a "frame" of assumptions through which the other—patient or client as the case may be—might be approached. For the question must remain forever open: how do we respond, what do we need in order to respond, to the mysterious, disturbed, and disturbing other, with whom we rub shoulders and who may have come to us, if we are psychotherapists, teachers, doctors, nurses, members of the "caring professions", for help and recognition? Can we, what is more, bear the confrontation with our own, internal "otherness"—our own disturbance, violence, envy, lust, greed?

Like all great art, the portraits open a space for thinking, for us to make use of if we choose. This, I believe, was also Géricault's purpose. In this sense, among others, he might justifiably be thought of as a sort of painter-analyst. "I do not find the circumstances right for thought," W. R. Bion is reputed to have said in the middle of the chaos of a large group conference (cited in Symington, 1986, p. 278)—thereby creating precisely the circumstances for the possibility of thought. At the time Géricault painted the pictures, in the increasingly reactionary climate of the restored French monarchy, circumstances for thinking in public were almost as unfavourable as they had been in the darkest days of the Revolution; the canvases were rolled up, probably not long after they were completed, and as far as we know not seen again for another forty years. In painting them Géricault was keeping a thinking space open for himself and, most likely, a small circle of friends; he was perhaps keeping alive the very possibility of a meeting with the face of the other—to use the language of the philosopher Emmanuel Levinas—during a period in history in which looking other people in the eye might not always have felt advisable.

There is another sense in which Géricault might be described as a painter-analyst. He does not psychologise: he does not present us with preformed ideas or theories about what made his sitters tick, or not tick. Nor does he moralise. He approached his task as a painter, allowing a sense of each sitter's living individuality to come through, and avoiding, as far as anyone ever can, imposing on them his ideas about who, why, or how they were. Although there must have been constraints and injunctions, self-imposed or imposed from the outside, as to how he should paint the people before him (was he for example instructed to pose them in the way he did?), he would have come to his work with two related painter's concerns in the forefront of his mind—if this is quite the right way of putting it. It might be better to say that he used the resources inherent in painting itself as a way of thinking, feeling, and registering a sense of the person in front of him: the weight and consistency of oil paint on brush as it meets canvas; mass, modelling, shape, texture, colour, light and dark, foreground and background, visual rhythm, slant of shoulder, eye, mouth, the subtle interrelations and modulations of all these things. He did all this, in these portraits, with the supreme and intuitive assurance of experience. In this, perhaps, he resembles the analyst, whose field being the aural rather than the visual, listens for the weight, texture, rhythms, pauses, hesitations, interrelations, the "music"of the patient's words. "… please give more attention to the text than to the psychology of the author," exhorted Jacques Lacan. "Don't try to understand!" (Lacan, 1988, p. 153; 2007, p. 394). Like "good" analytic interpretations, or like Constable's more or less contemporary studies of clouds, the portraits are attempts to catch the fleeting and mobile in the faces of his sitters. They are living descriptions, mediated through the mind and body of the painter/ painter-analyst in his meeting with another, living, mediating mind-and-body.

Géricault was very much a man of his time and culture, not least in his sense of his own alienation from it. Such though was the quality of his attention as a painter, of his temporary abstinence from other kinds of attention, his success in leaving other interests and concerns behind, that he is able to offer us an extraordinary and mysterious experience: we come to see the sitters not merely as events out there in our optical field, but as the engaging, generative "authors" of their own appearances. But they refuse to buttonhole and meet us halfway. They insist, unsettlingly, on their sheer separateness, and throw us back on our own most primitive sense of aliveness.

* * *

The book starts with the portraits' rediscovery in the mid-nineteenth century and with some of the questions they raised then and raise now. Further to address these questions, we shall look at Géricault's life, in the hope of getting a sense of its particular trajectory and of his developing beliefs, values, and desires, and of the political and cultural circumstances in which he lived. There follows an extended excursion into the history of attitudes and approaches to insanity in modernity, and an examination of the directions the treatment of the mad was taking in Europe and France before and during Géricault's lifetime, including, crucially, the development of the idea of "monomania". This history is essential for an appreciation of the moment of cultural transition and the complex contingencies that helped shape the portraits, and it is, inevitably, intertwined with the political and social history of the period. As Laure Murat has explored in a recent book (2014), the early alienists articulated their own ideas on the relationship of madness to historical experience; the doctors with whom Géricault was in contact tended to be on the liberal end of the political spectrum, and we shall go on to explore the portraits as essays in recent and current history, which subtly gather multiple themes that would have been alive in contemporary minds. This, to borrow Mikhail Bakhtin's phrase, is their "dialogic" dimension (Bakhtin, 1981): they were invitations to a conversation. Finally, before reaching out for some conclusions, we shall look at how the portraits exceed all these accounts of them, and point towards some of the roots and values of psychoanalysis.

* * *

Some introductory reflections on the history of madness might be helpful here—for as its most eminent specialists agree, it is a history fraught with difficulties and imponderables. Madness is "a fundamental puzzle", writes Andrew Scull (2015, p. 411); Roy Porter called it a "mystery of mysteries" (2002, p. 1). Does it even make sense to think there could be such a thing as a "history of madness", or is it, as Laure Murat asks, just a quest for a "phantom discourse", as vain as all attempts to pin down an abstract category? Could such a history ever be more than the history of psychiatry, "insofar as it depends on the sufferance of psychiatry to deliver the material for its analysis and evolution" (Murat, 2014, p. 20)? There can be no doubt that medical advances have brought incalculable relief, enabling, for example, those suffering from the last stages of syphilis or from Alzheimer's disease to be distinguished from the mass of the insane who were historically confined in cells or back wards. But even those like Edward Shorter, who argue from this basis that the medical psychiatry of our own era is therefore simply the greatest advance to date, accept that the history of madness is "a minefield" (Shorter, 1997, p. ix). Andrew Scull, no psychiatric fundamentalist, but equally impatient with the idea that it is all relative, a matter of social construction or labels, provides a working definition of madness as a phenomenon of all societies and ages that, as far as it goes, is as good as could be hoped for. The mad are those

> who do not share the common-sense reality most of us perceive
> and the mental universe we inhabit ... who act in ways that are

profoundly at variance with the conventions and expectations of their culture, and are heedless of the ordinary corrective measures their community mobilises to induce them to desist; those who manifest extremes of extravagance and incoherence … (Scull, 2015, p. 11)

Our historical ideas about madness depend on our understanding of the criteria by which a given era, society, or culture sought to comprehend, manage, or neutralise the incomprehensible, unmanageable, and unwelcome, and/or to celebrate and harness the ecstatic and revelatory, the intuitive and uncanny—this would be the culturally relativist view. Following this line of thought, we might want to consider "mad" to be the default category that a given culture and society has to create in order to try to rid itself of its own worst doubts and nightmares about itself, although it might also work as the means by which a culture expands and enriches itself: hallucinatory experience, for example, in many tribal cultures. We might think of madness as the outer limit of a culture's regime of sense and meaning, the need for sense and meaning being one constant that we can surely take for granted across time and place. One thing is mandatory, however: that we are circumspect about projecting and back-projecting our own values and ways of thinking, so that we do not, for example, attribute the idea of "mental illness" to the thought-systems of cultures which have or had no such concept, or describe as manifestations of "mental illness" behaviours or experiences that might predate the idea that there could be such a thing: the visionary and certain corporeal experiences of medieval Europeans, for example, which would typically betoken divine or demonic involvement. For most of human history structures of sense, and identity itself, were supplied by religion and myth. In the classical world, for example, belonging and identity were contingent upon loyalty to the god of the family and hearth, in the person of the father, the *pater familias*. "Patriotism", by extension, became identification with the city, and to be without this, "to be anything less than an active citizen, was to be an idiot", a non-person. Exile from the *polis* was a fate worse than death—it was total loss of human belonging (Siedentop, 2014, p. 25).

Mainstream psychiatry has been soundly critiqued over the last half-century, notably from existential/phenomenological and post-structural positions, with the most powerful philosopher's and historian's voice undoubtedly being Michel Foucault's. In the more extreme versions of this account and critique, which also tend to draw on Marx and (the Dionysian) Nietzsche, madness is a projection of the dark, unknowable core of us all. David Cooper, a leading figure, along with R. D. Laing, in the anti-psychiatry movement of the 1960s and '70s, states the position in his introduction to the first English edition of Foucault's (1961) *Histoire de la folie à l'âge classique* (*Madness and Civilization*):

> Foucault makes it quite clear that the invention of madness as a disease is in fact nothing less than a peculiar disease of our civilization. We choose to conjure up this disease in order to evade a certain moment of our own existence—the moment of disturbance, of penetrating vision into the depths of ourselves, that we prefer to externalise onto others. Others are elected to live out the chaos that we refuse to confront in ourselves ... one is awakened to a tragic sense of the loss involved in the relegation of the wildly charismatic or inspirational area of our experience to the desperate region of pseudo-medical categorization ... (Cooper, 1967, p. viii)

Madness, enlisted as oppositional and countercultural, is all that which, in bourgeois, capitalist society, with its premium on instrumentality, functionality, and efficiency, is non-productive, "dysfunctional"; contemporary psychiatric treatments and "mental health" policies are forms of torture instituted not by deliberate sadists but by the woefully blinkered, or wilfully self-blinded. Other spokespersons for this broad view would include Thomas Szasz, and the psychiatrist and historian Klaus Dörner, whose *Madmen and the Bourgeoisie* (1981) was first published in German in 1969. It is a view that has continuing currency in the fields of literary and cultural studies. The critic and historian Marina van Zuylen, for example, referencing among others Baudelaire, Flaubert, and Mann, has gone so far as to revive and revise the term "monomania", in order to make a case for obsession and compulsion as weapons against the multiple, debilitating disorders of modernity (2005).

It is important not to allow heady rhetoric such as Cooper's, so evocative of its period and milieu (London in the late 1960s), to obscure the very substantial contribution of the "anti-psychiatry" movement to thinking about madness, to the possibility of an engagement with sufferers which might take place outside the discourses of psychiatry, and to the idea that the acts and utterances of those designated as insane might be understandable. Informed by psychoanalysis, but drawing for their methodology on Sartre and phenomenology, R. D. Laing and Aaron Esterson were able to demonstrate "that the experience and behaviour of schizophrenics is much more socially intelligible than has come to be supposed by most psychiatrists". Their detailed descriptions of interactions within the families of people diagnosed as schizophrenic embodied and demanded a *"shift of point of view that ... has a historical significance no less radical than the shift from a demonological to a clinical viewpoint three hundred years ago"* (Laing & Esterson, 1964, p. 27; their italics). This is a powerful assertion; conceptually and ethically, Laing and Esterson's researches are a formidable challenge to stubbornly tenacious ideas of madness as both a medical problem and something fundamentally, constitutionally alien (this challenge continues to be taken up, at the time of writing, in remarkable seminars conducted in London by the historian and analytic and existential psychotherapist Anthony Stadlen).

If Freud primed the canvas, Laing and Esterson's view that madness is, in the final analysis, socially and interpersonally comprehensible is the underpainting, albeit mostly unseen, for everything that follows. It might be helpful at this point to sketch out my own view. It makes sense to follow Scull in seeing "madness" as that which exceeds the social norms prevailing at any particular historical juncture, whether or not this excess is deemed to be threateningly transgressive, or a cause for celebration, or simply to give pause for thought; as such it is always, like any other state of mind or behaviour, a product of the interpersonal and social. The interpersonal and social are, in my psychoanalytic understanding, internalised unconsciously in each of us; this is universal, and it happens in the first instance through the enigmatic message transmitted by the (m)other. This way of thinking comes from the French psychoanalyst Jean Laplanche (1924–2012). The enigma of the other, specifically the enigmatic message or "signifier" emanating from the other, is first encountered in the earliest physical and emotional contact with the caregiver. The message of the adult other impels the newborn to "translate" it. This message is transmitted through sights, words, and noises, and through the body of the caregiver; it is itself partly unconscious, and thus sexual in content; it necessarily overwhelms the newborn's capacity to assimilate or translate it. This for Laplanche was originary, anxiety-generating trauma, and we all undergo it. The unassimilable residue of the message is repressed, and anxiety is thereby sufficiently "bound up" for development to continue;

this moment of repression is the founding, generative moment of the unconscious, and kick-starts the drive to symbolise and speak (see, for example, Laplanche, 1999, pp. 138–195). The paintings, I believe, can get under our skins—resonate unconsciously—because they replicate this process of trauma and inscription.

What we might call "madness" results from enigmatic messages that are so overwhelming to the pre- and perhaps too to the post-verbal child that the translations and repression they generate can only be partial, and inadequate to the task of "binding up" the anxiety the messages generate. This anxiety can now only take the form of thoughts, speech, and behaviours that are at great variance with the norm but that are nevertheless accurate, however encoded, in their registration of trauma. Such messages would typically have been transmitted through physical, sexual, or emotional violence, including the Laingian mixed message or the classic Batesonian "double bind".

Psychoanalysis has various ways of conceptualising and modulating this process. Kleinians would emphasise the subject's innate capacities for translation, while Winnicottians would be mindful of the nature of the impinging message of the other. Lacanians would stress the mediating role of the symbolic father, which Laplanche, arguably, understates; the definitive account in English of a Lacanian understanding of insanity, which also gives great importance to the experience of being addressed, interpellated, is without doubt Darian Leader's masterful *What is Madness?* (2011). For present purposes, the Laplanchian schema offers an accessible way of encapsulating something on which all psychoanalysts would agree: if madness presents itself as mysterious, often profoundly so, it is far from an unapproachable "mystery of mysteries". It is the outcome, rather, of ultimately comprehensible, inter- and intrapsychic, processes.

Another powerful analysis, with the potential to throw considerable light on such questions, has been developed in authoritative detail by the psychiatrist and neurologist Iain McGilchrist. In his *The Master and his Emissary* (2009), McGilchrist offers a history of the world as structured by the shifting tension and interplay between left and right brains, between—vastly to oversimplify—the "irrational", intuitive right hemisphere (the Master), and the questing, rationalising left brain (Emissary). The general tendency, currently, is towards the creation of a disastrously left-brain-dominated world: the Emissary, in a metaphor McGilchrist borrows from Nietzsche, has lost touch with the Master and is running amok, creating an inhuman society of rigid bureaucracy and narrow self-interest, dominated by a mechanistic view of who we are. This world would find its apotheosis in a reductionist, diagnosis fixated, pharmaceutically driven psychiatry. The Romantic era, with its complex, critical relationship to the Enlightenment, the preceding "Age of Reason", exemplified a redressing of the balance in favour of the right brain, and in favour of communication between the hemispsheres; this line of thinking has been powerfully developed in Rod Tweedy's recent study *The God of the Left Hemisphere*, which centres on the work of William Blake (Tweedy, 2012). The Romantic era, argues McGilchrist, was a narrow window of opportunity for Western humanity. His work makes available a flexible conceptual tool both for historical understanding and for thinking about the present and the future; his prognosis is not rosy.

Laplanchian "translations" of course have many modes. The idea that madness, in particular the kind of state designated as schizophrenia, can be the result of *too much* reason—or to put it slightly differently, to claim with Dostoyevsky, and McGilchrist, that "too much consciousness might be a thoroughgoing illness"—was the basis of an extraordinary book of the early 1990s by Louis A. Sass, *Madness and Modernism*, which discerns "schizoid" experiences at the heart of modernist and postmodernist art. "What if madness were to involve not an escape from but an exacerbation of that thoroughgoing illness ...?" Sass asked (1994, p. 4). The early nineteenth-century French alienists might not have put it quite like this; their view tended to be that it was too much, or misdirected, passion that deranged people. There is a tension, however, that is worth acknowledging here so the reader can keep it in mind, between the two broad directions of medical and Romantic thinking: where the Romantic might critique the Enlightenment for elevating reason at the expense of feeling, the general direction of the philosophically minded alienists' thinking would seem to be in the opposite direction. Until, that is, we grasp that more often than not, for Pinel, Esquirol, or Georget, it was the dominance of a *single* passion or preoccupation that was the dangerous basis for much of the sufferer's reasoning, leading it astray. In this sense, the view that too much or falsely directed reason is a form of madness is implicit in the early alienists' understanding.

All these frameworks, the anti-psychiatric, the phenomenological, the psychoanalytic, and McGilchrist's, have their own histories, of course;

they are themselves part of history. All, ultimately, are outgrowths of Enlightenment and Romanticism, of Enlightenment science tempered by radical, humanising, critical Romanticism. They too are products of the period under examination here.

* * *

By the first quarter of the nineteenth century, "madness" was assuming its modern, medical patina. The "gradual secularisation of both the signs and the experience of madness was accompanied by a growing professionalisation of treatment", as the divine gave way to the medical man (Ingram, 1998, p. 2). Historical accounts of the beginnings of psychiatry and the birth of the asylum in France overlap and diverge; this is contested ground. Foucault saw the Pinelian attempt at dialogue with unreason as the institution of a new and more insidious confinement, and provided a touchstone which no subsequent account has been able to ignore. In the French sociologist Robert Castel's critique, in *L'ordre psychiatrique: l'âge d'or de l'aliénisme* (1976), the new science of psychiatry was a response not so much to insanity in itself as to a legal problem arising from the bourgeois revolution: how to deal with undesirable behaviour which does not justify incarceration under civil or criminal law? The answer: the institution in medical psychiatry of a system of guardianship, *une relation de tutelle*, fully enshrined in the law of 1838 (*la loi Esquirol*) in which the aberrant person might be treated as a dependent minor whose ordinary rights and responsibilities as a citizen were suspended. The American sociologist Jan Goldstein, in *Console and Classify. The French Psychiatric Profession in the Nineteenth Century* (1987), focused on an imperative also explored by Castel: psychiatry came into being on the back of the interests of medical practitioners who wished to carve out a new sub-profession for themselves, in relation and in tension with the clergy and the legal profession. The American historian Dora B. Weiner, in *The Citizen-Patient in Revolutionary and Imperial Paris* (1993), located the new treatment of the insane within the context of the reform programmes in public health and welfare which got underway in the early years of the Revolution: the Rights of Man and of the Citizen included a right to health, which was also extended to the insane. The French historian Jacques Postel has further demystified, demythologised, and contextualised the activities of the early alienists (Postel, 2007).

Biographical accounts of the main protagonists also diverge. Was Philippe Pinel an Enlightenment and revolutionary hero, a disinterested yet philanthropic product of the Century of Light whose efforts led to the establishment of that humane branch of medicine we call psychiatry? Or was he, at the other extreme, a southern provincial with a chip on his shoulder who took advantage of the revolutionary upheaval to further his own career, and in the process establish and promote the interests of a whole new, nefarious practice? Or was he a bit of both, a well-intentioned friend of the people who became the unwitting founder of a regime of mastery that was to lead to the great asylums of the nineteenth and twentieth centuries, to ECT, lobotomy, and the psychiatric prisons of totalitarianism? Pinel is a key figure in the background of the portraits, and where we stand on these questions will inform how we approach and interpret them.

A tentative overview of historical developments may help the reader to find a way through some of the sections that follow, and to be primed for certain problems and questions. The evolution of the care and treatment of the insane as a medical specialism in France, in Pinel's hands and those of his students and successors, rested on three conditions, deriving from the Enlightenment and the Revolution: a philanthropic impetus, a wish to improve the lot of the unfortunate; a philosophic impetus, that is, a need to bring order to chaos; and a legal grey area. One mainspring of the philosophic impetus, which also helped maintain the philanthropic, was the observation that insanity could affect only part of the sufferer, leaving a "reasonable" part intact. Important consequences flowed from this. There was a clinical emphasis on what became known as the "moral treatment", that is, on enlisting and speaking to the sane part of the patient (but how best to do this)? The idea of partial madness also contributed to the establishment of a professional identity for the doctor-alienist. Subtending this was a primacy placed on vision itself, as essential aid to diagnosis and classification: possession of a trained, expert eye was key to the alienist's unique expertise. But problems arose. What sort of a doctor is it who does not treat the body? What, in addition, was to be the relation between alienists and lawyers: were they in direct professional competition—now that the power of the Church to arbitrate on these matters had waned—over who held the criteria for determining if a person committing a crime were responsible or mad, and for deciding what should then become of him? Or did alienist and lawyer, as Castel argued, tacitly serve the same social and political ends? In the West, psychiatrists won the dispute over professional boundaries, becoming expert witnesses in the courtroom while retaining absolute authority in the asylum. When Géricault made the portraits, all these questions were still open.

A demanding but in the end clarifying way of thinking about the larger historical picture has been provided by the French political philosopher Marcel Gauchet and the psychiatrist Gladys Swain, who in 1980 published a detailed study of the beginnings of psychiatry in the first years of the nineteenth century in France, *La pratique de l'esprit humain. L'institution asilare et la révolution démocratique*, translated as *Madness and Democracy* (Gauchet & Swain, 1980; 1999). There is, they wrote, a history of the division of the subject, which can be traced back to the division of the world between the secular and the sacred, "between visible reality and invisible forces, between the natural and the supernatural—along with the obligatory consequences of that division for the representation of human experience". The history of the modern division of the subject, conceived in terms of psychopathology, "is nothing but the other side of the history of a reduction, precisely, in that division of the world", as it was gradually incorporated and finally, around 1800, absorbed into madness (Gauchet & Swain, 1999, pp. 269–270).

Gauchet and Swain also chart a history of the evolution of insanity in the West along another axis, that of conceptions and experiences of otherness. In writing such a history they would seek to trace a *lessening* of a sense of otherness between people and groups, feudal distinctions between lord and serf, for example, in which one was almost a different species to the other. Within this structure of otherness the insane were *radically* other, and could be accepted as such; their difference was part of the preordained order of things. But this difference gradually dissolved over historical time. At the same time, and as part of the same process, there took place a "reduction of invisible alterity", that is, waning belief and investment in spirits, gods, angels, and the devil, the forces of good and evil. Alongside this came an internalisation of experiences of (formerly invisible) external forces: from the divine conceived and experienced as residing within, to the development of the idea of personal moral responsibility. How, Gauchet and Swain go on to ask, "could such a general and large-scale process have failed to affect the very manifestations of the rift within the self we call insanity?" (1999, pp. 275–276). This broad theoretical framework allows for historical nuance and subtlety, and deals, at a stroke, with the question as to whether or not "illnesses" such as "schizophrenia" have been ubiquitous and universal, but only misunderstood as, for example, possession. It is, instead, an account which registers the dynamic and dialectical complexities of interactions between people and the cultures which they have shaped and been shaped by. Gauchet and Swain's approach "recommends itself as a way to engage historical writing in a project of human self-understanding that lies forever before us, rather than as an appeal to the past to stand witness to a knowledge we think we already possess" (Seigel, 1999, p. xii).

Gauchet and Swain's analysis countered what they saw as the overarching style of Foucault's theorising. Yet the importance of Foucault's *Histoire de la folie* should not be underestimated: it elevated madness "to a prime vantage point for observing the birth of the modern individual" (Murat, 2014, p. 14). Gauchet and Swain refined and developed the view from this vantage point. They were concerned, like Castel, with the place of the insane within a post-Revolutionary society of citizens; crucially, their interest was in how the democratic revolution irrevocably changed the face of insanity. For it now became conceivable for the mad person to cross from object to subject status. Romantic "appeal to the reflections of the heart", in Mme de Staël's phrase (Quetel & Morel, 1979, p. 239), legitimated a new openness to the humanity of unreason, and the unreason at the heart of humanity—an openness notably shared by Géricault's older Spanish contemporary Francisco Goya, the great artist of our shadow selves. The revolution in the care of the insane that was underway around 1800, and the shift in attitudes it implied, involved a development of the very idea of what it means to be human. The processes at work were lending impetus to the idea of the individual as free and equal to other individuals, yet simultaneously subject to strange forces from within; they were giving birth to modern Western subjectivity itself. The new conception of the human subject as constitutionally split, which this history reveals, finds its echo in the portraits.

Here too psychoanalysis has its roots. Is it, as a Foucault or Castel would argue, a repressive practice obliged by some logic of history to follow docilely in the footsteps of the irredeemably normalising psychiatry of the 1800s? Or is there another psychoanalysis, marking the fuller emergence of the subject-to-be-listened-to and engaged with, part of "a project of human self-understanding that lies forever before us" (Seigel, 1999, p. xii)?

* * *

To return to the portraits, McGilchrist sums up the task ahead: how to see what they are.

> Body and soul, metaphor and sense, myth and reality, the work of art and its meaning—in fact the whole phenomenological world, is just what it is and no more, not one thing hiding another; and yet the hard thing is the seemingly easy business; just "seeing what it is". (2009, p. 452)

A painting is not time-bound like a piece of music or a play; it does not (necessarily) require sequential reading like a poem or a novel. It has immediate impact. Like, as some argue, a patient in analysis, it gives you everything all at once, simultaneously, on first meeting—if only you could apprehend it. The actual experience is not only like this, of course, for meanings develop and change over time; they unfold, leap into focus and dissolve, or get created anew in and as a result of every encounter. So we must, viewers of paintings, therapists, or patients, follow Wittgenstein's advice to philosophers: "Give yourself time!" (Wittgenstein, 1980, p. 80, cited in Parsons, 2014, p. 193). The immediacy nevertheless persists; it can repeat itself each time we look.

Gregorio Kohon has approached the aesthetic experience in a way that might help us make some sense of this. A work of art, he writes,

> does not communicate to the subject a meaning that is already given. There is nothing intrinsic or given or natural to the aesthetic object: the aesthetic object itself generates the conditions for meaning to be created ... the work itself creates ... unconscious perceptions that did not exist previously. (2016, p. 18)

He continues: "If we are going not so much 'to understand' the artistic object or the literary text as to allow ourselves, instead, to become involved with it, there will be a demand for uncertainty to be tolerated: uncertainty, opaqueness, doubt ..." (ibid., p. 19).

The task of trying to convey this involvement in discursive words, in art criticism as in an analysis, can never be wholly satisfying or complete: analysis interminable. Once this is accepted, however, the process has a good chance of becoming enlivening and regenerative in itself. The pages that follow are a record of my own involvement and explorations over time. They are, necessarily, provisional, and, it is hoped, open to the patient reader's own fresh discoveries.

CHAPTER ONE

Illustrations

This chapter gathers together twenty of the images discussed in the book: ten paintings and a sheet of drawings by Théodore Géricault, a painting by Jacques-Louis David and another formerly attributed to him, a painting by Eugène Delacroix, a lithograph after a painting by Horace Vernet, three engraved book illustrations, by Ambroise Tardieu, including one made after a drawing by Georges François Marie Gabriel, a drawing by this same Gabriel, and a plate from a book by Charles Bell. The reader might care to linger on these for a while, in as open-minded and free-associative a way as possible, before reading on.

Illustration 1. Théodore Géricault. *Monomane du vol d'enfants (Monomaniac of Child Abduction)*. *c*.1822–1823. Oil on canvas. 86.8 × 54 cm. Museum of Fine Arts, Springfield, MA.

Illustration 2. Théodore Géricault. *Monomane du comandement militaire (Monomaniac of Military Command)*. *c*.1822–1823. Oil on canvas, 81 × 65 cm. Collection Oskar Reinhart "Am Römerholz", Winterthur, Switzerland.

Illustration 3. Théodore Géricault. *Monomane du vol (Monomaniac of Theft)*. *c*.1822–1823. Oil on canvas. 61.2 × 50.1 cm. Museum of Fine Arts, Ghent, Belgium.

Illustration 4. Théodore Géricault. *Monomane du jeu (Monomaniac of Gambling)*. c.1822–1823. Oil on canvas. 77 × 64 cm. Musée du Louvre, Paris.

Illustration 5. Théodore Géricault. *Monomane de l'envie (Monomaniac of Envy). c.*1822–1823. Oil on canvas. 72 × 58 cm. Musée des Beaux-Arts, Lyon, France.

Illustration 6. Théodore Géricault. *Chasseur de la Garde.* 1812. Oil on canvas. 349 × 266 cm. Musée du Louvre, Paris.

Illustration 7. Jacques-Louis David. *The Oath of the Horatii*. 1784.
Oil on canvas. 329.8 × 424.8 cm. Musée du Louvre, Paris.

Illustration 8. Théodore Géricault. *The Race of the Barbieri Horses*.
c.1817. Oil on paper marouflé on canvas. 44.5 × 59.5 cm.
Musée du Louvre, Paris.

Illustration 9. Théodore Géricault. *The Raft of the Medusa*. 1819.
Oil on canvas. 491 × 716 cm. Musée du Louvre, Paris.

Illustration 10. Théodore Géricault. *Expressive Self-portraits as Sailor*.
c.1818–1819. Graphite, pen, and brown ink on brown paper.
21 × 26.2 cm. Museum of Art, Baltimore, MD.

Illustration 11. Théodore Géricault. *Guillotined Heads.* c.1818–1820.
Oil on canvas. 50 × 61 cm. Nationalmuseum, Stockholm.

Illustration 12.
Théodore Géricault.
Mazeppa. 1823.
Oil on canvas. 28.5 × 21.5 cm.
Private collection.

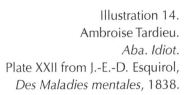

Illustration 13.
Charles Motte,
after Horace Vernet.
La folle par amour. 1819.
Lithograph. Plate XXVI,
volume 1, *Galerie
lithographiée de son
Altesse royale
Monseigneur le
Duc d' Orléans.*
Paris: Bureau de la
Galerie, 1830[?].

Illustration 14.
Ambroise Tardieu.
Aba. Idiot.
Plate XXII from J.-E.-D. Esquirol,
Des Maladies mentales, 1838.

Illustration 15.
Ambroise Tardieu, after
Georges François Marie Gabriel.
Démonomaniaque. Plate VI
from J.-E.-D. Esquirol, *Des
Maladies mentales*, 1838.

Illustration 16.
Anon. The Maniac.
Plate from C. Bell, *Essays on
the Anatomy of Expression
in Painting*, 1806.

Illustration 17.
Georges François Marie Gabriel.
Officier, devenu fou, par opinion politique. 1813. Bibliothèque Nationale de France, Paris.

Illustration 18.
Ambroise Tardieu. *Manie.*
Plate VIII from J.-E.-D. Esquirol, *Des Maladies mentales*, 1838.

Illustration 19.
French School, formerly
attributed to J.-L. David.
Half-Length Portrait of a Woman,
known as *La Maraîchère*
(*The Market Gardener*). *c*.1795.
Oil on canvas. 82 × 65 cm.
Musée des Beaux-Arts, Lyon,
France.

Illustration 20. Eugène Delacroix. *Liberty Leading the People*. 1830.
Oil on canvas. 260 × 325 cm. Musée du Louvre-Lens,
France.

The works above, together with other images referred to in the text, can also be viewed on my website: robertsnellpsychotherapy.uk. Click on "Illustrations".

CHAPTER TWO

The canvases unrolled

In 1863 Louis Viardot, journalist, translator, and former director of the Théâtre des Italiens in Paris, was party to the discovery of some rolled-up canvases in a trunk in an attic in Baden-Baden: five bust-length, life-sized portraits in oil, three of men and two of women. They belonged to a retired doctor named Lachèze. Viardot himself had recently moved to the spa with his wife, the legendary singer Pauline Garcia, as a voluntary exile from France. An opponent of the autocratic regime of Napoleon III, Viardot was also an art critic; he recognised the paintings as the work of Théodore Géricault.

Géricault's reputation in France, then as now, was colossal. He had died at the age of thirty-three in 1824 and was, with Delacroix (who himself died in 1863), a figurehead of the Romanticism of the previous generation, and of liberal opposition and dissent. His massive *The Raft of the Medusa* had been bought for the Louvre shortly after his death, where it still hangs; by the mid-century its status as a national icon was firmly established. In a long letter to the eminent critic Charles Blanc, written from Baden-Baden on 6 December 1863, Viardot produced the first account of the newly discovered Géricaults; it was published in Paris the following month.

He confidently identified the portraits as representing "five types of monomania, perfectly characterised": a monomaniac of child abduction (*le vol d'enfants*) [Illustration 1], a monomaniac of military command [Illustration 2], a monomaniac of theft [Illustration 3], a woman who "had been ruined by the lottery and, in her grief, lost her reason" [Illustration 4], and a monomaniac of envy [Illustration 5] (Michel, Chenique, & Laveissière, 1991, pp. 322–323). Having been hidden away for thirty-nine years the portraits were, Viardot wrote, as fresh as the day they left the artist's studio. Their impact is undiminished.

All five figures seem to share our physical space. They are close up; the foreheads of all five press against or come close to the plane of the picture surface. There is a sense of air around and behind them, but there is isolation and claustrophobia too. The heads, framed within off-white collars or bonnets, seem lifted out of the darkness (Wedekind, 2013, p. 73). Each painting makes use of a restricted palette of dark browns, muted greys, and dusty whites, with sparing passages or dashes of red or yellow; all the figures are seated or standing—it is not always easy to tell—in a gloomy interior, and more or less dramatically illuminated by a single source of light. In none of them are hands visible; even the presence of arms is barely indicated beneath their winter clothes, except in the case of the military commander, who has ample white shirt sleeves. Each seems securely held within the picture frame, bound by gravity, yet there are moments when they can also seem barely confined by the edges of the canvas, so alive are they. The body language of each, the tilt of a head and counter-tilt of a torso, seems a promise of communication. But they do not meet our eyes. Three of them look obliquely out of the frame, to the left; envy and the child abductor look to their right, which, given our Western tendency to read paintings from left to right, seems to make it even harder for us to follow their gazes and imagine what might be in their minds—as if they oppose and obstruct our wish to "follow" them. Each is lost in his or her experiences and thoughts. All the figures convey a powerful sense of underlying anatomy; in all of them the bony dome of the skull is strikingly apparent. All five pictures are in a traditional, vertical, portrait format, although the sizes and dimensions of each canvas are slightly different, ranging from sixty-one by fifty centimetres (theft) to eighty-six by sixty-five (commander). Within this relative uniformity, however, each is the unique evocation of an individual, and each is a variation within a sophisticated painterly language.

The woman ruined by the lottery, who has ever since been known as the monomaniac of gambling, the *Monomane du jeu*, might be looking sideways and up towards an unseen attendant, whether a persecuting or a comforting one is not clear. She seems in doubt herself (the ragged monomaniac of theft conveys similar ambiguity). Is she poised to spring, or cowering? For Viardot she was simply "a poor old woman without malice, forever absorbed in calculations of doubles, triples and quads" (Michel, Chenique, & Laveissière, 1991, p. 322). Her upward look is unsettling. She seems to have hypertropia, a kind of strabismus, so that while her left eye is directed upwards her right almost, but not quite, meets the viewer's. The left side of her mouth curls upwards, as if pushing up the eye; the two halves of her face are like two different faces, one in relative repose, and the other in an uncomfortable contortion. There is something mousy about her, with her dull grey hair and greyish complexion; no accents of colour relieve the olive greys and greeny browns of her three layers of heavy clothing; there is only the expanse of off-white linen covering her breast, and her nondescript white cap. She is the most weighed down of the sitters, and her portrait is the most austere. Her head sinks into her shoulders and into the coarse material of her cloak. The triangle formed by a large lapel on her right side seems to wedge her in to the picture; she is trapped, crushed, immobilised, an impression firmly reinforced by the presence—hers is the only one of the portraits to show such features—of brickwork dimly visible in the wall behind and above her to the left, the harsh straight line of a chair or bench-back to her right, and a diagonal crutch sealing her into the picture below her to her left. The folds of her clothes form long, shallow curves, echoing the plain oval of her face; the rhythm of the painting is slow, almost leaden. In a more ancient classification and iconography, she would undoubtedly be a melancholic.

The *Monomane de l'envie* is the most compositionally elaborate. The pattern of folds in her dress works with her white bonnet to frame her slightly downturned face in a loose oval, in a system of cradling, upward curves. She too is seen from a higher viewpoint than the three men, so that we look slightly down on her. In contrast to the slow, heavy curves of the gambler, the nervy, complex, tighter, rippling lines of the edges of her white bonnet and the bottom of her shawl, together with the thin, straggling bonnet ribbons and wisps of escaping grey hair, set up a faster visual rhythm which suggests physical and emotional lability. The red "V" of a scarf, the largest area of near-primary colour in any of the paintings, covers her breast and works like the warning "V" of a viper. In places her clothes are thinly and quickly brushed in, and rapid strokes of thin paint energise the background, especially above her right shoulder. Also known as the "The Hyena of the Salpêtrière", she seems to exude spite; she is on the manic end of the spectrum. Where the woman addicted to gambling is weighed down by her obsession, the monomaniac of envy seems tormented by life itself. Is she too about to spring, but more dangerously, quivering like a cat? Or is it merely shrewdness we can discern in that red-eyed, penetrating, downward glance? Perhaps she is on the point of speaking—it seems she might be ready to spit out some words. The portrait moved Viardot to cite Voltaire, in his characterisation of envy: "sad lover of the dead, she hates the living". He may also have been drawing on Lachèze's personal recollections of the patient.

> This unfortunate woman could not, for example, see someone else receiving a caress without falling into an internal rage, which would express itself in a grinding of her mouth and an injection of blood into her eyes. It is marvellous to see with what power and felicity, and without exaggeration, but on the contrary by means of barely accentuated effects, the painter has reflected, on the mirror of the features of her face, these convulsions of a deranged soul. It is frightening and magnificent. (Michel, Chenique, & Laveissière, 1991, p. 322, translated for this edition)

The *Monomane du vol d'enfants*, the child abductor, is infinitely stiller. His head fills a larger area of the canvas proportionately to the others. He looks with huge sadness to his right, and here there is little doubt that it is what is behind rather than in the sight of those watery eyes, particularly the left, that preoccupies him. There is longing and regret. Is there some insight into himself in that sadness? Something feels infinitely lost; his lips and chin seem to tremble, as if he were on the permanent verge of tears. At the same time he may be waiting for his punishment. He age is hard to determine; the complexion of the cheek closest to the viewer seems remarkably clear. His mouth is turned down; his collars droop. His cap looks as if it could be velvet, and his clothes, which might be those of a slightly better class of person, seem to be of similar texture, in shades of dark brown, the colour perhaps known to contemporaries as "merdoye" (Cobb, 1978, p. i, Glossary). We view him at eye level; although his shoulders seem to sag, his posture is more upright than that of either of the two women, and his head sits at the apex of the shrouded pyramid of his upper body. In this painting the play of light and dark, *chiaroscuro*, is at its most intense; the far side of the child abductor's face is in deep shadow, suggestive perhaps of shame, while the large surface of his forehead is brightly lit, as if to underline the sense of internal activity. Of all the portraits this is the most Rembrandt-like. It has a distant echo of Rembrandt's *A Scholar seated at a Table*, of 1634 (Národní Galerie, Prague), with his velvet hat (Bikker, Weber, Wieseman, & Hinterding, 2014, p. 217); Géricault would have known the *Philosopher in his Chamber* of 1632, which is in the Louvre, a seated figure also distinguished by a large forehead in strong highlight.

The *Monomane du commandement militaire* is an older man, and he wears a jaunty cap with a tassel. A large tin number tag ("121") hangs from his neck like a medal. He is in a different and, once again, more manic register. The hat is a "bonnet de police", the cap worn by Napoleonic veterans retired on half pay under the Restoration (Boime, 1991, p. 89). The number tag might be a hospital tag, or, as Viardot thought, a "médaille de commissionnaire", a messenger's or courier's identification. The man looks out to his left, and slightly upwards, with a mixture of apprehension and grim fortitude: it might be towards an unseen enemy. This is what Viardot thought too:

> he believed he was a Marshal of France, manoeuvring battalions from morning to evening, and winning at least a battle a day. He is proud, this one, arrogant, and as radiant as Caesar must have been after the battle of Pharsalus. (Michel, Chenique, & Laveissière, 1991, p. 322, translated for this edition)

Pharsalus was Julius Caesar's famous victory against Pompey in 48BC. It is interesting that Viardot, exiled from Napoleon III's France, avoids the more obvious reference to Napoleon I; the portraits subtly implicate us in the political from the start. Of all the sitters the military commander is perhaps the only self-conscious one; he does seem to be striking a pose, as if saying to himself: "Future generations will surely admire the steely resolve with which I am at this very moment impressing the painter of my portrait." He too is in *chiaroscuro*, although less deeply than the child abductor; his broadly and confidently painted white and dove-grey linen sleeves also have distant echoes of Rembrandt, of *Aristotle* of 1653 (Metropolitan Museum, New York), or the Trip portrait of c.1661 (National Gallery, London; Bikker, Weber,

Wieseman, & Hinterding, 2014, pp. 106, 216). The composition is the most geometrical of the five. The commander's head is level and erect, his eyes are horizontal, parallel to the top and bottom of the frame, and a near-vertical line runs from the bridge of his nose to the cleft of his chin; it is echoed in another line running downwards through the tassel of his cap to a pronounced fold in his left sleeve. A diagonal line also extends from this sleeve to the point between his eyes, making a triangle with the central vertical; this in turn is echoed in the smaller triangles of the tip of his hat and the string around his neck from which the medallion hangs. Battles were still matters of geometry and triangulation, of straight ranks trained to wheel in arcs or advance in straight lines. The commander is thin-lipped, on the alert. Yet the portrait conveys something else too: suppressed terror, a sense of trauma barely survived, a hint, in the eyes, of the unendurable horrors of a battlefield, of things seen and perhaps still being seen in his mind's eye that this man wishes he had never seen.

The *Monomane du vol*, the thief, was also, for Viardot, caught up in a kind of conquest. The youngest and the most evenly lit of the sitters, he has a reddish nose, a slightly bloodshot right eye, a scraggy beard, and thick, badly cut, tousled hair; unlike the others he has no hat. The viewpoint has changed; he is also the only one to be seen slightly from below, so that he appears to be popping up like a jack-in-a-box, his head tilting. His collars stick out and he appears startled, on edge; the top half of his body seems to be recoiling involuntarily from something slightly to his left, in counterpoint to the turn of his head. Providing a degree of stability, the nearly vertical lines of his lapels make a column topped with his lightly patterned cravat and white collars, a sort of capital supporting his head. Each lapel is also one side of a triangle, the other two sides being the slant of his sleeves and the bottom of the frame. They hold him securely in place, captive—but not without protest. His raised eyebrows suggest superciliousness. His downturned mouth conveys displeasure. His lower lip is thrust forward in a defiant pout. Viardot was struck by his rather handsome features, which seemed to him to denote "intelligence and resolution no less than guile"; he had

> the equivocal look and hesitant mouth of a scoundrel up to no good and anxious about being discovered. The painter has marvellously rendered this disposition of depravity mixed with audacity and fear. (Michel, Chenique, & Laveissière, 1991, p. 322, translated for this edition)

He looks as if he might dart out of the frame at any second; there is a suddenness, an impulsiveness about him, emphasised by the marked tilt of his head. Unless, of course, he is frozen like this, in a blank stupor. Is he a danger, a threat? At some point in the painting's history the man acquired the title "the mad murderer" or "murderous madman" ("le fou assassin"): might he hurt us if we get too close? Or—the more you look the greater the mix-up—is he the vulnerable one?

The immediacy of the portraits seems bound up with their manifest artifice and materiality as paintings. Just as you are struck by the life and individuality of the sitter, you meet the skein of brushmarks and small whirls and knobs of oil paint through which this human presence makes itself felt. The *Monomane du vol* and the *Monomane de l'envie* are lit from top left. Flecks of white bring life to the eyes, only to one of the child abductor's eyes, however, since the right side of his face is in shadow. The *Monomane de l'envie* has yellow, ochre, and pink on her forehead, and under her eyes. So does the child abductor. As one modern critic, Gregor Wedekind, has written, we are invited to look close-up, at

> the agitated brushstrokes, the scarified surface, the use of pigment as virtuosic overpainting or pastose crust, and the colours which at times include suphurous yellow, scarlet red and poisonous green, particularly prominent as facial tones.

For Géricault "resorted to such artistic artificiality to achieve the very opposite: truth and proximity to life" (Wedekind, 2013, p. 176). The sitters' pulsing vitality seems to push against the paintings' surfaces as well as their frames, against the constraining, sensual materiality of canvas and paint themselves. One of Géricault's finest twentieth-century commentators, the art historian Lorenz Eitner, noted that the portraits must have been painted at speed, in single sittings, without preparatory studies, from life, in the way a landscapist painting in the open air might work. The inclinations of the heads, the fall of the light, "seem to have been a matter of spontaneous decision; perception, choice and representation occurred almost simultaneously. Yet", Eitner continues, "the execution is by no means hasty or uneven, but of a deliberate, masterful economy; there is not one wasted stroke, useless flourish, or laboured passage." Nothing, for Eitner (1982, p. 247), equals the paintings for firmness and fluency in the whole of Géricault's work. With Eitner we are drawn to an appreciation of Géricault's sheer artistry.

As for the sitters, Viardot's confidence in giving them their labels must have come from his conversations with Dr Lachèze. Adolphe Lachèze would also have been the source of Viardot's assertion in his letter to Charles Blanc that there were originally ten portraits, that they were painted between 1820 and 1824, and that an important part in their creation was played by Géricault's childhood friend, later a celebrated alienist, Etienne Georget. Géricault, Viardot wrote, would often visit Georget in his hospital, the Salpêtrière; the portraits were likely to have been made "either at the express desire of Dr Georget, or for [Géricault's] own artistic satisfaction". Georget too had died young, in 1828; the ten portraits, according to Viardot, were shared between Lachèze and another intern, named Maréchal; both had become friends with Georget. Five of the portraits ended up in a town in Brittany; Viardot did not know their whereabouts in 1863, and their fate is still unknown. Lachèze became a specialist in plague and travelled widely in the Middle East before returning to France and finally settling in Baden-Baden. Viardot notes that the two young doctors had admired the paintings not as connoisseurs of art but as students of faces, "curieux de physionomies" (Michel, Chenique, & Laveissière, 1991, p. 322). Lachèze was, however, hardly a total philistine, his neglect of his five portraits notwithstanding; in his later life he had painters among his friends, and seems to have been a man of wide culture. What Viardot touched on was the major problem the portraits presented to a mid-nineteenth-century sensibility. What was their status? How were they to be approached? As art or medical illustration? Viardot himself felt that they would be equally at home in the Ecole de Médecine or the establishment of Dr Emile Blanche, the best known psychiatrist of the period—or next to the *Raft* in the Louvre, where one of them, the *Monomane du jeu*, does indeed now hang.

Viardot tacitly registered such problems of seeing and interpretation in his very first reactions. In his descriptions of the portraits he comes to a point at which matter-of-factness ("here are five studies ...") flips into a vividness which he seems unable to help. Presumably following Lachèze's recollections, he recounts in the manner of a case description how the child abductor would approach a child he saw alone on the street or in the country, pet him or her, and furtively take him home, believing himself to be the father. But the next sentence belongs in a different and fresher register: "C'est, en effet, une figure tout à fait paterne ...", the tipping point being the "en effet". "Actually, he is an altogether paternal figure, with his rounded forehead, kindly eye, and engaging mouth" (Michel, Chenique, & Laveissière, 1991, p. 322, translated for this edition).

Another contemporary, Théophile Thoré, a republican, one of the most politically liberal art critics of the era and the writer, twenty years previously, of a brief biography of Géricault, simply sidestepped the question of the status and artistic merit of the paintings precisely because of their subject matter, before he had even seen them (if he ever did). "Where would you put such things?" he wrote in reply to a letter from Viardot in 1864. Would Dr Lachèze care to come to Paris, bringing one of his "terrible madmen" with him? "I shall offer him a complete consultation and precise information. Alas! It's less the quality of the painting that gives it its value than its subject or charm. The humblest *Camargo* would be worth more than the most handsome madman from Bicêtre" (Marie Anne de Camargo was a famous eighteenth-century dancer; prints after a painting of her by Lancret were popular in the mid-century (Wedekind, 2007, p. 112, note 39)). Thoré valued Géricault's paintings, unseen, at a modest 500 francs apiece (probably about 1000 euros today) (Michel, Chenique, & Laveissière, 1991, p. 323). Later nineteenth-century commentators assessed them by similar criteria; for the critic Maurice Hamel, writing in 1887, they were merely representations of human nature "fallen into bestiality" (cited in Miller, 1940–41, p. 152).

Did the existence of the paintings somehow compromise Géricault's status, in Thoré's mind, as a liberal hero? For Thoré they crossed a boundary to which he was as alert as any of his educated contemporaries could have been. If a portrait was a record of some allegiance or membership—familial, social, ecclesiastical, political, military, commercial, professional, academic—or an exploration of psychological depth, of personality and merit, and insanity was a medical and social category designating precisely a lack of position, depth, and identity (although not necessarily of merit), then a *portrait* of the *insane* was a contradiction in terms (see too Bryson, 1983, p. 143). If we consider that a twenty-first-century socio-diagnostic title for the portrait of the child abductor would be *The Paedophile*, we have an up-to-date way of registering the gap, the tension, the disjunction, which Thoré felt at the prospect of portraits of the insane. It is a gap familiar in fairly recent British memory from the furore around the portrait of the child murderer Myra Hindley, shown at the Royal Academy's "Sensation" exhibition in 1997. A search on Google images will turn up plenty of reproductions of four of the Géricault portraits. Although he can eventually be found, the *Monomane du vol d'enfants* does not exist on many of the fine-art-based sites on which he might be expected to appear. "This portrait hits a raw nerve today," wrote a critic in 2000. "Its assertion that deviant desires are betrayed by the face might appeal to many who wonder how to identify the monster in our midst. What is more challenging is Géricault's compassion for this man" (Jones, 2000). The Louvre was not interested when it was offered the paintings by Lachèze's friend the landscape artist Henri-Joseph Harpignies in 1866. Géricault's biographer Charles Clément seems only reticently to have appended them to his catalogue of the artist's work in 1868.

It is not that the ground was totally unprepared, from at least the mid-nineteenth century, for a warmer appreciation.

> … you must consider no one too lowly, no one too ugly, only then can you understand them; the most ordinary of faces makes a deeper impression than any contrived sensation of beauty, and you can let the characters' own being emerge quite naturally without bringing in anything copied from outside where no life, no pulse, no muscles surge and throb. (Büchner, 1839, p. 150)

Thus wrote Georg Büchner in the 1830s, in *Lenz*, his novella about the late eighteenth-century poet J. M. R. Lenz, who died insane. Büchner gave the words to his character Lenz, but they are certainly also a statement of his own aesthetic. Courbet himself, the founder of Realism in painting, never put it better.

Here is Ruskin, who is unlikely to have known anything about Géricault's monomaniacs, writing in 1870. The real strength of a great artist, Ruskin said,

> … is tried to the utmost, and … never elsewhere brought out so thoroughly, as in painting one man or woman, and the soul that was in them; nor that always the highest soul, but often only a thwarted one that was capable of height; or perhaps not even that, but faultful and poor, yet seen through, to the poor best of it, by the masterful sight … the mind of man never invented a greater thing than the form of man, animated by faithful life … (pp. 120–121)

Viardot would have concurred, as did an artist called Charles-Emile Jacque, a painter of animals and a friend of Millet, who finally bought the portraits following their rejection by the Louvre. They were sold again in 1878, and dispersed among private collections. For several decades they disappeared from sight once more. One by one, between 1908 and 1947, they found their ways into public museums (Michel, Chenique, & Laveissière, 1991, pp. 244, 406–407). Only very gradually, echoing the history of the mad themselves, did they cease to languish as mere aberrations or curiosities (Edridge, 2002, p. 4).

Housed as they are in major art institutions, nowadays the portraits seem to present no difficulty in allowing themselves to be seen as works of art. Yet they are still perhaps not as well known, given their extraordinary quality, as they deserve to be. All five have only been shown together once, in Paris in 1924, at the exhibition commemorating the centenary of Géricault's death, at the Galérie Charpentier. The last time four of them appeared together was at the great 1991 Paris exhibition at the Grand Palais. Nowadays only three can travel; the man with ideas of military grandeur is confined to his Swiss billet under the terms of a legacy, and the child abductor is too frail to leave Springfield, Illinois.

Perhaps their subject matter still means that they are felt to have a rather specialist status, with the result that maybe even more sympathetic non-psychiatric viewers have deemed it somehow outside their competence to speak about them. The first, and very fine, scholarly article on them only appeared in 1941 (Miller, 1940–41), and there was nothing to compete with it until the early years of this century. An extensive exhibition at the Musée des Beaux Arts in Lyon in 2006, *Géricault, la folie d'un monde,* presented the *Monomane du vol,* the *Monomane de l'envie,* and the *Monomane du jeu* as expressions of Géricault the history painter and social and political commentator. Other ways in which they have recently been contextualised by art historians and curators seem rather to have underlined their "psychiatric" status—the *Monomane du vol d'enfants* was shown in London at the Hayward Gallery's 2000–2001 exhibition *Spectacular Bodies: The Art and Science of the Human Body from Leonardo to Now,* and the *Monomane du vol,* the *Monomane de l'envie,* and the *Monomane du jeu* appeared together in the 2013–2014 exhibition *Géricault: Images of Life and Death* (Schirn Kunsthalle, Frankfurt and Musée des Beaux-Arts, Ghent); both exhibitions framed the portraits within the context of medical and scientific discourse and anatomical illustration. Historians of psychiatry and madness, meanwhile, have tended to mention them only in passing, if at all; perhaps from their point of view too the portraits step outside a familiar professional frame in ways that seem to place them beyond their field of competence. Perhaps the portraits are victims of the proliferation of specialisms that was just beginning to make itself felt at the time they were made, before the sharp art/science distinction with which we are familiar was firmly established.

So how are we to see them—both the canvases and the people they represent? A modernist interpretative lens might want to focus on the anti-illusionism of the paintings, on the way in which the painter has drawn attention to the material bases of his work and, as a contemporary Brechtian and Marxist critic has put it, torn away a sanctifying veil of aesthetic form (Schwarz, 2009, p. 85). The sitters are clearly poor; yet they are not presented to us as picturesque low-life, in the mould of seventeenth-century Dutch, Italian, or French genre painting. They are straight portraits that take their sitters seriously, at face value. In this reading, as Thoré had intuited, Géricault was undermining the integrity of one of the academically sanctioned artistic genres; in this way too he can be enlisted as a forerunner of modernism, taking his place near the head of a lineage that runs through Courbet and Realism to Manet and the Impressionists and beyond; the 1991 Grand Palais exhibition promoted him as a "subjective Realist" (Michel, Chenique, & Laveissière, 1991, pp. XV–XVI). His likely friendship with the physician Etienne Georget, who espoused an advanced, materialist philosophy, might also lend weight to the view that Géricault intended to draw attention both to the portraits' tangible nature as artefacts and to the material conditions of the lives of his sitters.

But this does not sufficiently account for their continuing power to disturb, their uncanniness. In part this may derive from their stand-alone nature. Portraits had been made of people in extreme physical and mental states before; one example, possibly known to Géricault, would be Greuze's bust of a paralytic, now in the Musée Fabre in Montpellier, of the early 1770s, which bears a chilly resemblance to one of several paintings Géricault made of guillotined heads. But Greuze's paralytic was a preparatory study, not a finished work in its own right, for a large-scale, morally edifying painting, *La Dame de Charité* of 1775 (Museé des Beaux-Arts, Lyon). Later nineteenth-century painters such as Jacque, forerunners of the Impressionists and pioneers of a freer and looser way of applying paint, would have had no difficulty in seeing the portraits as finished works in their own right. Yet they might, especially the kleptomaniac, still be taken for studies—Viardot indeed described them as such, "études", in his letter to Blanc.

The difficulty lies perhaps in how few encouraging signposts—beyond their forbidding titles, evoking a long-defunct diagnostic category—they offer the modern viewer. With the exception of the military man again, the sitters are without identifying attributes. The gambler has a crutch; otherwise Géricault does not in any obvious way seem to lead us into a game of social or political complicity. From the Renaissance onwards, conventional subjects of portraits (those of Moroni or Titian, for example) invariably convey a sense of their relationships to their costumes, accessories, and settings, even to their own poses, from pride and ownership to, less usually, degrees of awkwardness or ambivalence. With the exception of the military man Géricault's sitters seem quite unconcened about how they might be seen, in themselves and in their relationship with the human and physical environment. But perhaps what Géricault was registering was a common human response to being interned and disenfranchised: the sitters' withdrawal from contact may have been strategic, the only authentic or dignified option open to them.

Nor is there the satisfaction of allegory. Do the portraits harbour distant echoes of the Seven Deadly Sins? Envy (*invidia*) was certainly one of them; the envious woman also seems full of Wrath (earlier epochs might have identified her as a witch). Greed (the kleptomaniac, the gambler), Lust, possibly combined with Sloth (the child abductor), and Pride (the military commander) are also present. But it is a distant echo; there is no sense that Géricault was engaged in anything as programmatic, nor self-consciously playing with such iconography and inviting us to join in a guessing game. Might the paintings be satirical? "Only the insane take themselves quite seriously," quipped Max Beerbohm (2015), and the sitters do indeed seem to do take themselves very seriously. Are they mirrors of a "serious", self-absorbed, self-seeking society? Yet they are absent, as if drugged. They are not court or holy fools innocently showing up the world's follies and errors. Where Goya, drawing on Hogarth and eighteenth-century British caricature, more clearly corralled the mad for purposes of satire in his painting *The Madhouse* of 1816 (Real Academia de San Fernando, Madrid), not even Géricault's man in his military grandeur can readily be taken to have any ironic or satirical intent. He is who he is.

Yet he and his companions come to us with no names. Being insane in the eighteenth and nineteenth centuries might indeed mean losing one's name, perhaps, if one were of a certain class, because family honour was at stake. It was also perhaps because in madness "one existed only for oneself ... [one] no longer had to know others or to situate oneself in relation to them" (Gauchet & Swain, 1999, p. 112). We have only the archaic diagnostic label of "monomania", and this hardly works the usual defensive magic of such labels, to protect us from anxiety. Far from shielding us, it underlines and seems to confirm the sitters' gripping otherness, the impossibility of their joining us on our familiar terms. How far do those eery titles still frame our responses? "Those faces look lived in," said a colleague who had never seen or heard of the paintings before and did not know what they were called. It is hard to sustain phenomenological innocence for long, however, once the titles are known, or even once it is known that these are "portraits of the insane". The titles invite us to view the figures as objects of a dispassionate, appraising, Foucauldian gaze, with which, especially those of us who are psy-"clinicians" of one persuasion or another, we may be familiar from other settings—invitations to distance ourselves. Later in the nineteenth century, at the hospital which almost certainly housed Géricault's two female sitters, the Salpêtrière, Jean-Martin Charcot famously commissioned photographs of his hysterical patients, sufferers under the diagnostic banner which superseded monomania. Do the portraits perhaps have no more to teach us than they taught Charcot, that is, as some historians have claimed, *"how to make images produce already established readings*, how to institute a system of perceptual codes" (Isaak, 1996, pp. 159–160; Isaak's italics)? Is the *Monomane de vol's* wild hair merely a visual trope of madness that will flourish, for example, on Jack Nicholson's head in Milos Forman's *One Flew Over the Cuckoo's Nest?* The sitters, with the possible exception of the military man, seem unlikely to have had much say in how they were to be represented. Were they posed and framed so as to conform to an idea of what madness looked like, and to show how it might be recognised?

For all their degrees of motility they also seem frozen in time—as if the regime in power in the early 1820s, the restored Bourbon monarchy, in its attempts to put the clock back to the years before 1789, had at last succeeded in making time stand still. They breathe the atmosphere of the post-Revolutionary period. Like characters from Balzac, the sitters might be its residue, surviving human figments from the Revolutionary and Napoleonic dream. They are, like the records Laure Murat trawled her way through in the Parisian hospital archives for her remarkable book on early psychiatry, "ledgers … of social wretchedness" (Murat, 2014, p. 18).

Contemporary accounts suggest that there was an increase in delusions of military grandeur under Napoleon (Miller, 1940–41, p. 163, note 1). It is very possible that the monomaniac of military command thought, like some of his fellow patients, that he *was* Napoleon—who was, after all, a usurper himself, and widely believed, not just by his enemies, to suffer from pathological delusions of grandeur. In which case the *Monomane du commandement militaire* would have been "a usurper who thought he was a usurper, and a megalomaniac who thought he was a megalomaniac". The portraits open up the broadest questions about identity, subjectivity, and projection,

> … within the gap between *being* and *imagining, believing, claiming,* or *thinking oneself to be.* Hence the real question might not be the classic Who am I? but rather Am I who I think I am? (Murat, 2014, pp. 107, 134).

It is the question constantly faced by both psychoanalyst and patient, and it could hardly be expressed more clearly.

* * *

The canvases have left biographers and historians with questions since they were first unrolled (Athanassoglou-Kallmyer, 2010, p. 189; Clément, 1868; Miller, 1940–41); the darkness of their backgrounds is both literal and figurative. There is no documented record of them before 1863. The question of what they are, exactly, was present from the moment of their discovery. Even their dating is controversial. That Géricault's friend the alienist Georget was somehow involved is generally accepted, although even this has not been universally agreed (see Kromm, 2002, p. 238). Even the titles are questionable; we only have Lachèze's word for it, as reported by Viardot, nearly thirty-five years later. Lachèze was not an alienist; was he merely calling up the dominant category of the day? Why were the canvases rolled up? Had Lachèze forgotten his paintings, was he just not very interested in them, or was there some other reason? Let us start by turning to Géricault's life.

CHAPTER THREE

Géricault, a biographical sketch

> Simple and modest, he admired others and was rarely content
> with himself. He did not *pose*, he did not think of playing a role,
> and one would be tempted to believe he did not know himself.
> If he thought of posterity, it was to fear that he had not deserved
> his name to be recorded. In studying this unostentatious life,
> I had on more than one occasion to ask myself if I were not the
> plaything of an illusion, if it really was a great artist I had before
> my eyes … (Clément, 1868, p. 1, translated for this edition)

So wrote Charles Clément, who published the first book-length
biography of Géricault in 1868. The Géricault myth is familiar, and the
painter became a key contributor to the mythology of the Romantic
artist: passionate, troubled genius, ahead of his times, his life, like those
of his British contemporaries Keats, Shelley, or Byron, cut tragically
short. His career as a painter lasted only eleven years, and we need to
keep in mind that the man before us never stops being a young man,
still finding his way, at times reaching his goals with supreme flair and
acumen, and at times floundering, without, in either instance it would
seem, a particularly developed self-awareness or secure sense of himself. We know that he brought determination, courage, and energy to

29

virtually everything he did, and that he was also subject to crushingly severe emotional crises; that he revelled in his own physical and athletic prowess, admired Michelangelo above all other artists, and, as a mere glance at his work will confirm, loved horses. "Horses, as he himself confessed, just made him crazy … so much was his passion for the horse akin to madness," recalled a cousin in the 1860s. "An excellent rider, his greatest pleasure was to gallop wildly through the countryside" (Athanassoglou-Kallmyer, 2010, p. 15). A startling film, *Mazeppa*, made in 1993 by the French horse-trainer Bartabas, is a colourful and highly visual account of him, and it centres on this passion (Bartabas & Karmitz, 1993). There is not much dialogue, but the film does contain the line: "Learn from your horses, not your mentors." It is suggestive of the nature of Géricault's originality; while he certainly had mentors and learnt from them, what distinguished him was his willingness to give himself over to his subjects and as it were be taught by them, to the point of self-effacement, or even self-loss. He was extraordinarily open to the emotional currents around him.

Jean-Louis-André-Théodore Géricault belonged to a generation that was almost but not quite too young to participate in the Napoleonic adventure. Born in Rouen in 1791, he was the son of a lawyer who had married into a bourgeois family, the Caruels, with profitable interests in the tobacco trade. There can be little doubt that the family wealth rested on slavery. In 1795 or 1796, after the fall of Robespierre and the triumph of the bourgeois revolution, the Géricaults moved to Paris, where the family tobacco business thrived. Géricault attended the prestigious Lycée Impérial (known after 1815 as the Lycée Louis-le-Grand, Delacroix's school, and then Baudelaire's). He was the sole inheritor of his mother's fortune when she died in 1808; from the age of sixteen he was guaranteed an independent future. Determined to be a painter, he entered the studio of the history and battle artist Carle Vernet. Vernet was fascinated by English sporting art, and no doubt Géricault's passion for horses was stimulated by his experience at the studio, particularly through his friendship with Vernet's son Horace. He then studied with Pierre-Narcisse Guérin, a pupil of Jacques-Louis David and one of Napoleon's official painters. Guérin's studio meant systematic exposure to the grammar and syntax of Davidian neoclassicism, the dominant idiom in French art. He was to meet Delacroix there some years later. He copied in the Louvre; like any contemporary he would also have been steeped in the martial imagery of Napoleonic propaganda, particularly that of its leading exponent, another former student of David, Antoine-Jean Gros.

If Géricault had military dreams of his own, they were perhaps, like Stendhal's Fabrice von Dongen's in *The Charterhouse of Parma*, "fed on showmanship and mirages" (Athanassoglou-Kallmyer, 2010, p. 30). In 1811, as was common practice for bourgeois families who did not want their sons conscripted, Géricault's father paid for a substitute to go in his place. This young man, who was called Claude Petit, died of his wounds the following year, probably one of the 300,000 French casualties of the Russian campaign. How much might the guilt accruing from this, and maybe too from his family's implication with slavery, have driven him? It certainly seems that he was touched by a recognition that art was the expression of something more material than "mere figmentary inspiration" (Brown, 1938, p. 61). In the social and political climate of the Empire a young artist of Géricault's education and disposition could hardly fail to be aware of art's relationship to the rest of society, and to want somehow to develop it.

In 1812, aged twenty-one, in the year of the retreat from Moscow, Géricault received a gold medal for his first exhibit at the Salon, the breathtaking, life-sized *Chasseur de la Garde* now in the Louvre [Illustration 6]. The painting shows a cavalry officer from the most renowned regiment of Napoleon's Imperial Guard, his sabre drawn, resplendent in the furs and gold brocade of his full uniform, turning in the saddle of his rearing horse to look behind him. The picture straight away presents us with uncertainties and ambiguities. It exerts both a forward and a backward pull. Is the rider advancing or in retreat? He seems to be charging into the inferno of battle. But his sabre is in the defensive position. Is the painting really the thrilling portrayal of heroism that it might at first seem? Or is there irony in the splendid uniform, a suggestion, as one biographer has put it, that the French, including perhaps the painter himself, required a substitute for thwarted masculinity? In this reading the officer is a Romantic anti-hero, "melancholic and doomed, the imaginary creation of a generation nurtured by … Goethe's *Werther* and Benjamin Constant's *Adolphe*" (Athanassoglou-Kallmyer, 2010, pp. 32, 37–38).

The painting registers the sheer scale and bloodiness of Napoleonic ambitions. With its dramatic composition, it shows a moment of extreme physical and emotional tension, of danger and excitement. Yet there is also, in the face of the officer, a strange, reflective stillness. "He turns towards us and thinks," wrote the great nineteenth-century historian Jules Michelet (cited in Michel, Chenique, & Laveissière, 1991, p. 30). What could he be thinking about other than death? In reality the sitter for the painting, a lieutenant named Alexandre Dieudonné, was also to perish in Russia, in December 1812. How much was Géricault identifying with him: Théodore/Dieudonné ("gift of God")? In one sense, the lieutenant is an exemplary Cartesian, demonstrating his aliveness, his continuing being, in his act of thinking. Yet a terrifying sense of the transience of the moment underlines the limits to thought's mastery.

In the Salon booklet the picture was, interestingly, listed as a portrait (it was given as *Portrait équestre de M. D. ****) (Michel, Chenique, & Laveissière, 1991, p. 338). Dieudonné's face, which occupies a tiny proportion of the canvas but sits at the top of an oval formed by the curve of the sabre and the haunch, belly, and head of the horse, is indeed the focal point; the painting's listed title underlines the fact that it is a picture of a unique individual, not a generic hero. Like the protagonists of the great proto-republican moral constructions of David and his school—*The Oath of the Horatii* (1784) [Illustration 7], *The Death of Socrates* (1787), and *The Lictors Bring to Brutus the Bodies of His Sons* (1789)—he is an individual at a moment of crisis, and like them he is thinking. But the Horatii, Socrates, and Brutus were engaged in internal, moral struggles, winning over their ordinary human frailties and family sympathies in favour of higher interests (patriotism, duty, going off to die for one's ideals); they are wholly identified with their own conscious resolve. The possibility of the Horatii being swayed by feeling or the irrational is hived off to the right, into a group of resigned, repining women. Dieudonné exercises no such total mental control. He may be master of his immediate feelings and of a powerful horse, but this is as far as his power to dictate events and outcomes goes; the horse too, with its terrified eye, is in the thrall of forces beyond its control; one of its most vulnerable parts, its anus, is in the foreground of the picture.

The thinking being in this most un-Davidian composition embodies not the triumph of reason and reflection but their crisis. There is no rational ordering of space in depth, but rather deliberate confusion and spatial indeterminacy; the composition is built on a system of sweeping curves rather than right angles; if there is a logical narrative unfolding, its conclusion, horsemen and cannon in a conflagration, is far removed from any Davidian statement of stoical dignity. Even dead, David's Marat, painted in 1794, occupied the centre of a decorously spare and mathematically proportioned world; if this, in David's mythologising, was a world partly of the austere Marat's creation, the living, sensitive, and reflective Dieudonné, with whom Géricault invites the viewer to identify, gathers around him destruction and chaos. It is, moreover, a world of materiality as well as mentality, of heat and energy, weight and musculature, the sensuality of fur and fabric, metal and flesh; it embraces too the possibility of erotic, homoerotic, engagement. Géricault's Rubens-like reliance on colour, so often noted by contemporaries and historians as a distinguishing feature of Romantic as opposed to Classic art, was itself of course based on the idea, espoused by Romantics from Stendhal to Delacroix to Baudelaire, that colour speaks directly to the emotions and the body. Géricault introduced, into the mainstream of French painting of contemporary events and moral and political pre-occupations, precisely that recognition of the power of the embodied drive—that which links us to the animal like a rider to his horse—which Freud was also to formulate at the heart of his understanding of the human subject.

Géricault was disappointed that in spite of his medal the painting was not bought by the state, and even more disappointed at the relative failure of his next large-scale, single-figure military "portrait", *The Wounded Cuirassier*, to have a big impact at the Salon of 1814, which was delayed until November due to political events: Napoleon had abdicated in April and departed into exile. Monumentality and emotion now take the place of furore and dynamism, as the art historian Gregor Wedekind has observed. Both paintings use a single figure, and a solitary horse, to represent historical forces "manifested as individual psychological experiences and physical postures" (Wedekind, 2013, p. 28). Each registers a different moment of check and reversal.

On the return of the Bourbon king Louis XVIII in 1814 Géricault enlisted in the mounted National Guard, shortly to become the alto-gether more swaggering "Les Mousquetaires du Roi". The subsequent period of Napoleon's brief return to power after his escape from Elba, the so-called Hundred Days which ended at Waterloo, was the subject of a novel of 1958 about Géricault, *La Semaine Sainte*, by the poet, com-munist, and former Surrealist Louis Aragon (Aragon, 1958). Géricault accompanied the king on his flight from Paris; his motives during this short military interlude have been a matter of speculation for historians. Was he, as some early biographers felt, swept along with other mem-bers of the *jeunesse dorée* on a kind of costumed equestrian pleasure trip

(Blanc, cited in Michel, Chenique, & Laveissière, 1991, p. 271)? Aragon makes use of the fictional Géricault in his novel to explore a maturing self-consciousness: his character comes to a sense of the lives of others, and to an awareness of time and history, in a way that opens the possibility for fuller political as well as artistic engagement. Géricault indeed seems, to the end of his life, to have been in search of purpose and belonging. He was also from now on increasingly subject to periods of serious depression, alternating with manic activity. "Géricault was quite dark in mood; he rapidly exhausted enjoyment and pleasures and often sought to escape from himself," recalled a contemporary; he was subject to "moral lassitudes that at times laid him low" (Michel, Chenique, & Laveissière, 1991, p. 271, translated for this edition).

Having failed in 1816 in his candidature for the prestigious Prix de Rome, the means by which aspiring artists could study in Rome at the French Academy, he travelled to Italy anyway. He was also attempting to escape from a hopeless love affair, with his maternal aunt Alexandrine-Modeste Caruel, who was to bear him a son in 1818. In Rome, often profoundly depressed, he produced another image of the relationship between horse and man, the *Race of the Riderless* or *Barbieri Horses* [Illustration 8], in one version of which, against a stage-like background which directly alludes to a Davidian neoclassical schema, the horses' energy is barely contained by semi-naked men who prevail, if they do, through sheer physical force as much as mind.

In Italy Géricault was "transfixed by the way Michelangelo gave life to sculpted bodies" (Jones, 2000). For his older contemporary Stendhal, who published his *Histoire de la peinture en Italie* in 1817, Michelangelo was the exemplary man of his time: Michelangelo drew from antiquity, but infused it with the passions and concerns of his era (Athanassoglou-Kallmyer, 2010, p. 56). The nineteenth century, wrote Stendhal, after two centuries of passion repressed and stifled by codes of etiquette, "… is going to restore these passions to their rightful place. If a Michelangelo were born in our century, imagine what heights he might achieve!" (1817, cited and translated in Stendhal, 1973, pp. 80–81). Géricault may never have read this passage; he was nevertheless casting himself in the role of a modern, Stendhalian Michelangelo. "The truly gifted individual does not fear obstacles, because he knows he can surmount them; indeed … the fever they are able to incite in his soul … often becomes the cause of the most astonishing productions," he wrote in Italy, in an unpublished manuscript. In their explosive physicality and earthy sexual explicitness, his drawings took Michelangelo's *terribilità* to new domains of experience. A painting of a Neapolitan tarantella is a "modern dance of Dionysian maenads" (Athanassoglou-Kallmyer, 2010, pp. 59, 60); and while the riderless horses and related works showing cow herders, cattle markets, and butchers evoke a kind of timeless antiquity, they also resonate with a determinedly modern heroism: they show heroes of and from the people, as Gregor Wedekind has put it. Géricault followed Stendhal in seeing history taking place in an embodied present (Wedekind, 2013, p. 32). And the social climate could intoxicate. It was, as Byron explained in a letter to John Murray in 1820, "not English, nor French—nor German", but generated by

> a people—who are at once temperate and profligate—serious in their character and buffoons in their amusements, capable of impressions and passions, which are at once *sudden* and *durable* … Their best things are the Carnival balls—and masquerades—when every body runs mad for six weeks … (Byron, 2015, pp. 351–352)

Italy was also a seat of political liberalism, and in the throes of resistance to Austrian domination. It is not known how far Géricault, like Stendhal, may have had friends or acquaintances among patriotic liberals or members of the secret societies—the largest and most influential being the Carbonari—which proliferated in the first two decades of the century. In the minds of Stendhal and others, political resistance was associated with assertions of freedom from the constraints of rule-bound, backward-looking classicism in the arts, in other words with nascent French Romanticism. What is clear is that from around 1818 until his death in 1824, "ideologically militant Romanticism", in his biographer Nina Athanassoglou-Kallmyer's phrase, became the driving force behind Géricault's art (Athanassoglou-Kallmyer, 2010, p. 86).

By late November 1817 Géricault was back in a politically restless Paris. Waterloo, and the Congress of Vienna that settled the new balance of European powers, had signalled the victory of something quite new in Western history, "a coherent and coordinated project for a return to the past"; at the same time it marked the end of the period it hoped to revive (D'Eramo, 2015, p. 79). Bourgeois Parisian youth, as the painter Henry Scheffer recalled in his middle age, "nursed defiance and hatred" against the restored royal dynasty, "which was to become a general eruption in 1830. From the first years of the Restoration young people wanted to outstrip popular feeling and make it explode. Conspiracies and secret societies took shape ..." (cited in Chénique, 2006). Indeed, the generation that was coming of age around the end of the Empire, whose parents' destinies had one way or another been shaped by the Revolution, was probably the first in modern history to be conscious of itself as a potential political force, and an embodiment of hope for the future (see Spitzer, 1987). It was also, as Balzac noted in *Illusions perdues*, a generation of young men "who did not know what to do with their strength ... [and] harnessed it not only to journalism, political conspiracies, and the arts, but to strange excesses as well ..." (Balzac, 1837/1843, p. 463, cited and translated in Spitzer, 1987, p. 259).

Géricault moved into 23 rue des Martyrs, on the hill up to rural Montmartre, the house of a Colonel Bro, who was a veteran of the Grande Armée and the landlord of Géricault's father. He was now next door to Horace Vernet and his family, and found himself among a little community of friends. He painted Vernet's daughter Louise, with a knowing, quizzical look and a faintly sinister cat; he made enigmatic, unsentimental portraits of the daughters of his friend the architect Pierre-Anne Dedreux, and their gaze too seems to indicate a nascent sexual and social consciousness, all the more disquieting for its refusal to be dominated by the viewer's (Germer, 1999, pp. 86–90).

Liberal and Bonapartist sympathies united the group of friends. The liberalism of this circle is likely to have embraced a range of political views. "Liberal" did not necessarily equate with anti-monarchist and republican; under the Restoration republicanism could not be professed except clandestinely. Nor did "Bonapartist" necessarily mean republican. To be liberal might simply mean identification with the royalist opposition, and support of the rights enshrined in the Charter of 1814 to which the monarchy was supposedly bound (Berthier, 2008, p. 51 n. 1). It might mean being a plotting, anti-royalist Carbanaro, like Henry Scheffer and his brother the painter Ary. It might also mean opposition of a more unfocused kind, and this would probably describe Géricault's position in 1817/1818. Bro's house and Vernet's studio, like, a little later, Corréard's bookshop "At the Wreck of the Medusa" (Barnes, 1989, p. 127), was a magnet and safe haven for young radicals from across the spectrum. Vernet, who was a freemason and Carbanaro as well as a fashionable man-about-town, commemorated his studio in a painting of 1820 that is packed with Napoleonic emblems. Among its cast are former Napoleonic officers, a horse, and Géricault's students in boxing gear; in the centre the fashionable and well-connected Vernet himself, palette and brushes in one hand, fences with a former army lieutenant. There are no women present; the painting is a self-conscious and unequivocal celebration of the masculine. It makes explicit the heady conjunction of oppositional politics, sporting skill, and a profession of painting outside the walls of the academy, that coloured Géricault's emotional and social landscape.

Between 1818 and 1820 he produced a series of lithographs on Napoleonic themes, scenes of military life and of the plight of the thousands of veterans on half-pay—*demi-soldes*—who still lived in inactivity and often semi-penury in the capital, and could be perceived as threats to the regime and to public order (Athanassoglou-Kallmyer, 2010, p. 90). Lithography allowed rapid responsiveness to events. As oppositional artists such as Raffet, Charlet, and Lami grasped, it lent itself perfectly to reflections of the public mood, and to attempts to create it. Napoleonic themes in particular were "metaphoric vehicles for libertarian impulses worldwide, for *la liberté des peuples*" in Latin America, Spain, Greece, or Haiti (ibid., pp. 95–96). Géricault produced lithographs depicting the South American revolutionary generals José de San Martin and Manuel Belgrano, and made drawings for a project commemorating the short-lived triumph of liberalism in Spain in 1820. There are drawings showing the black Haitian warriors of Saint-Domingue, former slaves fighting French colonial forces for the island's independence (ibid., pp. 106, 113). He projected a painting based on the murder of a liberal *député* and former Jacobin by one of the gangs of right-wing extremists who roamed France during the so-called White Terror of 1816–17 (ibid., pp. 119–122); in the early 1820s he was to plan a major work dealing with the slave trade.

In 1817 Géricault found the subject that would define his career, in a contemporary event with tremendous resonances for his liberal circle and for the public at large. On 2 July 1816 a French frigate, the *Méduse*, ran aground off the coast of Senegal; the incompetent captain was a royal appointee. A large raft was built to carry 150 or so crew members and soldiers to shore, but after a few days it was cut loose from the boats towing it. Géricault's monumental painting *The Raft of the Medusa* [Illustration 9], to which he devoted most of the following year, dramatised the horrible fate of the raft's passengers, who during thirteen days adrift in the Atlantic witnessed or joined in both a violent mutiny and acts of cannibalism. He made numerous oil sketches, depicting different phases of the survivors' travails, adjusting and refining his composition until it seemed to him to subsume their experiences with maximum visual and emotional impact. Géricault met with some of the ten survivors, notably the ship's surgeon, Henri Savigny, and carpenter, Alexandre Corréard, whose published account of events threatened to bring down the government. Géricault had discovered a subject that allowed him to explore some of the major preoccupations of his life: abandonment, suffering, survival, and extreme physical and emotional states. The painting's political dimensions extended beyond the indictment of official corruption. The three black figures on the raft, one at the very apex of the pyramid of bodies, waving to a tiny, distant ship, signalled outrage at France's continuing involvement with slavery; for the flotilla led by the *Méduse* aimed to wrest formerly French Senegal away from the British, with the aim of resuming the lucrative trade in slaves (Wedekind, 2013, pp. 37 etc.). There may have been an echo of personal guilt. Géricault also aimed to bring to his painting an awareness of history-in-the-making, and to bring to life in the viewer a whole gamut of recognisably modern and familiar feelings, from hope—a sail on the horizon—to despair and grief, all to be registered in the body and the face. In the foreground, almost sharing the spectator's physical space, was mourning: the expression of the father who cradles his dead son speaks of inconsolable bereavement.

The undertaking was also the opportunity for a definitive engagement—a measure of Géricault's artistic ambition—with the European, Renaissance tradition and, through the construction of a large multi-figure painting with powerful moral echoes, with the dominant neoclassical current in the nation's art. To modern eyes those polished bodies resembling ancient sculptures can seem at an unaccountable remove from the real horrors Géricault was evoking; we must consider, however, that for contemporaries classicism in painting carried the stamp of the highest, ethical authority; the neoclassical body, in the words of Milton Brown, carried "an aspect of 'goodness' as well as 'beauty'" (Brown, 1938, p. 26). "Beauty is truth, truth beauty," wrote Keats in 1819, who was undergoing his own political awakening (Motion, 1998, pp. 394 etc.). At the Salon of 1819 the *Raft* competed for attention with a strange and insipid work by David's former pupil Girodet, *Pygmalion et Galatée*; the *Raft* was an attempt to re-establish the more vigorous outlines of the Davidian revolutionary tradition.

In 1820 Géricault and Vernet visited the exiled David in Brussels, a mark of their allegiance to the artist who had almost single-handedly established these outlines. But Géricault also loosened the "restraining tenets of classicism" (Brown, 1938, p. 80) to allow a far greater range of physical posture, an enrichment of classical body language beyond a conventional rhetoric of gesture and expression; he extended the depth and range of its emotional possibilities, testing it to its limits. He painted both as a *citoyen* and a *philosophe* (Brown, 1938, p. 17): the painting was to be readable as a statement about humanity in general, which would speak to ordinary people; it also plumbed humanity's madness, and, in spite of everything, the individual and collective will to live.

None of this, for Géricault, was just academic. His work on the vast canvas involved a monk-like commitment; he shaved his head, and attempted to parallel and recreate the experiences of the survivors for himself, to gauge them in his own person [Illustration 10]. He studied the suffering of dying patients at the Hôpital Beaujon near his studio, visiting the dissecting room and the morgue, and making oil studies of severed limbs and the heads of the recently guillotined (Eitner, 1982, p. 245) [Illustration 11]. The purpose of these visits was not only to study the hues of dead and decaying flesh; they were also part of a pro-gramme of deliberate self-mortification and identification (Eitner, 1972, 1982; Miles, 2007); he sought, in Julian Barnes's phrase, "to infiltrate the air with mortality" (1989, p. 126).

The "still-life" paintings of severed limbs are literal *natures mortes*, body fragments and limbs seen close-up, larger than life, and, as Gregor Wedekind observes, bathed in a flickering light which works "to permit life to show through even in death, the unscathed person in the body fragment ... horror is not rescinded, but it is imbued with a strength and beauty" (Wedekind, 2013, p. 93). For Delacroix the still life with arms and legs in Montpellier was simply "the best argument for the Beautiful as it ought to be understood" (Delacroix, 1980, p. 644). Like all students at the Ecole des Beaux-Arts, Géricault attended anatomy classes conducted by professional surgeons; but he brought to his studies a particular fervour and sensibility, an eye for clinical detail, and an interest in how skeletal and muscular structure determines external form; life may not be what immediately meets the eye. More than fifty drawings, some large-scale, of human and animal anatomy by him exist, and he was as dispassionate as a surgeon: his friend Alexandre Dumas reported him observing an operation on his own back with the help of a mirror, in furtherance of a wish to make "an anatomical study on a live individual" (Athanassoglou-Kallmyer, 2010, pp. 152, 196–197).

The heads of the guillotined also reflect a particular interest in the last glimmering of the spirit at the moment of death. The paintings register "the monstrous contrast resulting from the fact that what was once still living should now be forever dead" (Wedekind, 2013, p. 132). A taste for horror and the uncanny was, of course, linked to the English fashion for things "Gothick" and to the spooky, other-worldly stories of E. T. A. Hoffmann; the theme was taken up by Nodier and Balzac among other French writers, and formalised by Victor Hugo in the preface to his play *Cromwell* in 1827—a signal of rebellion against both classicism and political conservatism (Athanassoglou-Kallmyer, 2010, pp. 118–119). It had subtler and more powerful effects too. Disgust undermines sympathy, which is linked to the viewer's secure position at a remove from what he sees; the barrier between imagination and reality, nature and art, is removed, and the possibility of our remaining detached is undermined. Disgust in the way Géricault exploited it generates a closer and challenging approach to reality, making it as hard as possible for the viewer to evade (Wedekind, 2013, pp. 132–139).

The physician's clinical gaze combined with that of the politically astute philanthropist (ibid.): the heads may have served yet another purpose. Several of Géricault's friends and members of Vernet's circle, including Vernet himself, were members of a liberal grouping called the Société de la Morale Chrétienne (one of many such societies, pressure groups and *cénacles* that formed themselves during the period), which was committed to Greek independence, prison reform, and the abolition of the slave trade. They also advocated the repeal of the death penalty. Alongside the argument that the guillotine was an engine of repression—an astounding number of executions took place under the Bourbon Restoration, sometimes three or four a week—was the view that it was also an instrument of torture, a cause of unspeakable suffering; there was reputable medical opinion to attest that the head continued to feel and perceive for some moments after its separation from the body (Athanassoglou-Kallmyer, 2010, p. 148). In what minimal circumstances, Géricault might have been asking himself, can life and consciousness subsist?

Critical opinion, across the spectrum from conservative to liberal, understood the *Raft* as an attack on conservatism in all its aspects. Géricault was both disappointed and perturbed by public and critical reactions, and troubled by the notoriety the painting unleashed; he threw himself, already exhausted, back into a dissolute, partying life (Eitner, 1982, p. 242; Michel, Chenique, & Laveissière, 1991, p. 286). In the autumn of 1819 he became very disturbed while in the countryside near Fontainebleau, with delusions of persecution: he seems to have thought the Seine boatmen were conspiring to kill him. "Pauvre raison humaine!", remarked the former schoolteacher he had gone to visit (Wedekind, 2013, p. 186). He was brought back to Paris by his friend and former comrade in the Royal Musketeers Auguste Brunet, who may at this point have consulted his friend, a fellow member of the Société de la Morale Chrétienne, the alienist Etienne Georget. One plausable view is that Géricault was persuaded to spend some time in the clinic of the second most eminent specialist in insanity of the day, Jean-Etienne Esquirol, where Georget also lodged (Sells, 1986). His friends recounted that Géricault felt nothing was worthwhile; he was repulsed by the sight of his earlier canvases and had the *Chasseur* and the *Cuirassier* rolled up (Athanassoglou-Kallmyer, 2010, pp. 152, 196). The fact that there had been madness in his family may have added to his fears: his maternal grandfather, and an uncle on his mother's side, had died insane, in 1779 and 1805, both in institutions (a cousin also later died insane, as possibly did his own son, the offspring of his relationship with his aunt (Eitner, 1972, pp. 245, 322 note 13)).

The following year he travelled to London and Dublin, exhibiting the *Raft* commercially, in the hope of lucrative returns. In this as in other respects, he was in touch with a new development—the rapid growth of an art market, in which artists might see themselves as entrepreneurs, producing for unknown buyers (Brown, 1938, p. 29). He was in London from April to June, visited the aged David in Brussels in November, and was in London again from January until December 1821. In the winter of 1821 he was ill, possibly with pneumonia, and had sciatica, which made riding painful; in early 1822, back in Paris, he was once more suffering from physical and emotional exhaustion. There were rumours of a suicide attempt: he may have tried to kill himself by inhaling the fumes of a coal stove (Athanassoglou-Kallmyer, 2010, pp. 154, 220–221). Suicide did perhaps fascinate him; in 1818 he had drawn Bro's friend General Letellier on his deathbed after he had shot himself in despair.

The British architect and archaeologist Charles Cockerill, another member of the Société de la Morale Chrétienne, was worried by

Géricault's sickly looks when he met him in London in 1820. He was also struck by his

> modesty so unusual and remarkable in a Frenchman, his deep feeling of pity, the pathétique [sic], at the same time vigour, fire and animation of his works ... profound and melancholy. Sensible singular life—like that of the savages we read of in America. Lying torpid days and weeks, then rising to violent exertions. [R]iding tearing driving exposing himself to heat and cold violence of all sorts. (Athanassoglou-Kallmyer, 2010, p. 154)

Indifference to heat and cold, and to violence, was still popularly attributed to the mad.

In a letter to Dedreux from London in February 1821 Géricault gave this account of himself: "I work a lot in my room and then, for relaxation, wander about the streets which are so full of constant movement and variety ... I am getting wiser by the day" (ibid., p. 153). He filled sketchbook pages with drawings of the faces of passers-by, some overtly caricatural. In a new climate of anglomania in the early 1820s, which touched Delacroix and Stendhal, Géricault felt the particular appeal of English artistic freedom; the hierarchy of the genres in painting, so strictly respected in France, was shaken up in Britain through the imperatives of the art market (ibid., p. 15). He learnt from the relative informality and spontaneity of English portrait painting, and from the shift, discernable in English bourgeois portraiture from Hogarth onwards, from a focus on appearance to an interest in the inner life (Fornari, 2013, p. 163). He was impressed by Constable and Turner, and by animal painters such as Ward and Landseer; he painted horses at work as well as racing at Epsom.

Horses also re-enacted the great social disparities of British life (Athanassoglou-Kallmyer, 2010, p. 162), and Géricault's eyes were now more than ever open to the vulnerability of an impoverished and brutalised underclass. He drew the hanging of three of the Cato Street conspirators in May 1820, a group of radicals who, in 1819, following the Peterloo Massacre and subsequent repressive legislation, had planned to assassinate the cabinet. In a series of thirteen lithographs, like the elderly Goya a few years later in Bordeaux, Géricault turned his attention to the urban poor: a beggar, a paralytic woman—wearing a straitjacket, maybe the victim of paralysis-inducing madness (Athanassoglou-Kallmyer, 2010, p. 171)—street sweepers, itinerant musicians, a farrier, waggoners. The images avoided anecdote or didacticism (Wedekind & Hollein, 2013, p. 37); their call to the viewer relied solely on what they showed; they assumed an audience in solidarity. The English journey was a landmark in his life and his development as an artist. "In Italy he had learnt how to reconcile his academic training with naturalism. England enabled him to get rid of the last vestiges of classicism" (Athanassoglou-Kallmyer, 2010, p. 180).

Still fired with entrepreneurial enthusiasm on his return to France in late 1821, Géricault invested in a factory for the production of artificial stone; his friends the Dedreux brothers also had a share. The scheme failed, leaving him in debt. He lost another large part of his fortune in August 1823, to a dishonest broker. His health continued to falter, and he seems to have become increasingly reckless (ibid., pp. 180, 186). It is, I believe, most likely that the portraits of the insane were made now, in late 1822 or early 1823. Others argue for 1819, when he may have been a patient in Esquirol's *maison de santé* (ibid.; Kromm, 2002). Eitner notes their richness of colour and touch; in spontaneity and format they are like a "common English type of informal portraiture", especially that of Thomas Lawrence, whom Géricault had met in London, and all this would place them after the English and Irish journeys. Probably, to judge by the clothing of the sitters, they were made in the winter, but whether at the start or the end of the year is not known, although Eitner (1982, pp. 248–249) persuasively suggests the earlier part of the year. If it was at the end, Géricault would have been recuperating, no doubt in considerable pain, from the effects of three serious riding accidents earlier in the year. These were followed by now almost permanent illness; syphilis seems one possibility. One of his falls had resulted in a tubercular abscess on his spine, possibly Pott's disease; he had fallen on his back, his lower vertebrae catching a knot in his trousers (see for example Du Camp, 1882–1883, pp. 230–231). Agonising operations, including the one he observed himself, ensued. In 1823 he was declared bankrupt, and may have tried to kill himself again. He died aged thirty-two in January 1824.

* * *

A quasi-religious aura developed around him after his death. For the Salon of 1824, Ary Scheffer depicted the deathbed scene as a sort of Lamentation, with ministering doctor (Biett) and weeping friend (Pierre-Joseph Dedreux-Dorcy, who, like Scheffer himself, had been a student at Guérin's studio). The painting was widely reproduced as a lithograph in the 1830s, the cult image of a Romantic martyr. Géricault's death mask and the plaster cast of his hand were also venerated relics. His reputation as a liberal and Bonapartist did not however endear him to the new king, the reactionary comte d'Artois, who became Charles X in 1824. His body had no permanent resting place until the reign of Louis-Philippe, the so-called bourgeois monarch, for whose regime the Napoleonic legend was an ideological keystone. In 1841, the year after Napoleon's remains were returned to France and interred in the Invalides, a monument was finally erected on Géricault's grave at the Père Lachaise cemetery. The current monument, conceived by the sculptor Antoine Etex in the early 1880s, shows the artist not in the full health and vigour on which he prided himself, but haggard and suffering, his brush and palette nevertheless firmly in his hands. The first biographies appeared in the 1830s and '40s, and established his nineteenth-century reputation. In 1843, Thoré declared naturalism to be the key to Géricault's modernity, and naturalism was to be the immediate future. In 1846 Michelet singled him out, in a lecture on national identity in support of the Polish revolution, as a genuinely French artist, and in a subsequent lecture, before he was sacked from the Sorbonne as a dangerous radical, he used the *Raft* to illustrate France itself as corrupt and adrift (Athanassoglou-Kallmyer, 2010, pp. 211–216). Such was the Géricault no doubt who inhabited Viardot's mental landscape in 1863.

CHAPTER FOUR

Madness in modernity, 1656–1789

That mad *people*, at any particular historical juncture, had their own personal stories can usually, as Laure Murat has pointed out, only be read between the lines of things written by other people who had power over them: edicts, legal or ecclesiastical documents, medical or philanthropic reports (Murat, 2014, pp. 15, 20). What physicians (or priests or witch-hunters) made of madness, and what those designated as suffering from it made of it, might be "two sides of a pattern that ultimately fails to cohere" (Ingram, 1998, p. 9). There are a few, surprisingly few, powerful visual images—Hogarth, Goya—but they are generic, contain multiple figures, and typically serve satirical rather than documentary agendas. We have to work to imagine what the person historically classed as insane might really have been like to meet, although there are occasional, tantalising glimpses, the eighteenth-century encounter between the philosopher Diderot and the nephew of Rameau, for example (Diderot, 1805). There is a distinguished handful of fictional and real individuals, from the Old and New Testaments and from Greek tragedy, and from the late Renaissance onwards (Don Quixote, Lear, Smart, Cowper), some of whom, like Gérard de Nerval (1855) or less fêted figures like Hannah Allen or James Tilly Matthews (Ingram, 1998; Jay, 2012), left their own accounts of their experiences.

Perhaps the discourse of "madness", as Murat wrote, "can no more be circumscribed than can the discourses of 'the people' or 'homosexuality'". At the end of his life Michelet regretted his failure to make the tongue of "the people" speak (Murat, 2014, pp. 20–21)—as if it were singular or monolithic. Géricault's portraits are silent (and the blame for their silence can hardly be laid at his studio door); their sitters left no testimonies which might tell us something about their individual lives—their families, their work, their friendships, their pleasures, their losses—and we know nothing about what happened to them next. Their portraits, nevertheless, suddenly propel them onto the historical stage and into our imaginations as flesh and blood people in their own rights, anonymous, certainly, and portrayed by someone else, but not performing, not putting on a display, not, apparently, making anyone else's point for them, or indeed any special point—at least, not in any way that is immediately obvious. For it is suffering more than illness that seems to be written all over their faces. How did they come to find themselves here, represented in this way?

* * *

The beginnings of a modern, institutionalised madness can, in Michel Foucault's account, be specifically traced to the mid-seventeenth century, and in particular to the absolutist France of Louis XIV and an edict of 1656 which marked the start of what Foucault called "the Great Confinement": the establishment of the *hôpital général*. In the middle of May 1657, begging and alms-giving in Paris were banned, and beggars and vagrants, who made up about a tenth of the city's population, and were seen as a kind of plague, were rounded up by paid enforcers and disappeared from the streets overnight. The *hôpital général*—a collection of prison-hospitals in all but name—consisted of a number of affiliated insitutions, including Charenton, Saint-Lazare (which originally housed lepers), and the Hôtel-Dieu (the oldest charitable foundation in Paris, a hospital which did retain a medical function); their role was to accommodate the poor, the disabled, the insane, orphans, abandoned children, the destitute, the elderly, prostitutes, and women deemed to be of easy virtue. At the heart of the new system were Bicêtre, for men, a former orphanage originally built as a military hospital, on the southern outskirts, and the Salpêtrière, south of the river to the east, for women. The Salpêtrière, constructed on Louis XIV's orders of 1656 by the architect Libéral Bruant, stood on the site of a former gunpowder factory; it was expanded in 1684. Both institutions were staffed by lay rather than religious personnel, but they were organised on principles established by St Vincent de Paul: division into "good" and "bad" poor. At the Salpêtrière women who could work, prostitutes, women confined by royal *lettres de cachet* or convicted by tribunals, and the mad, were confined in separate quarters; for the latter it was the dreadful *basses loges*, where they were treated as animals (Foucault, 1967, pp. 70–71; Hazan, 2010, pp. 16, 153; Woshinsky, 2010, pp. 162–163).

"The Great Confinement" marked the beginnings of the establishment, in Foucault's analysis, of the restrictive conditions necessary for the unimpeded future functioning of the clinical gaze. It coincided with the rupture between subject and object instituted in philosophy by René Descartes. Following Descartes, object was irrevocably separated from subject; it was what perceiving subject required in order to define itself: the evaluating "I". Reason could thus more clearly be distinguished from unreason. Awake or asleep, wrote Descartes in the first of his *Méditations métaphysiques* in 1647, we are subject to mistaken impressions and to dreams, but never so much that we cease to doubt and question the truth of what we are experiencing. This is just what the mad do not do; while the sane wake up, the mad remain imprisoned in falsehood and illusion. Madness lost the untamed, revelatory status and the critical and tragic dimensions it had retained from classical and medieval times; if previously the mad had been kept at a remove, cast adrift, or left to wander, they were at least a feature in a shared landscape. The imprisonment of which Descartes spoke was, for Foucault, contiguous with the literal incarceration of the mad during the age of reason, and it marked the final break with the ancient possibility of intercourse between reason and unreason (Murat, 2014, pp. 12–13).

Other historians contest the real impact of "the Great Confinement". Records show that the total number of incarcerated people in the seventeenth century, as a proportion of the overall European population, was relatively small (Scull, 2015, pp. 125–127; Shorter, 1997, pp. 5 etc.); it makes even less sense to imply a pre-industrial, pre-capitalist Golden Age in which the mad frolicked happily on village greens. The reality, in tightly knit, tradition-bound village and small town communities, was that looking after the mad was by and large a domestic and family affair; the deviant and useless, if they were too violent and uncontainable to be allowed to run loose or wander the roads, were tied or chained up in isolated rooms, pigsties, pens, stables, or outhouses. Where there was public provision, stark contrasts existed between what Protestant and Catholic countries might offer:

> ... monastic orders had specialised in psychiatric nursing, but in Protestant countries the Reformation had disbanded these. In some cases, national institutions developed, as in the Holy Roman Empire; in others, notably in Great Britain, the mentally ill languished in the poorhouse until the eighteenth century. (Weiner, 1993, pp. 251–252)

Across Europe, those whose families could afford the fees might be installed in private madhouses, which proliferated in the eighteenth century and could be anything on a spectrum from comfortable homes to dungeons. In cities, asylums had also existed since the Middle Ages, often with custodial rather than therapeutic functions. Bethlem in London ("Bedlam") was founded in 1247 as the Priory of St Mary of Bethlem, in Moorfields, and provided, like other religious foundations, "asylum" for small numbers of travellers, pilgims, and the destitute, including the insane; by the reign of Henry VIII Bethlem seems to have been entirely given over to the insane (Shorter, 1997, pp. 2–5). In Germany *Tollhäuser*, fools' houses, had also been in existence since the Middle Ages. In *ancien régime* France, alongside *dépôts de mendacité* (workhouses), *hôtels dieux* (hospices), and the *hôpitaux généraux*, there were also the notorious *maisons de force*, in which the insane, who might include commercial or amorous rivals or unwanted family members, could find themselves confined against their wills on the strength of a *lettre de cachet*, a letter with the royal seal signed by the king or a royal minister, which permitted incarceration without trial or appeal. The wealthier mentally ill thus confined might be cared for by the Brothers of Charity and similar orders, "under forms of strict but thoughtful supervision which predate the 'supervised freedom' inaugurated by the Quaker William Tuke at the York Retreat in the 1790s" (Weiner, 1993, pp. 251–252). In all the above the medical doctor's role was merely one among other caring, supervising, or custodial functions.

Up to 1800 and beyond, treatment, where it was administered at all, remained much as it had been since classical times, whether offered by monks, nuns, physicians, attendants, or family members, under the umbrella of medical or folk wisdom. It might consist in attempts to restore balance by evacuating malign spirits or unhealthy humours, or to relieve the brain of the pressure of nervous fluid, and there were various means for this: the use of purgatives, emetics, sudorifics or diuretics, or bleeding, with the help of a scalpel or leeches. There was also a whole technical paraphernalia, which continued to be central to the therapeutic-disciplinary arsenal well into the nineteenth century. Mechanical devices such as rotating machines used centrifugal force to achieve the expulsion of harmful fluids, through every orifice. Baths might be used for soothing, water showers or ducking stools to shock or discipline. Far from inviting universal enlightened censure, such devices and practices were by-products of Enlightenment rationality and its inventions and discoveries. Thus from the late eighteenth century, electric currents might be applied to the skull. Is it any wonder that patients like James Tilly Matthews imagined elaborate "influencing machines" (Jay, 2012)?

Opium ranked highest among drug treatments, most commonly, from the late eighteenth century, in the form of its alcoholic extract or tincture, laudanum, although it might also be mixed with anything from mercury to cayenne pepper. Other treatments, most in use since antiquity, included stramonium (extract of thorn-apple), henbane, and belladonna, all with a supposed calming effect; camphor (as a sedative), castoreum, musk, asafetida, valerian, mistletoe, and peony (antispasmodics), rhubarb, senna, jalap (purgatives), ipecac, and tartar (emetics), hellebore, mandrake, and theriaca Andromachi (Venice treacle, for sundry purposes). Paracelsians—followers of the sixteenth-century Swiss empiricist Paracelsus—favoured copper ammoniate and zinc oxide as antispasmodics; further stimuli to evacuation included cauterisation, moxibustion (processed mugwort burnt onto the skin or applied with needles), blistering, and the application of setons (fine cords tied around raised areas of flesh) and cups, as close to the brain as possible. Actual brain surgery—trepanning (removal of a section of skull), or the insertion of thin, sharp instruments through the temples—had also been part of the therapeutic armoury since ancient times. "One concludes", writes Dora Weiner, "that the absence of doctors from eighteenth-century asylums may in fact have promoted the patients' recovery!" There were Enlightenment minds, Diderot's for example, which would have agreed (Quetel & Morel, 1979, pp. 67–140; Weiner, 1993, pp. 254–255).

Conditions in hospitals/asylums/prisons in the late eighteenth century could be unspeakable. At the "terrible Bicêtre—haut lieu de l'horreur carcérale", criminals locked up for correction mixed with the scabied, the venereal, prostitutes, delinquents, and the mad, who, regarded as incurable, received no treatment of any kind (Quetel & Morel, 1979, p. 150). In 1788 the chronicler Sébastien Mercier called it

> a dreadful ulcer on the body politic; a deep, wide suppurating ulcer that can be viewed only by averting your eyes. Even the air of the place, which you can smell from eight hundred yards away, tells you that you are approaching a place of force, an asylum of wretchedness, degradation and misfortune. (cited in Murat, 2014, p. 47)

But at least Bicêtre had a fresh water supply and because of its higher location was open to fresh breezes. The Salpêtrière, low-lying, by the Seine, subject to flooding, was surrounded by stagnant water, open sewers, and rubbish dumps; the river Bièvre passed right by it, carrying waste from the Gobelins tapestry factory. When water levels rose in winter, the cells of the *basses loges* became

> a refuge for a swarm of huge rats which during the night threw themselves on the unfortunates confined there and bit them wherever they could reach them ... mad women have been found with feet, hands and faces torn by bites which are often dangerous and from which several have died. (from a report cited in Foucault, 1967, p. 71 and Quetel & Morel, 1979, p. 152)

Things could be as bad elsewhere. At the York Asylum (not to be confused with the Quaker York Retreat, which was opened partly in reaction), patients were raped and murdered (Scull, 2015, pp. 192, 418 note 10). The physician Johann Christian Reil, founder of a humane and distinctively modern psychotherapeutics, had this to report on the state of the incarcerated mad in Germany in 1803 (the passage was cited by Esquirol, writing on French asylums, in 1819):

> These unfortunates are thrown like common criminals into the bottoms of pits, into cells where a humane eye never penetrates. There we let them rot in their own filth, weighed down by chains which tear their limbs. Their physiognomy is pale and haggard, they wait only for the moment which will bring their misery to an end and cover our shame. They are displayed for public curiosity,

and greedy attendants show them off like rare beasts. These unfortunates are thrown together pêle-mêle; terror is the only means
known for maintaining order among them. Whips, chains, cells are
the sole means of persuasion adopted by employees who are as bar-
baric as they are ignorant. (Quetel & Morel, 1979, p. 143, translated
for this edition)

Less violent and frenzied inmates were, in the eighteenth and early
nineteenth centuries, simply crammed together into chambers or wards
of varying sizes. Those considered dangerous were routinely chained to
walls and beds (Foucault, 1967, pp. 71–72).

The fate of women was especially dire. The degradation of female
inmates as reported by a visitor to the Salpêtrière at the end of the
eighteenth century could not contrast more powerfully with the idealised image of genteel, bourgeois womanhood which was developing
in the same period:

> ... madwomen ... chained like dogs at their cell doors ... separated
> from keepers and visitors alike by a long corridor protected by an
> iron grill through which food is passed, together with the straw
> they sleep on; rakes are used to clear out some of the filth that sur-
> rounds them. (Foucault, 1967, p. 72; Ussher, 1991, p. 65)

Such practices, as Foucault pointed out, owed their violent intensity
less to a desire to punish or correct than to a persisting image of the
animality of the mad. This did not so much connect the mad person
to "the familar strangeness", the "menacing marvels" of the animal
world, as establish her or him "at the zero degree of his own nature",
irredeemably dispossessed of what was specifically human (Foucault,
1967, pp. 72–74). Mad men and women were thus considered to be
immune to extremes of cold and heat, and this idea was still current
into the nineteenth century; protected from disease, the mad, in this
vision, were curiously restored in their animality to the kindness of
nature (ibid., pp. 74–75).

Displaying the insane for an entrance fee—a usual way in which
keepers sought to meet the expenses of their upkeep—was a practice
that seems to have survived until as late as 1815 at Bethlem, "a favou-
rite excursion spot for Londoners, who came to stare at the madmen
through the iron gates" (Alexander & Selesnick, 1966, p. 114). (Do we

see survivals, or revivals for the digital age, in TV programmes such as Louis Theroux's *By Reason of Insanity*, BBC, 29 March and 10 April 2015?). In France, until the Revolution, it was common for Parisians to make Sunday excursions to Bicêtre, where the keepers put the inmates through their tricks, making them dance and do acrobatics with the flick of a whip (Foucault, 1967, pp. 68–69). By the end of the eighteenth century the mad were also encouraged to exhibit and display each other; where the jesters of the Middle Ages and Renaissance had mimed madness, "now it was madness itself, madness in flesh and blood, which put on the show", most famously at the asylum at Charenton, under its director Coulmier, where, to public mockery, the mad played both actors and spectators (as re-imagined in 1963 by the German playwright Peter Weiss, in *Marat-Sade. The Persecution and Assassination of Jean-Paul Marat as Performed by the Inmates of the Asylum of Charenton Under the Direction of the Marquis de Sade*). Madness, wrote Foucault, "became pure spectacle, in a world over which Sade extended his sovereignty and which was offered as a diversion to the good conscience of a reason sure of itself" (ibid., pp. 69–70).

"There is no surer indication of attitudes towards madness than the instinctive popular tendency to set it up as a curiosity," wrote Gauchet and Swain—the mad person thus as irredeemably external, a figure in whom no one could recognise anything of him- or herself. The shift away from making a spectacle of insanity "is one of the most reliable indicators we have of the content and impact of the psychiatric revolution" (Gauchet & Swain, 1999, pp. 260–261). In the years around 1800 the iconography of madness was defining a new and unsettling thematic register (Stoichita & Coderch, 1999, p. 147), most manifestly perhaps in the work of Goya. We might wonder, with Gauchet and Swain, about just what it was that was unsettling. In their engagement with Foucault, Gauchet and Swain propose that what was taking place was a reduction rather than an increase of alterity and "alienness", of a sense of the otherness of the other. This sense was, rather, coming home to roost in the individual, to reside in the viewer as much as in the object of the spectacle. Rather than there being foreclosure of the possibility of dialogue between reason and unreason, unreason was coming to be felt at the core of the observing, speaking subject himself.

* * *

The grounds on which it was possible to think about the relationship between psyche and soma were also changing. The nature of this relationship taxed inquirers then as now; Roy Porter was hardly exaggerating when he wrote that it presented "intractable, even maddening, dilemmas". The eighteenth-century British physician William Heberden spoke of our "great ignorance of the connexions and sympathies of body and mind" (Porter, 2002, pp. 60–61). Not all philosophers and medics were as undogmatic.

Divine or demonic explanations of insanity did not disappear with the dawn of modernity—exorcisms were still being carried out in the late eighteenth century and beyond—but they began to lose their force among the educated and enlightened, as physical, material accounts of the human being gained credibility; religious fervour itself could qualify as madness (ibid., p. 31). If, as Descartes maintained, consciousness is the same as rationality, then insanity and irrationality could only come from the body. For post-Cartesian, post-Newtonian philosophy, "mental illness" was a contradiction in terms; illness had to come from the body, since the soul was "definitionally inviolable"; the mad person must thus be "a disordered sensory-motor machine". The influential Dutch philosopher and physician Herman Boerhaave (1668–1738), for example, regarded as the founder of physiology, maintained that the mistaken beliefs characteristic of madness were the symptoms of physical disorder; melancholic lethargy, for example, resulted from evaporation of the volatile elements of blood and thickening of its earthy residue (ibid., pp. 124–125). Treatments followed suit. In the first half of the eighteenth century disorders of the "nerves" became all; the nervous system was key to the understanding of illness and the nerve-doctor the authority to whom appeal must be made; madness was, in the words of a governor of Bedlam, a "Machine out of Tune", a Newtonian universe in disarray (see Scull, 2015, pp. 162 et seq., 171–172).

One direction in which the emphasis on the power of the nerves led was that taken later in the century by Franz Anton Mesmer and his followers; in a sort of meeting between the Catholic exorcist and the Newtonian physicist, Mesmer claimed to have discovered invisible electric and magnetic forces in the form of a vital fluid which ruled the human organism and mind; the power of "animal magnetism" could be manipulated and redirected by the skilled magnetist (Scull, 2015, pp. 181 etc.). If mesmerism was, in its way, an aspect of a wider theoretical transformation, a "psychological turn", around the middle of the century, the philosophy of John Locke provided firmer and more fertile ground (Porter, 2002, pp. 127 etc.). In his *Essay Concerning Human Understanding* (1690) Locke had suggested that far from containing innate ideas, as Descartes had maintained, mind was a blank sheet of paper, subject to sensory experiences which gave birth to ideas and, by the power of their association, to new and more sophisticated combinations of ideas; madness, he suggested, resulted from a failure in this process, leading to ideas becoming falsely associated. It was a process that could, through education, be put back on the right tracks; Locke's ideas, powerful as they were in their implications for education in general, also opened the way to a new therapeutic optimism. They were given more radical form in Enlightenment France by the *philosophe* Etienne Bonnot de Condillac, friend of Rousseau and Diderot; in his *Traité des sensations* (1754) Condillac concluded that all human knowledge, passion, imagination, and memory derived from the senses. In a famous image he pictured man as a statue endowed with a soul but no innate ideas; everything about him is derived from what he can experience from the outside through his five senses and the associations between them, in a process that Condillac carefully analysed sense by sense. We are shaped by environment, in ways that depend on the vividness with which we are able to feel; the senses can, however, be trained. Condillac effectively replaced "rational constructs with sense experiences and reflection" (Audi, 1999, pp. 170–171), for he also thought, crucially, that mind has the inherent creativity to compare and analyse the sense impressions it receives. This was to have major future implications.

In Britain the Lockean view of mind was developed by the philosopher David Hartley, who also put the association of ideas derived from sensation at the centre of an account of human memory and emotion. This was taken up in medicine by the Scottish physician William Cullen, a friend of David Hume and Adam Smith, and a leading figure of the Scottish Enlightenment. Cullen's model of madness remained grounded in physiology: it was the result of "some inequality in the excitement of the brain" and nervous system; he coined the term "neurosis" to describe this. This led the patient to produce false judgements and "disproportionate emotions", and it was these, and the behaviour flowing from them, that the physician must address. Madness was a mental disorder, albeit coming from the body; Cullen's achievement, in the forefront of European thinking, was to reintegrate the mental into medical discourses (ibid., p. 128).

This called for a case-history approach and the systematic observation of the ideas and behaviours of individual patients; an interest in the journey of the unique individual was paralleled in the contemporary growth and popularity of the novel. There is also a sense, in the later eighteenth and early nineteenth centuries, that madness was a topic of some urgency. In Britain, it was at the forefront of the public mind thanks not only to the madness of King George III, who first succumbed in 1788, but also to that of other political figures: both William Pitt the Elder, in the 1760s, and his rival Charles James Fox, in the 1780s, suffered collapses into insanity. Satirists such as James Gillray and Thomas Rowlandson, following in Hogarth's footsteps, found in Bethlem the perfect setting for their strictures (Arnold, 2009, pp. 136–137). Madness was perceived as a scourge of the age, rather perhaps—although such comparisons must always be treated carefully—as cancer is today: both a product of the pressures and corruptions of modern life and an offence to people's ideas of what an advanced civilisation should be able to master. In the late eighteenth century the physical world was, after all, being transformed in all kinds of ways—canal building, massive urbanisation, the creation of new plants and animals through selective breeding—and the idea that anything was immutable was open to unprecedented questioning (Scull, 2015, p. 159). All this lay behind an outpouring of publications on insanity after around 1770, most, like Cullen's former student Thomas Arnold's *Observations on the Nature, Kinds, Causes and Prevention of Insanity, Lunacy or Madness* (1782–86), or Alexander Crichton's *An Inquiry into the Nature and Origin of Mental Derangement* (1798), basing themselves on Locke's philosophy of mind and informed by the hopes for cure it engendered.

If madness was a mental disorder, and mental conditions were acquired not inherited, it was the mind that the physician or guardian must address. There ensued "a remarkable marriage across enlightened Europe between psychological thinking and reformist practice in what has been called 'moral therapy'" (Porter, 2002, pp. 129–130). Cure was to be effected through humane management, although, as we shall see, this did not preclude judicious use of fear. Force was, except as a last resort, to be avoided, and the key therapeutic agent was the character, expertise, and moral example of the doctor himself. The spread of the moral treatment was a Europe-wide development, albeit with regional variations. In London William Battie (1703–1776), a critic of the inhumane regime of Bethlem, had stated as early as 1758, in his *A Treatise on Madness*, that management did much more than medicine (ibid., p. 102). Francis Willis, William Cullen, and John Haslam were active in this respect in London; probably the most influential philanthropic initiative, quickly to have an international reputation, was that of the Quaker William Tuke (1732–1822), who opened the York Retreat in 1796. In France were Jean Colombier and Jacques Tenon; at Chambéry in Savoie there was Joseph Daquin (1732–1815), whose *Philosophie de la folie* was published in 1791, and at the Providence Hospital in Avignon a Dr Gastald, who took up a post at Charenton in 1797. In Italy, presiding over the Bonifazio Hospital in Florence, Vincenzo Chiarugi (1759–1820) published his *Della pazzia in genere e in specie* (1793, rapidly translated as *On Insanity*, in three volumes, in 1793–94); Chiarugi posited a mediating "sensorium commune" between body and mind, intellect, and senses, another psychological solution to Cartesian body–mind dualism. Geneva had Abraham Joly (1748–1812), Prague Jan Theobald Held (1770–1851), and Moscow, a little later, V. F. Sabler (Postel & Quetel, 2012, p. 152; Weiner, 1993, p. 255). In Halle in Germany Johann Christian Reil (1759–1813), who probably first coined the term *Psychiatrie*, in 1808, advocated psychological treatment in an extraordinary book of 1803, *Rhapsodien über die Anwendung der psychischen Kurmethode auf Geisteszerrüttungen* (*Rhapsodies on the Application of the Psychic Cure Method to Mental Disorders*). Reil maintained that while madness might have physical causes, it could also be the result of a loss of *Gemeingefühl*, of a basic feeling of things hanging together, thus a response to social conditions. He also however recommended a formidable and ingenious array of strategies, stimulating excitement, terror, and pain in a kind of therapeutic theatre, in order to subject the patient to the asylum director (Weiner, 1993, p. 269). Alongside works by Johann Christian August Heinroth (1773–1843) and Karl Wilhelm Ideler (1795–1860), who paid special attention to the life of the emotions and recommended cure by "psychic self-activity", Reil's *Rhapsodien* is a key text of what might legitimately be termed a "Romantic psychiatry" (Ellenberger, 1970, pp. 211–213).

The eighteenth century's interest in the relations between mind and body, psyche and soma, represent more, however, than just a "psychological turn" within medicine. "Body" was something undeniably shared by all humanity, while the Cartesian *cogito* might seem to reinforce a conclusion that "mind" was the possession of a privileged elite. "Je pense, donc je suis": only in so far as I can show that I can think can I be conceived of as human in the fullest sense, to exist as a "je", a grammatical and existential subject. Only in thinking do I prove my existence to myself, and if the other does not give evidence that he too thinks, then I have no reason to think of him as a subject too, even, necesarily, as a fellow human (a position skewered with extraordinary prescience by Jonanthan Swift in the Houyhnhnms passages in *Gulliver's Travels*). Only in rational discourse do I have proof of fellow subjecthood. Hence the development and prestige, in the seventeenth and eighteenth centuries, of academies, clubs, learned and "corresponding" societies, salons, and masonic lodges, indeed of the whole Enlightenment drive towards social perfection and individual cultivation, self-mastery, and excellence (as wonderfully manifest in *The Magic Flute*).

Mind–body debates worked to undermine and break down such convictions, and had an implicit levelling, democratising effect. We are all possessed of "animal spirits" or, in the eighteenth century's formulation, of "nerves". If madness had meant having no mind, to be mad was to be virtually all animal and body, so it was easy to conclude that the mad would be impervious to heat and cold, voracious, driven, and likely to be dangerous, if not merely bovine—indeed it would be irrational to conclude otherwise. The more closely theoretical links were drawn between body and mind—they were being drawn above all by physicians, and the nature or veracity of these links is less important than the fact that they were being made at all—the harder it was to see anyone, not just the mad but also people of colour, women, the deaf and disabled, as beyond the pale, excluded from human discourse and community. Such developments were given particular stimulus, and found a special resonance, in Revolutionary and post-Revolutionary Paris.

CHAPTER FIVE

The Revolution, Cabanis, Pinel, the asylum

Citizens and public health

In August 1789, within weeks of the fall of the Bastille, the social and administrative foundations of the old regime in France were being comprehensively dismantled. The National Assembly, which now held most of the reins of power and had transferred them from the royal court at Versailles to Paris, was undoing royal, feudal, and church powers and privileges; in passing the Declaration of the Rights of Man on the 26th, it proclaimed the principle of equality: social equality, equality before the law, equal liability to taxation, and equality of opportunity. At a stroke the nobility lost its automatic monopoly of the higher offices of state. "All citizens", decreed the Declaration, "without distinction of birth, are eligible for all offices, whether ecclesiastical, civil or military" (Hardman, 1998, p. 112).

A special commission of the Assembly, the *Comité pour l'extinction du paupérisme*, was investigating the problem of beggary and poverty, in order "to apply ... to the protection and preservation of the non-propertied class the great principles of justice decreed in the declaration of the rights of man and in the constitution" (Miller, 1940–41, p. 154). But the Declaration of the Rights of Man included no provision for

59

health. Within a few months, thousands of poor, sick, and unemployed people were petitioning the Assembly, prompting the committee's chair, the liberal aristocrat the duc de la Rochfoucauld-Liancourt, to proclaim that society owed the poor and ill assistance that was "prompt, free, assured, and complete". The *droit d'assistance* assured free medical treatment for anyone unable to pay for it, and it was to be "avilé ni par le nom, ni par le caractère de l'aumône" ("debased neither with the name nor the character of almsgiving") (Miller, 1940–41, p. 154). For the first time in Western history a nation faced an obligation to compensate for the disadvantages, including the physical illnesses and imperfections, of its citizens (Weiner, 1993, pp. 3–4, 276). Patients were being transformed from Christians relying on Christian charity, "meekly accepting pain and suffering", into citizens, in the full meaning of the word, with duties as well as rights: to maintain, once they were recovered, hygiene in their persons and homes and, later in the decade, after the Consulate had set up a public health programme, to protect common resources such as water, be vaccinated, and report health hazards to the police. Old distinctions between the respectable and the undeserving poor disappeared in the face of Equality (Weiner, 1993, pp. 6, 8).

The Revolution's emphasis was on *santé*, the "most perfect state of life" in the *Encyclopédie* definition. Although enlightened physicians such as Joseph Ignace Guillotin, professor at the Faculty of Medicine and a member of the Assembly, played key roles, the early revolutionaries seem to have had more time for the word *santé* than they had for *médecine*, which had overtones of élitism and charlatanism; they preferred *officier de santé* to *médecin*. Over the next few years a *Comité de Salubrité* or *Comité de Santé* was the main point of referral, where health and medical matters were concerned, for successive governments. The promotion of *santé* was consistent with the Enlightenment ideal of the perfectible New Man; it contributed to the light of a new historical dawn (time itself began anew in 1792, Year I of the Republic), and the future realisation of the ideals of social perfectibility and progress towards general happiness espoused by the *philosophes* (Crosland, 2004, pp. 229–244; Gauchet & Swain, 1999, pp. 64–67).

The mad, however, presented special difficulties. Were they a public health problem or, unable to take up their duties as citizens, a legal problem, a threat to public morals and safety? Were the insane in confinement victims of injustice and tyranny, or of illness? Or might they be fugitives from justice, enemies of the people, merely feigning madness? It is important in this context not to *over*estimate the democratic views of the French revolutionaries, who, in the words of one historian, "inherited from the *philosophes* a hostility to what they saw as the superstition, ignorance and conservatism of the bulk of the population" (Black, 1991, p. 179). Philanthropy towards the mad, particularly the pauper mad, did not always preclude suspicion or disdain.

On 27 March 1790, the Assembly abolished the infamous *lettres de cachet*, the most potent symbols of tyranny after the Bastille itself. For Robert Castel, the history of psychiatry in France really begins here. Indeed, for Castel, the whole modern problematic of madness, with its tension between treatment and questions of civil liberties and human rights, unfolds from this point. With the collapse of royal authority, a former balance of powers for dealing with the insane, between royal administration, legal system and family, was upset. It was now left to judges, local administrators, and doctors to fill the gap. A long process of transformation in the practices of each of these agencies and their relations with each other was required. In 1785 Louis XVI's finance minister Jacques Necker had commissioned a review of the kingdom's hospitals and prisons and, for the first time, there followed official state recognition of the competence of doctors to organise a system of general assistance for the mad, with simultaneous acknowledgement of the mad as ill. Yet medicine did not yet have a monopoly over questions of health nor, certainly, of insanity. Only when it succeeded in establishing itself as the keystone of the system, in the late 1830s in France, was a new equilibrium possible (Castel, 1976, pp. 9–10, 61–62). The promotion of a *philosophical* medicine, distinct from former, less well-reputed medical practices, was a key part of this process.

Following the Declaration's assertion that no person could be deprived of his freedom arbitrarily and without legal cause, the various institutions of the *hôpital général* were also to be abolished, or, perhaps more accurately, "examined for their utility within the context of the new laws" (Dörner, 1981, p. 119). The picture of actual provision for the indigent insane within and without the *hôpital général* was never clear-cut or one-dimensional. The National Assembly's committee on *lettres de cachet* was quick to assume the innocence of those jailed on the pretext of madness, and decreed in March 1790 that each inmate should be questioned by a judge and visited by a physician; they were surprised when the Commissioners reported back that Charenton, still run by the Brothers of Charity, was a model institution and that each of the eighty-seven inmates was patently mad, with not one asking to be released (Weiner, 1993, p. 253).

Other Commissioners, from the Poverty Committee, one of whose members was the *philosophe* and doctor Pierre-Jean-George Cabanis, were tasked with inspecting the two huge custodial institutions of the *hôpital général*, Bicêtre and the Salpêtrière, and they were generally appalled by what they found (consider that these were men probably accustomed to the perfumes and fine fabrics of the late rococo *salon*). The duc de la Rochefoucauld-Liancourt reported that:

> The house at Bicêtre contains paupers received for nothing, paupers en pension (and there are four different kinds of pension), men and children who are epileptic or scrofulous, paralytics, mad people, men locked up by order of the king, or by decrees of Parliament, and these are both with and without pension; children arrested on the orders of the police or sentenced for theft or other offences, children without vice or illness admitted gratis; finally men and women treated for venereal disease. So this house is at one and the same time hospice, Hotel-Dieu, pension, hospital, detention centre and house of correction. (cited in Castel, 1976, pp. 88–89, translated for this edition)

The disturbed and deranged made up a considerable proportion of the population; the 200 or so insane men housed in Bicêtre, in their own ward, seemed, however, under the management of a superintendent named Jean-Baptiste Pussin and his wife, to be decently fed and accommodated. They had, for example, single beds, rather than sleeping three or more to giant cots as was the practice elswhere in the institution; they were treated with kindness, and, provided they were not violent, allowed to wander in the courtyards in the day (Weiner, 1993, pp. 61, 253).

Conditions at the Salpêtrière, nearly twice as big as Bicêtre, were worse. The Salpêtrière was in fact a city within a city, made up of about forty-five buildings with streets, squares, gardens, and a church (Ellenberger, 1970, p. 93). By the late 1780s it was probably the largest hospital in the world. It could accommodate a staggering 10,000 people, together with some 300 prisoners. An earlier official report, of 1788, Jacques Tenon's *Mémoires sur les hôpitaux de Paris*, had described the Salpêtrière as populated by "agitated madwomen, imbeciles, epileptics, paralytics, the blind, cripples, patients with ringworm, all kinds of incurables, children with scrofula ...". In 1790 it contained 6,704 destitute women, mostly aged and infirm, alongside 1600 abandoned girls, from toddlers to teenagers (some accommodated above the hospital pigsty and dissecting room), and about 100 prostitutes, who were frequently paired with convicts and forcibly expatriated to New France. A special section housed some 100 indigent married couples. In the centre of the hospital was the prison, comprising a common jail for the most unruly inmates, a reformatory for less serious offenders, a lock-up for women brought in under *lettres de cachet*, and maximum security cells for branded criminals. Five hundred and fifty women were chained, in new purpose-built cells. The hospital incorporated a profitable market, selling everything from bread, brandy, and wine to pig-feed, for the hospital also raised its own livestock. The Commissioners of 1790 concluded that the despotism of the officials was "more active, harsh and vexatious" at the Salpêtrière; while at Bicêtre, ouside Pussin's ward at least, "Laziness, vice and villainy prevail ... bitterness, envy and corruption permeate the Salpêtrière. Idleness debilitates the men at Bicêtre, forced labour kills the children at the Salpêtrière" (Weiner, 1993, pp. 63–67).

If the asylum/prison was an abomination in enlightened minds, it still had a role to fill which no other agency could—not the family or the community. For "... to the extent that the contractual structure of society becomes generalised, rejection of those who are unable to play by its rules is required. Liberal society and total institution function well as a dialectical pair" (Castel, 1976, p. 80). Cabanis had tacitly understood this as early as 1790; along with like-minded contemporaries he regarded the hospital less as a bastion of absolutism to be eradicated in one fell political swoop, than as a cause of suffering brought about by bad management, therefore amenable to reform: the problem was technical rather than political. Cabanis was also a doctor, but one who had devoted more time to translating Homer and attending parliamentary assemblies and the Enlightened salon of Mme Helvétius, widow of the Swiss *philosophe* Claude-Adrien Helvétius; the emphasis of Cabanis's report on conditions at the Salpêtrière in 1791, "which no humane administration should tolerate", was not just on improving physical conditions but on the need to classify and group the inmates, and establish observational techniques for doing this. He recommended the appointment of an *officier de santé* to each section, with all sections subject to the inspection of a doctor-in-charge. "The asylum provided the specific setting in which its reduction to medical knowledge and its practical management could go hand-in-hand." What were now needed were efficient and humane managers. Cabanis and his colleagues on the *Commission des hôpitaux* found their man in Philippe Pinel (Castel, 1976, pp. 80–85).

Citizen Pinel

Philippe Pinel has traditionally been celebrated as the father of modern psychiatry, which he supposedly founded at a stroke: removing the chains of the inmates of Bicêtre and the Salpêtrière. This mythical view is enshrined in two later nineteenth-century paintings, which are housed at the heart of the medical establishment: Charles-Louis Muller's *Philippe Pinel fait enlever les fers aux aliénés de Bicêtre en 1792* (*Philippe Pinel has the mad freed from their chains at Bicêtre in 1792*), of 1849, in the Académie nationale de médecine, and Tony Robert-Fleury's *Le docteur Pinel faisant tomber les chaînes des aliénés à la Salpêtrière* (*Doctor Pinel striking off the chains of the mad at the Salpêtrière*), of 1878, in the Bibliothèque Charcot at the Salpêtrière-Pitié (for a full discussion see Swain, 1977, pp. 119–171). In fact, the revolution which Pinel brought about centred, as Cabanis had prescribed, on administration and housing rather than questions of restraint; nevertheless Freud was right to call it the most humane of all revolutions (Appignanesi, 2008, p. 59).

Born in 1745, Pinel was the son of a barber-surgeon from rural southwest France; he studied mathematics and theology in Toulouse, and was a seminarian and tonsured cleric before, aged twenty-five, giving up a religious career for medicine. He was a student first in Toulouse, then, in a course of self-directed study, in Montpellier, the gateway through which Arab medicine had entered Europe in the Middle Ages, and France's second seat of medical learning. In 1778 Pinel set out on foot for Paris to establish a professional career. His provincial and social background, together with highly restrictive rules as to who could practise medicine, made this difficult under the *ancien régime*; he wrote in a letter to his brother, in 1778, that he found in Paris only "meanness and scheming". According to his nephew Casimir Pinel, Philippe Pinel was of less than average height, shy and awkward, with an austere manner, a weak voice, and a speech impediment, something he shared with his contemporary Jacques-Louis David (Brookner, 1981, p. 50; Murat, 2014, p. 35). He was to be a beneficiary of the Revolution, if a more circumspect participant than David. He failed three attempts to win a grant for the Faculty of Medicine, was turned down for a royal appointment (as physician to Mesdames, the king's aunts), and toyed with the idea of emigrating to America. He made a living as a private tutor in mathematics and as a journalist, publishing articles and translations; in 1784 he became editor of the *Gazette de Santé*, and got a job as a consultant at one of Paris's eighteen private *maisons de santé* (Weiner, 1993, p. 252), run by a former mirror dealer who, Pinel discovered, had little interest in curing his fee-paying clientèle (Murat, 2014, pp. 35, 73). It was here nevertheless that Pinel began to interest himself in madness.

Was devoting himself to the welfare of the insane merely a shrewd and expedient career move? It probably satisfied more profound emotional and intellectual needs in him too. It seems to have been the theoretical and literary side of medicine that had most engaged him at the start; the death of a friend in 1783, insane "through an excess of enthusiasm for glory" and let down by physical treatments, led Pinel to "renewed respect for the wise precepts of the ancients" (Pinel, 1801, pp. 50–51). He was steeped in the classics, and admired Hippocrates above all ancient medical writers (Postel & Quetel, 2012, pp. 134–135). Like his Greek and Roman predecessors, "… he regarded insanity as a 'natural', not a 'spiritual' problem, and their observations formed the basis of his own theories," as a glance at the opening pages of his famous *Traité* of 1801 confirms. His ideas, in so far as they were revivals of classical knowledge (Miller, 1940–41, p. 155), were in alignment with the ideals of the early Revolution: revolution as re-volution, a coming round full circle to the highest achievements of the classical past (for the politicians, the Roman Republic) (Starobinski, 1979).

This certainly did not mean the mad must be bombarded with a more or less random array of time-honoured physical treatments. Pinel was, as he reaffirmed in the *Traité*'s second edition of 1809, dismissive of "the harsh ordeals of confused polypharmacy managed in an empirical manner". Rather than having blind faith "in a sumptuous array of medicaments", physicians needed to recognise medication merely as an opportune and rare secondary means, for dissections revealed no structural abnormalities which might have warranted physical intervention (Porter, 2002, p. 132; Scull, 2015, pp. 208–209).

Like so many of his class and generation, Pinel had early felt the liberating force of Enlightenment, of Rousseau and the *philosophes*, not least the conviction that the instilling of reason through education could transform society and promote universal justice and happiness: "L'éducation peut tout," wrote Helvétius (Scull, 2015, p. 161). Through his friendship with Cabanis, Pinel became a regular at the "société d'Auteuil", Mme Helvétius's salon, which embraced the thinking of Locke and Condillac and welcomed Lavoisier, Condorcet, and Benjamin Franklin, along with others who were part of the circle later known as the *idéologues* (Castel, 1976, p. 85; Goldstein, 1987, p. 69). Helvétius himself, following Locke, had regarded the sensations as the bases of all knowledge, but stressed too that knowledge is subject to social determination; the passions, and the wish to maximise pleasure and avoid pain, are what point us to seek knowledge in the particular directions we do (Appignanesi, 2008, p. 58; Audi, 1999, pp. 506 et seq., 170–171, 374–375). This was to remain an essential part of the background to Pinel's thinking; his Lockeanism emphasised the affective as much as the intellectual side of psyche (Porter, 2002, p. 132). Here too were roots for the idea that social and environmental factors, not just spiritual, hereditary, or biological ones, play a part in madness.

Contact with this circle confirmed Pinel in his anti-clericalism, which was to be lifelong, and in his insistence on observation and description in medicine rather than on dogma or untested theory. He had translated Cullen's *Institutions of Medicine* and some of the Royal Society's Transactions in the 1780s (Appignanesi, 2008, pp. 57–58); adherence to the values of European Enlightenment also underlay his belief in words as agents for change. He insisted on a medicine grounded in philosophy, without which no principles could exist for arranging observed data (Goldstein, 1987, pp. 50–51, 77); the important medical taxonomies which he produced were based on the principles laid down earlier in the century by the great Swedish botanist Linnaeus. Pinel's major treatise, published in 1801 with a second edition in 1809, was entitled *Traité médico-philosophique sur l'aliénation mentale ou la manie*: the medical and the philosophical are conjoined (Appignanesi, 2008, p. 59). He was a thoroughgoing product of *les lumières*.

There is no reason to suppose that Pinel did not greet the Revolution with enthusiasm, touched by the sense of solidarity and goodwill, the "bliss in that dawn to be alive" famously recorded by Wordsworth. Cabanis and his circle were acutely aware of "the revolutionary character of their new professional opportunity, and current conceptions of liberty and individualism took on specific meaning to them" (Miller, 1940–41, p. 155). Pinel would have been alert to medicine's potential new political influence and social role; an article of 1790 in the *Journal de Paris*, in which he linked the health of the "body politic" to that of "the body of the individual", catches the social optimism and intellectual excitement he almost certainly felt (Murat, 2014, p. 36).

Appointed a municipal officer, a local representative, he attended meetings of the Legislative Assembly, and as an official Citizen under Arms from his district was present at the execution of Louis XVI on 21 January, 1793. Thanks to Cabanis, on 11 September 1793 he was appointed chief physician at Bicêtre, less than a week before the Jacobin Law of Suspects set in motion the period of mass killings known as the Terror. Pinel now predicted nothing but disaster, writing that "as a physician and philosopher, accustomed to meditating on governments ancient and modern, and on human nature, I can foresee only anarchy, factions, and wars that will be disastrous even for the victors ..." (Murat, 2014, pp. 33, 42–43). By June the following year victims were being dispatched by Dr Guillotin's device in batches of fifty or sixty; by July (Thermidor) Robespierre himself, the Terror's chief architect, had been executed.

Was the hospital a sort of asylum for Pinel too, in which he could maintain and practise his ideals, as the original altruistic unity of the Revolution broke down? The hospital can hardly have offered much guarantee of security. Only a year before Pinel's appointment to Bicêtre, on the night of 3/4 September 1792, following the massacre of imprisoned royalists, a mob from the surrounding Faubourg Saint-Marceau had stormed the Salpêtrière and released 134 prostitutes. It also murdered twenty-five madwomen, who were dragged into the streets, some still in their chains (Bosworth, 2001).

Conditions for the insane at Bicêtre were, as we have seen, rather better than elsewhere thanks to the presence of the Pussins. Jean-Baptiste Pussin was not a doctor but an experienced superintendent and manager of the insane. He had agreed with the inspectors in his firm opposition to harsh treatment and physical blows, dismissing attendants who protested against being forbidden to beat inmates. "I have always tried to impress [the patients]," he said, "and even to gain their confidence ... they are the first to protect me." Pussin was a former asylum inmate himself; following a practice common at the time he used recovering inmates for patients' daily care (Weiner, 1993, pp. 256–257). Probably unaware of developments elsewhere, he shared the humane, pragmatic outlook of the "moral" practitioner.

> One must ... treat them with as much kindness as possible, dominate them without mistreatment, gain their confidence, fight the cause

of their illness and make them envision a happier future. I have always fought this illness by psychologic means and thus known the happiness of some favourable results. (ibid., pp. 260–261)

It was Pussin who, by his account, first unshackled patients, at Bicêtre: "… in the month of Prairial of the Year V [May–June 1797], I managed to eliminate their chains (used until then to contain the furious) and to replace them with straitjackets that permit freedom of movement and the enjoyment of all possible liberty without any added danger." Pinel followed three years later at the Salpêtrière, rather later than the myth would have it (ibid., p. 257).

However, without Pinel's taking up the cause of the mentally ill, Pussin's intelligent stewardship might have remained unknown outside the inspectors' reports. It may seem remarkable that a highly educated forty-eight-year-old doctor should apprentice himself to a relatively unschooled superintendent, who was moreover also a former patient. Perhaps however it was more than just a mark of Pinel's democratic good faith (ibid., p. 261). Pinel recognised that he had much to learn from Pussin both as a manager and a man who could tell him what it was like to be a patient. The doctor, in turn, "philosophised" the pragmatism and *savoir-faire* of the lay healer (Goldstein, 1987, p. 77).

The career on which Pinel was able to launch himself after the Thermidorian reaction eventually led to him becoming Napoleon's personal physician. At end of 1794, following a reorganisation of the institutions of medicine, he was appointed professor of internal pathology at the new Ecole de Médecine; his teaching reached hundreds of students, for whom in 1798 he produced a textbook surveying the whole medical field, including madness, the *Nosographie philosophique, ou méthode de l'analyse appliquée à la médecine*. It went through six editions and was every French medical student's guide for a generation (ibid., pp. 264–268). In 1795 he became head physician at the Salpêtrière, a post he retained until his death in 1826.

At the Salpêtrière he found administrative chaos, and requested that Pussin join him. This request was not granted until 1802, and Pussin's arrival elicited acerbic comments from the hospital's comptroller, who wrote in his annual report:

… [Pussin] would like it known that M. Pinel only copied and wrote down his ideas which inspired the various works published by this great physician. Anyone who can tolerate his arguments for ten minutes will be convinced of the contrary … Imagine that such a man could restore their reason to persons who have lost it! (ibid., p. 270)

So much was the climate changing, as Pinel's prestige, and medicine's, rose. The *mythe pinelien* was perhaps already taking shape, and it required a devaluing of Pussin's contribution (see Postel, 2007). For medicine itself was undergoing a revolution in its institutional and social status; respect for practical wisdom was giving way to deference to professional expertise, to be claimed as part of the preserve of the new professional élite (Goldstein, 1987, p. 77). Although Pinel himself did not lose his scorn for physicians whose interactions with patients were limited to fleeting visits (Scull, 2015, p. 208), what the comptroller's comments also reflect is the central role of the head doctor, as Cabanis had recommended. The doctor united in his person several functions, but he was above all a doctor-*philosopher*, a master observer.

Vision and observation

"Observation" was the watchword of science, and the shibboleth of *idéologie* (Lane, 1979, pp. 165, 269). Michel Foucault stressed the institutional power vested in seeing and the central role played by a cultivated vision in the establishment of the new profession (Foucault, 1967, 1973). It was precisely on his acts of observation and classification that the alienist's particular claim to professional identity rested; observation was his defining skill.

Pinel wrote of the "confusion of objects", the "disparate and ceaselessly mobile picture" which confronted him when he was appointed doctor in charge of Bicêtre in 1793, and the "fluctuation of opinions, uncertainty and extreme discomfort" which this produced in him (Azouvi, 1980, p. iii in unpaginated introduction). Here is how he described what the hospital for mad people can be like:

> Only frequentation of insane asylums can give an idea of the difficulties of the service; constantly renewed disgust to swallow, dangers to run, continual vociferations and offensive cries to hear; often, acts of violence to repel; at one moment, the good offices one renders are rejected with savage misanthropy, at another there are treacherous and malicious tricks to be frustrated, basins of excrement ready to be poured over one's head, or even murderous blows

to avoid. How difficult it is for men of little enlightenment and little used to mastering themselves to see only blind and automatic compulsion behind these lapses, that one has no more right to blame the insane than to lose one's temper with the impact of a stone carried along by its own weight! (Pinel, 1801, p. 87, note 1, translated for this edition)

The doctor's experiences were to be mastered through strength of character buttressed and allied with education, experience, and enlightened insight; order was to be brought to violent chaos through the administrative arrangements he and his superintendents put in place. In this way the institution itself was to be transformed; it became a habitable, visual, experimental field in its own right. The well-regulated hospital allowed for observation and classification of its inmates (Appignanesi, 2008, p. 55). Thus an ever-expanding empire of order came into being, and the instilling of order, through regular routine and habits of work and recreation, was integral to treatment itself.

Pinel's work of ordering and classification distinguished melancholics from maniacs, and, crucially, both these categories from congenital "idiots", or those whose condition appeared to be the result of physical malformation or injury; patients were formed into "distinct species". Careful listening, observing, and the compilation of records and statistics, also increasingly delegated to trained attendants, enabled considerable refinement to be brought to the establishment of categories and principles: doctor and attendants sought to discriminate between continuous and intermittent states, looked for patterns of periodicity, noted the beginnings and ends of attacks and what they prefigured, recorded the sufferer's age and the violence of attacks, and established grounds for deciding on degrees of danger from which the hospital and the outside community would need protection. All this worked to underpin the biggest distinction of all: curable versus incurable (Weiner, 1993, pp. 258–260).

The observation of periodicity was central, and it led Pinel to an approach that was new to psychotherapy: to engage the patient in dialogue during periods of lucidity, and establish a relationship of trust, in what would now be called a therapeutic alliance, with the "healthy" part of the patient's personality in order to get a therapeutic process underway (Weiner, 1993, pp. 263–264). For insanity—this is crucial to the idea that it was curable—was rarely total. If Pinel retained the traditional categories of melancholia, mania, idiocy, and cretinism, he also developed new ones, including *manie sans délire*, which he later christened *folie raisonnante*, in which sufferers whose reasoning was otherwise sound might be mad on a single subject, a dangerous but nevertheless amenable, because partial, insanity (Porter, 2002, p. 132). He also alluded in the *Traité* to a class of melancholics who suffered from a dominant idea but otherwise had "free exercise of all the faculties of understanding", and to other mad people, "dominated by a kind of instinct of fury", who similarly showed "no lesion of the understanding" (Pinel, 1801, pp. 149–150).

There is another important implication in all this. Observation was the basis on which Pinel and his successors undertook classification and ordering of the human phenomena assembled in the asylum. But it would not be quite enough to say that they then built theories out of this; if "observation" was a shibboleth it was because it could mean much more. For the contemporary, Romantic mind, observation was in itself an act of theorising. Theory was "not something extracted from experience and separate from it (based on representation), but present in the act of perception"; phenomena were themselves the source of theory (McGilchrist, 2009, pp. 355–356). For Goethe, perception was thinking:

> My perception is itself a thinking, and my thinking a perception. Man knows himself only to the extent that he knows the world; he becomes aware of himself only within the world, and aware of the world only through himself. Every new object, clearly seen, opens up a new organ of perception in us. (cited in McGilchrist, 2009, pp. 359–360)

To observe was to make present. Such was the ethic that underlay Pinel's conception of nature as teacher, *la nature éducative*, and of *la médecine expectante* itself, watchful, waiting medicine. Sparing in its use of time-hallowed, physical remedies, cautiously optimistic about the prospects of cure, it was not founded in preconceived ideas and categories. Such too was the ethic behind Géricault's portraits. Vision and observation were central to the alienists' work, as, of course, they were to that of the artist, for whom painting was the supreme form of thinking, of making present.

* * *

In the air too was the premium that was now being placed on the gathering of statistics. This is an important marker for a wider shift of consciousness. The development of the science of statistics was undermining the determinism that had been a conceptual foundation of the Age of Reason: the conviction that an ideal observer would be able to discern the fundamental principle or formula that would explain all the forces in the universe, however apparently random or inexplicable. Nation states were increasingly finding it expedient to collect and tabulate numerical data on their citizens, in order, for example, to facilitate the *levée en masse* required to create a citizens' army, as was the case in Revolutionary France, or to police oppositional and deviant behaviours: suicide, crime, vagrancy, madness. It was not long before statistical patterns emerged, and these began to assume their own explanatory force; they pointed to the existence of statistical *laws* that could bring random events into a new kind of coherence, and be used to predict. In this way, the notion of the "norm" was born, and with it, the need to try to conform to it. The idea of an "everyman" was coming into being, whose efforts to make himself normal, in a feedback loop, in turn shaped perceptions and definitions of normality (Bostridge, 2015, pp. 360–364, and see Hacking, 1990).

The moral treatment

In designating his approach to treatment *le traitement moral*, Pinel was following and refining British precedents. It involved, as we have seen, order with a minimum of necessary restraint, and a kindly discipline, *douceur*, backed up where necessary by an imposing threat of repression (Appignanesi, 2008, p. 61; Goldstein, 1987, p. 86); this was not, however, to be accompanied by feelings of animosity or anger on the part of the physician or nurse (Pinel, 1801, pp. 46–47 et seq.). It did not preclude, indeed was often accompanied by, physical interventions which could vary in mildness from warm baths to lotions applied to the head to laxative drinks and bleeding. The philosopher Yves Bonnefoy has stressed that the word *moral* in *le traitement moral* had the connotation "wanting the good" (Bonnefoy, 2006, p. 71). Laure Murat has pointed to "the perversely double meaning" of the expression, which translates as both "mental" and "moral" therapy, "a mental orthopedics in which reason is connected to virtue" (Murat, 2014, p. 98); *le traitement moral*, in other words, was suffused with social values. It also rested on the perception, or assumption, that there was a part of the mad person available to be reached with words.

Each patient—this was Pinel's democratic and republican message—is worthy of sustained attention (Weiner, 1993, pp. 262–263).

In the tradition of Locke, for Pinel and his students environment, life events, and life history, including childhood, played major parts in the generation of the illness (Esquirol, 1838, vol. I, pp. 34–35). Pinel started to engage his and Pussin's patients in conversation—in their cells, perhaps, or on one of the benches in the courtyards—and Weiner reconstructs Pinel's questions on the evidence of the case histories in his *Traité* and on a text he wrote on the clinical training of doctors.

> He wanted to know how each inmate was feeling about himself, and about his life in the hospice. What had brought him there? When? From where? Where had he been born? Did he have a family? A wife? children? Had he ever been sick? With what illness? Had others in his family been sick? How had the Revolution affected his livelihood? his politics, his religion? his safety? What exactly had precipitated his psychologic illness and when exactly had it started? What were his symptoms? his fears? his hopes? (Weiner, 1993, pp. 262, 422, note 36)

In the two editions, 1801 and 1809, of his *Traité* he published case vignettes—*historiettes*—which were widely cited in the medical literature and beyond: a clockmaker obsessed with perpetual motion; a patient who imagined he had been guillotined but pardoned, and had the wrong head put back on him; a man who thought he was Louis XIV and gave out dispatches for his provincial governors; a white-haired seventy-year-old who believed he was a young woman; a man who believed he was commanded by heaven to bestow "a Baptism of Blood and merciless immolation" upon those whose happiness in the next life he craved (ibid., p. 262). The "moral treatment" was both a matter of general principles, and something bespoke. It involved the discovery that each mad person is mad in his or her own way, "with an original, unique madness" (Quetel & Morel, 1979, p. 240).

This "hygiène morale", as Pinel and Cabanis referred to it, was a "medicine of the imagination", and the ability to strike the imagination of the sufferer through all manner of theatrical means and subterfuges, many sketched out in the *Traité*, was a key part of the moral healer's repertoire, just as the *fêtes révolutionnaires*, designed by David and others, were part of the visual rhetoric of the Revolution. As Pinel's star pupil Jean-Etienne Dominique Esquirol later wrote, "Everything that might act upon the brain, directly or indirectly, and modify our thinking being, everything that might dominate and direct the passions, will be brought to bear in the Moral Treatment" (cited in Quetel & Morel, 1979, p. 233, translated for this edition).

The next generation, while it could now take the achievements of the revolutionary, Pinelian era for granted, also revealed its cultural and Romantic links, its allegiance both to the questing aspirations of philosophical Enlightenment and to a heightend sense of the power of feeling and human receptiveness to it. The doctoral thesis that the thirty-three-year-old Esquirol submitted in 1805 to the Ecole de Médecine (and dedicated to Pinel) has an exemplary title: *Des Passions, Considerées comme Causes, Symptômes et Moyens curatifs de l'Aliénation mentale* (*On the Passions Considered as Causes, Symptoms and Means for the Cure of Mental Alienation*). In his discussions of treatment he adds little that is new to the precepts of moral medicine already laid down by Pinel; his thesis is, however, a more succinct and emphatic exposition of the whole basis upon which the moral treatment rested. Its central assumption is that madness "is a total phenomenon that touches upon all aspects of the human personality ... yet [it] does not completely abolish the self; it allows the mentally ill to preserve part of their personality and presence to the world". Neither brain lesion nor failure of intellect, it is "a divisive force that affects the entire human being by turning the sick half against the healthy one" (Gauchet & Swain, 1999, p. 149).

Esquirol stresses the therapeutic value of isolating the sufferer from his or her family and old habits, a practice already established in England, France, and elsewhere.

> [Mental alienation] seems to break all the links attaching man to man. The most exquisite sensibility, the most delicate sentiments, the sweetest and most tender affections, having determined this illness, still exercise their dismal influence on it. The disorder of the sufferer's ideas will ceaselessly put him at odds with those with whom he lives, and with himself. (1805, p. 32, translated for this edition)

Familial kindness is not enough. Indeed the family may be the problem: "[T]he moral cause of alienation often exists in the bosom of the family." Former shocks or hurts sustained or first experienced within the family, which have impressed themselves on the nervous system, can be kept alive or reawakened in the old environment: in what Esquirol calls a "simultaneity of impressions" (post-Freudian commentators might have no hesitation in recognising a form of transference), external objects "recall a particular series of ideas which are associated, often or just once, with the first impressions, but with force and energy" (ibid., pp. 43–44). In the new and unfamiliar setting of the hospital, "… new objects, stimulating new impressions, will give birth to new ideas," and sometimes the displacement itself, together with the profound shock of finding oneself in a madhouse, is enough to restore the alienated person to reason (ibid., p. 34). Secondly, there is the application of the passions themselves. Sometimes it may be enough to appeal to his or her self-esteem by persuasion, or to counter despair with good news, fabricated or genuine: a priest thrown into melancholy by the destruction of religion in the Revolution is cured by being shown the new Concordat (Napoleon's with the Pope, of 1801) reinstating the faith (ibid., p. 76).

Generally, however, simple reasoning does not lead to cure.

> Are not alienation and all its variations passions carried to the extreme? To treat them with dialectical formulae and syllogisms would be to show a poor understanding of the march of the passions and the clinical history of mental alienation. (ibid., pp. 82–83, translated for this edition)

In these all-too-common circumstances, cure must be attained by "moral shocks"—"des secousses morales". It is necessary to provoke a crisis by shaking up the imagination—"ébranler fortement l'imagination"—and this more often than not means the judicious instilling of fear, perhaps with the help of the hospital's well-trained team of assistants (ibid., pp. 54–55), who, like the doctor, must proceed with kindness as well as firmness. Calming baths and soups, emetics, exercise, showers, strait-jackets and other humane restraints are also part of the establishment's therapeutic armoury—but less for their physiological or disciplinary than for their "moral" effects. The "sweet and harmonious impressions of well-played music" give rise to to pleasant sensations in the epigastrium and animate or calm the nervous system, or may be associated with happier times (ibid., p. 77). Other, convalescing patients might be recruited as part of the cure: a former soldier wrecks his room first thing every morning, until Esquirol persuades a woman patient to confront him (ibid., p. 76). He was on his guard against over-systemisation and what twenty-first-century practitioners (often uncritically) call manualisation: "When you want to combat mania you need to arm yourself against *l'esprit de système*". It is so easy, he went on, to be carried away in the face of the violence of the symptoms. "One must modify therapeutic outlook according to the individual"; a rational treatment is a different treatment for each circumstance, as he continued to maintain (Esquirol, 1838, vol. II, pp. 35–36). The moral treatment was nothing if not pragmatic and inventive.

The person of the doctor and emerging Romanticism

The personal presence, qualities, experience, and education of the healer were also crucial. Pinel insisted on an imposing manner, and an orderly mind; he cited the reforming English apothecary John Haslam, from Bethlem Hospital in London, on the primary importance of an ability to gain the patient's confidence (Pinel, 1801, pp. 195 etc.), and the already legendary Francis Willis, the exuder of quiet authority who had imposed his will upon George III in the late 1780s (Goldstein, 1987, p. 86). Esquirol, less wedded to fear than Pinel, expressed this clearly.

> While humane restraint may occasionally be called for to prevent injury, the doctor who treats a maniac must never seek to inspire fear in him … The doctor needs to be a comforting figure for his patients; he must skilfully find opportunities to show himself benevolent and protective, he must maintain a loving but grave tone, ally kindness with firmness, and command esteem. By means of this conduct he will gain the patient's confidence, without which there can be no cure; his bearing, his look, his words, his tone of voice, his gestures, even his silence, act on the mind or the heart of the maniac. (1838, vol. II, p. 34, translated for this edition)

The moral character of the doctor was also his protection: doctors, wrote Esquirol, owe their resistance to infection and "epidemic miasmas" to the courage and devotion that they bring to their ministrations (1805, p. 9).

Since it was directly to the passions that the doctor must speak, and the nature and state of the passions—their relative harmony or disharmony, regulation of deregulation, diffusion or focus—that engaged the alienist in his clinical writing, he also needed to have cultivated the attitudes of an artist, poet, and philosopher. Indeed, in contrast to the medicalised fever of contemporary British "delirium", French *délire*, a key word for the Parisian alienists, was something closer to "the ecstatic joy of the poet, the hashish smoker and the revolutionary rioter" (Appignanesi, 2008, p. 54). As Pinel put it,

> Can the doctor remain a stranger to the history of the most lively human passions, since in them lie the most frequent causes of the alienation of the wits ("l'aliénation de l'esprit")? And should he not therefore study the lives of men most renowned for their thirst for glory, their enthusiasm for the fine arts, the austerities of monastic life, the delirium of unhappy love? Will he be able to trace all the alterations and perversions of the functions of human understanding if he has not meditated profoundly upon the writings of Locke and Condillac, and if he has not made himself familiar with their principles? (1801, pp. 44–45, translated for this edition)

And does not the doctor who administers treatments without proper consideration deserve to be put in the patient's place? he asked (ibid., p. 40).

The moral treatment was saturated in Rousseau, the great expert, for the *idéologues*, on the passions; Rousseau's expertise had been cultivated through first-hand knowledge, as a melancholic himself. In his second *Discourse on the Origin of Inequality*, Rousseau saw passion not as the subverter but as the indispensible ally of reason, a view endorsed by Diderot. The moral treatment was also informed and inspired by Rousseau's ideas on schooling, in *Emile*, and the possibilities of re-education, in *La nouvelle Héloïse*. The moral healer's appeals to *sensibilité*, to the sufferer's tender fellow and family feelings, as a way of steering him away from vicious passions and restoring him to health and sociability, echoed the proto-romanticism of Richardson's *Clarissa* (1748), which was widely read and admired in continental Europe (Goldstein, 1987, pp. 97–98). Pinel's moral treatment was, indeed, "entirely suited to the general cultural trend of his day, to romanticism emerging out of Enlightenment" (ibid., pp. 117–119).

In *Des Maladies mentales* of 1838, which was a collection of the lectures he had given annually at the Salpêtrière since 1817 (Eitner, 1982, pp. 243, 354, note 33), Esquirol both located himself in the enlightened tradition of Locke (Esquirol, 1838, vol. I, p. 6) and continued to lend "expert" weight to the view, both ancient and thoroughly Romantic, that melancholy was "very appropriate for the growth of the arts and sciences" (ibid., p. 212). Among European precursors and contemporaries with whom he engaged was Schlegel (ibid., p. 372: he cites a work on "political medicine" of 1819); a hint of German *Naturphilosophie* as well as of Rousseau can now be felt. Esquirol more than once stressed the "natural history" of the illness, and the idea of the doctor as a respectful natural scientist, who contents himself, like Constable in his cloud studies, or Géricault in his portraits, with careful, attentive observation and description, as the servant of nature. Medical troublemakers, wrote Esquirol, who intervene too early, at the first symptoms, with copious bleeding, deprive nature of its course. They fail to understand that

> the doctor does not cure, that he is only nature's minister, that his mission is to remove the obstacles which might block its course, and to settle the patient comfortably in such a way as to facilitate the development of the successive symptoms of the illness, and to suffice to the critical efforts which must assess it ... thanks to the principles discovered by Pinel, one finds oneself today in a state of wise expectation, in which one keeps a watchful eye on nature's efforts, in order to support them rather than destroy them. (ibid., vol. II, p. 168, translated for this edition)

He reiterated, in the more sober language of the Restoration or the Bourgeois Monarchy, Pinel's profession of alienism as a human and "artistic", a pluralistic rather than a technical enterprise.

> You need, before any medication, to be quite convinced that this illness is resistant and difficult to cure; that moral medicine, which seeks the first causes of the trouble in the heart, which pleads, which weeps, which consoles, which shares in the sufferings and awakens hope, is often preferable to any other. (ibid., vol. I, p. 230, translated for this edition)

He was a doctor who would listen to his patients. Thus we hear, in *Des Maladies mentales*, snippets of what they said. Here is "P.J.D.", for example, a tradesman who entered Charenton in 1836 aged twenty-eight:

> In this state ... my intelligence is annulled; I do not think, I see and hear nothing; if I do see, I take things in, I keep silent, not having the courage to respond. This lack of activity is due to the fact

that my sensations are too weak to act on my will. (ibid., pp. 46–48, translated for this edition)

("At home", Esquirol added, with no obvious irony, "he was obstinately resistant to doing anything anyone wanted of him." He does not elaborate further, but when this particular patient speaks might we be entitled to hear a bit of a malingerer, a Harold Skimpole who has, moreover, learnt the doctor's language?)

Esquirol was also a doctor who would go through at least some of what his patients went through. According to Pinel he subjected himself to a "therapeutic" cold shower: a reservoir of water ten degrees colder than the atmospheric temperature was emptied over his head from a height of ten feet. "It seemed to him that a column of ice was breaking against that part," causing acute pain and leaving his head numb for more than an hour. This is the marker of a difference between the older type of philanthropist, who could still feel that the patient feels no pain, and the practitioner who wants to know how the patient experiences treatment, in order to help him develop and transform the principles governing medical practice (Gauchet & Swain, 1999, pp. 211–213).

The new figure of the alienist, as established by Pinel and developed by Esquirol, was an enquirer who, like Géricault, made use of himself, his own feelings and observations of himself. In this, self-consciously in a vanguard, he was aligned with contemporary developments in the wider cultural field, the birth of an artistic avant-garde and an evolving identity for the artist.

The socialising agenda of the asylum

Later eighteenth-century minds tended to take it as axiomatic that man is a social animal. For followers of Rousseau, man was perfectible only as such (Lane, 1979, p. 27). For Adam Smith, in *The Wealth of Nations*, we are mutually dependent, with our "general disposition to truck, barter, and exchange" (1776, pp. 120–121). The idea of the asylum as a means for reintroducing inmates to sociality was a dream of late Enlightenment. It had been announced by Jacques Tenon in the 1780s (Weiner, 1993, p. 270), and by Jean Colombier and François Doublet, two physicians commissioned by Necker in 1785 to produce a report which became an influential book, *Instruction sur la manière de gouverner les Insensés, et de travailler à leur guérison dans les Asyles qui leur sont destinés* (*Instruction on How to Govern the Insane and Work towards their Cure in Asylums Dedicated to Them*) (Castel, 1976, pp. 61–62). In the first years of the new century, Pinel, Pussin, and Esquirol were giving the idea extremely serious attention. "A house for the alienated is an instrument of cure; in the hands of a skilful doctor, it is the most powerful therapeutic agent against mental illnesses," wrote Esquirol (1838, vol. II, p. 398).

Confinement, in the Pinelian revolution, was elevated into a therapeutic requirement. At first the isolation of inmates from each other was retained as facilitating observation and seen as generally preferable to throwing them together indiscriminately; this gradually gave way to dormitories, and to freer association. "… how salutary to the return of reason", wrote Pinel,

> are the periodic gatherings of several people where they can converse freely about the interests of their families, whom they left behind several months earlier … Their days thus go by quickly, spent in communicating to each other their troubles and fears. (1809, p. 248, cited in Gauchet & Swain, 1999, p. 106)

The shift in emphasis can be traced between the two editions of Pinel's *Traité*, and the ascendancy of institutionalised treatment over individualised moral treatment was marked by Esquirol's appointment as "supervisor of the insane" at the Salpêtrière in 1811 (Gauchet & Swain, 1999, p. 145). It was "a transfer of the mainspring of moral treatment from the realm of personal relationship to that of inscription and immersion within a communitarian order". The asylum functioned as "a gigantic apparatus for socialisation, as a machine for reducing the insane person's highly resistant alterity" (ibid., pp. 45, 48).

In its early development, the very way the institution was set up enshrined a confidence that cure for insanity was possible. The asylum would not limit the amount of time the sufferer could remain before being consigned to the poor house, prison, or street; the institution would through its very existence proclaim that chronicity did not have to mean incurability (Azouvi, 1980, p. vi). At Bicêtre Pinel recorded an initial 20 per cent cure rate—at least forty men left the ward "to take charge of their lives as citizen patients" (Weiner, 1993, p. 263). Figures he and Pussin reported for the Salpêtrière for 1802-05 are also impressive: about 100 out of 156 melancholics, and 224 out of 452 maniacs, were sent home cured (ibid., p. 271).

The asylum was also a tacit social experiment; the principles and ground rules it worked out for itself pertained to a model society of well functioning social bonds, the ideal of the society to which it hoped to restore its inmates. As the century progressed, therapeutic optimism was tempered and expectations of cure were lowered; it was nevertheless still hoped that the asylum might do the work of restoring patients to sociality. It did both less and more.

> Asylums may not have treated the insane, but they *changed insanity* ... in the long run disciplinary and collectivist mechanisms that were implemented in the asylum context had the indirect but decisive effect of making evident, or at least perceptible, the fact that the insane were fit to live among other people, and that they continued to participate in the multiple networks of the social bond ... The asylum separated the insane from the rest of the world, but it also drew them out of the primitive abyss of their solitude ... it brought them out of their self-containment, from their confinement within their own bounds, from their inaccessible otherness ... No doubt the asylum left its inmates subjectively alone, if not in a state of intimate abandonment ... [But] though it failed to seize hold of souls, [it] at least succeeded in integrating individuals into a collective organisation. (Gauchet & Swain, 1999, pp. 100–101)

Birth of a profession

Ambitious, capable, open to the most difficult challenges, humane, literate, and politically canny enough to take advantage of his good luck, Pinel had been the right man in the right place. His character left a powerful imprint on his students and successors, and continued to do so right up to and beyond his death in 1826, two years after Géricault's (see Weiner, 1999). But it was also the articulation of a cluster of ideas and practices that brought the Pinelian alienists their power, prestige, and influence in the first third of the nineteenth century: preservation, expansion, and subdivision of the institutional space, and separation of the mad from other inmates; classification and ordering on the basis of observation; the development of a specific power relation between doctor and patient, the "moral treatment", founded in the perception or assumption that there was a sane part of the patient to be addressed. The alienist was a doctor who through his practice and person insisted on the solidarity between a certain knowledge and power, and the place in which he exercised and embodied this power, the hospital: "These three dimensions, none of which was in itself new, cause the transformation, by the very fact of being brought together." This is what assured the *mythe pinelien* and the pre-eminence of French psychiatry in the first half of the nineteenth century. In England, in contrast, there was a split between on the one hand the philanthropy of Tuke and other lay reformers, and on the other the prestige and claims to scientific knowledge of the medical establishment. Tuke was not a doctor, and the English alienists had difficulty bridging the gap in such a way that the moral treatment might be assimilated, as for a time it was in France, into medical technology (Castel, 1976, pp. 87–88, note 71).

The way the different aspects of the alienism project fitted together was esssential for the establishment of its credibility in the early years of the century. It was not uncontested. The Catholic Church and monastic orders had claims of their own regarding the care of the insane; smaller, private, establishments embraced a family model, notably, from 1821, that of Dr Esprit Blanche, which was later to welcome Gérard de Nerval (Murat, 2001). But it was enough to put the whole question of madness, and what thinking about it might have to offer, on the map in a new way. The work and prestige of Pinel and the alienists, as transmitted to a wider public by his publications, gathered and brought into focus questions and themes of urgent interest to contemporaries.

"Clear and unambiguous classification was a first crucial step in holding the line against insanity" (Ingram, 1998, p. 4). Pinel was a very different representative of Enlightenment from the character in *Le neveu de Rameau*, the "Moi" who in Diderot's dialogue is accosted and unsettled in a public place. As the nephew, "Lui", ducks and dives, the "Moi" struggles to speak for an integral, sincere, and unitary self. If Pinel opened up a dialogue with his distracted and alienated patients, it was in the closed confines of the institution and on his terms. The crazy person must not threaten to undermine him, his reason, his integrity, and his citizenship. For all his identification, he is insulated by his professional status, for he has established this status above all by postulating and indeed finding, in a supreme act of rational discrimination, a "sane" part in the madman. This postulation and therapeutic manoeuvre, however, open things up, in what Hegel would have termed an irony of history, in ways that neither Pinel nor Esquirol could have intuited.

CHAPTER SIX

A new account of the human: responses to Pinel's *Traité*

Precedents

In certain respects Pinel's and his students' approach to madness was nothing new. We have seen how his initiatives in moral treatment belong among Europe-wide developments. As long ago as the early seventeenth century the surgeon Pierre Pigray had extolled kindly words as far more use than physical remedies when working with the mad; Samuel-Auguste Tissot, in his influential *Traité des nerfs et de leurs maladies* (1778 onwards), was critical of doctors who were ignorant of the emotional lives (*le moral*) of their patients (Bernard, 2015). Rousseau had been acute to his own and others' internal discrepancies and self-deceptions.

> It is impossible for a man constantly putting himself about in society and ceaselessly engaged in dissimulating to others not to dissimulate a little to himself, so that when he did get time to study himself he would find it almost impossible to recognise himself …

he wrote in "Mon Portrait" (Rousseau, 1782, p. 162). This catches both the idea that social life can alienate us from ourselves and that we can be divided against ourselves in the first place; a part of us that wants to know ourselves does, however, survive. St Paul and St Augustine themselves are evidence that Pinel was hardly the first to entertain such thoughts.

In *The Anatomy of Melancholy* (1621) Robert Burton had affirmed that we are all capable of being "brain-sick", because we are all subject to falsehood and error; divine revelation was the only certain means of separating truth from illusion (Burton, 1621, vol. I, p. 25; Rosen, 1998, p. 117). Religious faith provided a secure frame of meaning; by the end of the eighteenth century, in the climate of Enlightenment anti-clericalism, the idea that everyone could go mad was securely linked to the conflicts and traumata of everyday, social existence. Such links seemed to be confirmed in the life of the English poet William Cowper, or the German poet Jakob Lenz (the subject of Georg Büchner's *Lenz*, of 1839), or in Wordsworth's portrayals of madness rooted in "the ordinary lives of the poor and the middle class" (*The Thorn, The Ruined Castle, The Idiot Boy*) (Rosen, 1998, pp. 117–118). In France, the aftershocks of the Revolution and the Napoleonic wars came to be seen as major causative factors.

As far as descriptions of madness itself were concerned, Diderot's and d'Alembert's great *Encyclopédie* might already seem to have had the last word, although these descriptions also enshrine some time-hallowed assumptions. In entries attributed to him on "Mélancolie" ("le sentiment habituel de notre imperfection", our permanent feeling of imperfection), "Mélancholie réligieuse", and "Mélancholie" (the last two with an h), Diderot drew on Hippocrates to make some fine nosological distinctions. Melancholy, he writes, anticipating Pinel's *manie sans délire*, is different from frenzy and mania in that it "centres on one or two determining objects", with no fever or fury. Sufferers show insurmountable sadness, are of dark humour, misanthropic, and seek out solitude; some imagine they are kings, lords, or gods, or that they have been turned into animals: wolves, dogs, cats, rabbits (they are lycanthropic, cyanthropic, gallanthropic). They fight with animals, they fear they will flood the world, that they are made of glass. The causes are the same as for mania: "chagrins, mental pain, the passions, especially love and unsatisfied sexual appetite … acute and continuous fear … impressions which are too strong", as well as excessive fear of punishment and of hell, inspired by religion. The cause may be liver, spleen, or womb problems, debauchery or "immoderate commerce with women".

> Sad, pensive, dreamy, anxious … [they are] tolerant of cold and
> hunger; their faces are austere, with knitted brows, weatherbeaten,
> brown in complexion; they are constipated … They behave and
> reason sensibly on all subjects which do not relate to the object of
> their delirium.

Diderot gives the example of a man who thought he was a rabbit, who was perfectly reasonable until a dog came into the room. No brain lesions are evident, but there are epigastric and lower belly disturbances, which influence the head; the effect of black bile is not, he writes, as ridiculous as some moderns have thought.

In the spirit of a practitioner of the moral treatment, Diderot insists that cure must start with the mind—"l'esprit"—"and then attack the vices of the body, when these are known". The physician must gain the patient's confidence, enter his idea, adapt to his delirium, appear persuaded that things are as he says, promise a radical cure, then offer singular remedies, employing ruse if necessary, such as pretending to remove an animal from the sufferer's body or head. Balls and theatre are curative distractions, and music above all can have "marvellous effects". Diet is better than pharmacy, and better still than surgery; wine, changes of air, riding, "rubbing the lower belly" and sexual exercise ("des exercices vénériens"), especially when lack of it or separation from a beloved has been the cause of the illness, are all indicated. Apart from the reminders of a mid-eighteenth century sexual frankness, which might not have chimed with the sensibilities of the post-revolutionary generation, there is little here that will not reappear in Pinel or Esquirol, from the epigastrium, to the idea of partial delirium, to the interest in physical appearance, to the notion of a cure which must start with gaining the sufferer's confidence (Diderot, 1762, pp. 307–310, translated for this edition).

Perhaps the most significant rival and forerunner to Pinel's *Traité* was the Savoyard physician Joseph Daquin's *La Philosophie de la folie*, published in 1792. Daquin's book was dedicated "To Humanity". It is written in a spirited style, fuelled by early revolutionary fervour. "Egoists, you may save yourselves the trouble of reading this … Anyone who sees a mad person without being touched by his state, or who makes amusement from him, is a moral monster." Can philosophy, that is, a love of wisdom, really be linked to madness? Daquin asks. His answer is that you can have a philosophy of anything, and that philosophy is perhaps the only resource in the treatment of madness. He called his book *La Philosophie de la folie* in recognition of the fact that "[O]f all the ills which can afflict us this is one of those that calls for the smallest number of remedies from pharmacy" (pp. i–vii, translated for this edition). Success with the mad is infinitely more sure when one approaches them with

> patience, enlightened prudence, little attentions, respect, sound reasons and consoling suggestions … offered during the lucid intervals which they sometimes enjoy. The bringing together of all these means is what I understand by PHILOSOPHY … and I maintain that moral approaches to helping should perhaps be the only ones that should be offered. (cited in Bernard, 2015, translated for this edition)

Stendhal and Hegel

Certain contemporary responses to Pinel's *Traité*—Stendhal's, Hegel's— show, however, that this was not just one more treatise among others; it marked a profound shift in contemporary consciousness. Pinel was an experienced writer who had honed his literary style to make his ideas accessible; but it was not just a question of style, or of enlightened philanthropy, or of new classifications, or of the equation of madness with the passions (this was ancient). The *Traité* obliquely drew attention, without reference to theology, to divisions in *everybody*, which were not merely contingent or periodic, but constitutive. At the same time it held out the possibility of fuller self-knowledge and self-mastery.

The *Traité* was translated into German in the year of its appearance, 1801, and into English in 1806, by which time, according to Stendhal who wanted his own copy, it had sold out in France. Contemporaries saw it as the work *par excellence* on the question of madness (Swain, 1977, pp. 39–40). For Stendhal, Pinel was essential reading, because this doctor had unparalleled access to the life of the passions, anatomising and elucidating them and their roots and causes. It was more than mere whim that led Stendhal, who was embarking on his own lifelong project to observe and understand himself and his society, to try to get hold of a copy in 1805–6 (Goldstein, 1987, pp. 64–65).

In 1805 he was still Henri Beyle; he was twenty-two, and trying to live as an independent man of letters. He seems to have first read the *Traité* in this year. He recorded in his journal that he found the library of the Ecole de Médecine closed when he went there in January to seek out the book. In the library of the Panthéon, he turned to another recently published and much discussed work, a book by Cabanis, *Rapports du physique et du moral de l'homme*; but he found Cabanis "general" and "vague". His reading, however, led him to the early statement of an utterly Stendhalian idea: "In the case of instinct as in all other cases, the individual again follows that which seems to him to lead him to his greatest happiness" (Stendhal, 1888, vol. I, pp. 195–196, translated for this edition).

In July, in self-exhortation, he cited and referenced a phrase from the *Traité*: "Extreme sobriety to boost one's moral faculties, Pinel, 54". The case vignette from which this is taken might be the sketch for a Stendhalian novel (his first, *Armance*, was only published in 1827). Under the heading "History of a mania in which Moral Treatment would have been necessary", Pinel tells the story of a young man of twenty-four, "gifted with an ardent imagination", who comes to Paris to continue his studies, believing himself "destined by nature to go on to play the most brilliant role at the Bar". The story ends badly; the young man's rigorous working regime plunges him into alternating heights of joy and depths of despair, migraines, nosebleeds, chest and intestinal pains, and flatulence, and finally into a persecuted delirium, profound melancholy, and a lonely death in a wood near his father's house in the Pyrénées (Pinel, 1801, pp. 54–57).

"Yesterday I observed storms of the passions," Beyle wrote in his journal in January 1806, "that the great passions can only be cured by the means indicated by Ph Pinel in *La Manie*" (as he called the book) (Stendhal, 1888, vol. I, p. 384). Four years later, in 1810, he noted that he had read the first pages of Pinel's *Nosographie philosophique, ou méthode de l'analyse appliquée à la médecine*. He promised himself to write his own "nosography of the passions and states of the soul", in the form of a journal with headings such as "Vanity" and "Avarice" under which he would record the features of each passion as he observed them. "These signs will strike my imagination and strengthen my wits" (ibid., p. 603). Medical works and those of Pinel in particular, as he wrote later in the year, were a key part of a self-training in literature; he grouped Pinel with Helvétius and Hobbes, Burke, Shakespeare, Cervantes, Tasso, Ariosto, and Molière, contrasting these writers to academically correct critics and dry arbiters of "taste". Pinel spoke to Beyle with trenchancy because he had studied the passions at close quarters and—this at least is the implication—experienced them himself. For, as Beyle wrote in the same journal entry, once again anticipating one of his later, key formulations, "… to depict them, you have to have felt them" (ibid., pp. 628–629). If the *philosophe* Pinel was a voice of reason, the centrality he gave to the passions removed him from the Romantic counter-charge that he was a representative of a form of reasoning which could stunt and make you mad, that with which the Stendhalian "jeune homme raisonneur", like Julien Sorel, was afflicted.

* * *

Hegel summed up Pinel's achievement with penetrating insight. Pinel understood that once the mad patient learns to respect his doctor, he becomes conscious of his own subjective state and its collision with an external reality.

> It is the merit of *Pinel* in particular to have conceived this residue of rationality present in the mad and the insane as the foundation of cure and to have conducted his treatment of the mentally ill in accordance with this conception. His publication on this subject must be declared the best that exists in this field. (Hegel, 1830, p. 127)

He wrote this in 1817, as part of a longer discussion of states of madness; it is one of six references to Pinel in Section One, "Subjective Mind", of Volume Three, *Philosophy of Mind*, of his monumental *Encyclopaedia of the Philosophical Sciences*. He preceded this appreciation of the discovery that the doctor could work with the healthy part of the patient's personality with an acute and incisive commentary. Psychological treatment, he wrote,

> can often be successful in the treatment of madness proper and insanity because in these soul-states a vitality of consciousness is still present, and alongside derangement related to a *particular* representation, in its *other* representations a rational consciousness still subsists, which a skillful psychiatrist can develop into a *power* over that particularity. (ibid.)

Hegel's understanding was not based on a naive, cognitive model which would oppose reason to unreason and attribute cure to the rational correction of mad ideas; his references to soul-states and vitality suggests the workings of something like an inherent therapeutic drive (see too Weiner, 1993, p. 264). For Gauchet and Swain, what Hegel found in Pinel was the very source of the subject's decentring, the "moment when the fundamental ambiguity of the proximity of man to himself became perceptible experience" (Gauchet & Swain, 1999, pp. 256–257).

The subject and the individual

The German satirist George Christoph Lichtenberg had predicted, around 1780: "From the folly of men in Bedlam, it should be possible to determine more about the nature of Man than has been done until now" (cited in Rosen, 1998, p. 118); 1800, wrote Gauchet and Swain, marks the beginning of the era "in which insanity was integrated into human organisation as a limit case" (1999, p. 258). The new alienism opened the way to awareness of changes that were taking place in Western subjectivity itself, that is, in ways in which people were now starting to experience themselves and each other.

The eighteenth century, in particular the philosophy of Condillac, had prepared the ground, and provided essential underpinning to Pinel's therapeutics. Condillac's statue, the individual, was both passive, a receiver of what impacted on his senses, and active and creative in constructing the world with the materials, the original sense impressions, to hand. It follows that he or she will come up against the constructions of others, which are likely to be more or less different. Such is the source of the misunderstandings and misrecognitions which drive Stendhal's novels and shape the destinies of his protagonists. Condillac's ideas and those of his followers, the *idéologues*, which so informed Pinel, were entering the mainstream of French educational, social, and political thinking during Stendhal's formative years; perhaps it took a novelist more fully to work out some of the implications, and to begin to grasp the new urgency of the question: what does the other think and want of me?

The relevance and usefulness of the Cartesian notion of a clear subject-object distinction, of mind or consciousness ranging freely over a given, immutable reality which was external to it, was also coming to seem more questionable than ever. Corresponding with this was a dynamic, social vision of the human, the human being as inherently changeable (or even, as for the *idéologues*, perfectible) through contact with other human beings, and thus through education, administration, and government. Hence too contemporary interest in the educabilility of those whose senses were impaired, the deaf, blind, and mute, and in the *enfant sauvage*, who could be seen as the exemplary living statue, a testing ground for the new philosophy. The fourth section of Condillac's *Traité des sensations* ends with a discussion of a "wild boy" who had been found living with bears in a Lithuanian forest. The most famous such child, the so-called "wild boy of Aveyron", was a focus of tremendous philosophical, medical, and public interest, including both Pinel's and Esquirol's, in the years immediately following his "discovery" in 1800 (Lane, 1979).

The moral treatment addressed a thinking and feeling subject, with a subjectivity of her own. For Gladys Swain, Muller's and Robert-Fleury's paintings commemorating Pinel's mythical gesture of unchaining are like screen memories for something otherwise impossible to picture (*infigurable*)—a major shift in attitude. The real revolution consisted in the fact that for the first time the mad person might be seen as a subject in her own right, aware or potentially aware of her state, conscious of suffering it (Swain, 1977, pp. 119–121). This is what was new and critical about the Pinelian/Esquirolian revolution and distinguishes it from a Diderot's or a Daquin's understanding of madness. There is no complete eradication of subjectivity; there is distance between self and illness. "The fundamental aspect of the Pinelian break consists in achieving an opening onto insanity from within that reveals the principle of 'effective' treatment" (Gauchet & Swain, 1999, p. 37). The subject was a *therapeutic* subject, able to respond to the moral treatment.

In contrast with the earlier eighteenth-century, empiricist attitude, which might justly be summed up as "madness incurable in theory but sometimes curable in fact", for Pinel and his followers madness was tractable and thus curable in theory—although, as they also recognised from the start, often incurable in practice (ibid., p. 36). The differences in Pinel's and his followers' approach to moral therapeutics, in contrast for example with that of Daquin, can now be understood more clearly. Daquin's enlightened *philosophie* was humanitarian and philanthropic in emphasis. Pinel's was closer to that of a natural scientist, in the spirit of detached, enquiring Enlightenment, with its promise of new knowledge. He uncoupled the action of the passions from morality; following Crichton, he viewed the passions simply as phenomena of the animal economy. His concern, as Beyle/Stendhal grasped, was with establishing a general science of the sources and laws of human behaviour (Pinel, 1801, pp. xxi–xxii). Just as political and economic phenomena were becoming "autonomous and intelligible domains entirely unrelated to moral precepts", with their own laws (of power, production, the growth and distribution of wealth …), so was the subjective field itself in the process of becoming constituted as a specialised science (Gauchet & Swain, 1999, p. 160).

Perhaps the most important difference with the older-style philanthropist lay in the question of the effects of the doctor's words and how the physician now envisaged these. Daquin only conceived of the sufferer's perfect blind adhesion to his madness, with no discordance between self and self, only occasional, unaccountable moments of lucidity; words could only offer reason and consolation. Skilled intervention by the Pinelian practitioner could, as Hegel saw, produce a "gap between the insane person and his insane convictions", indirectly, not by reasoning but by arousing an echo within the patient and "mobilising [his] invisible reserve" towards his chimeras so that he might perceive a sudden distance. Pinel gave the example of the inmate of Bicêtre who thought he'd been guillotined and given back the wrong head. Another, convalescing, patient was enlisted to tell him the story of St Denis carrying and kissing his own head after his decapitation; the watchmaker took this seriously, comparing the saint's with his own sad predicament. But when the other patient burst into laughter and mocked him for his credulity, it worked to shock and embarrass him out of his delusion, of which, Pinel says, he never spoke again (Pinel, 1801, pp. 66–70). Crucially, change only came about when, in one way or another, the patient's feelings were engaged. This, wrote Gauchet and Swain,

> under its crude cloak … signifies a major discovery, one that was found fascinating in its own time, and for good reason. Pinel's example marks the advent of a fundamental possibility: the power to manipulate an internal difference that has not been absolutely eliminated in the insane person, appearances notwithstanding. (Gauchet & Swain, 1999, p. 215)

Pinel could not quite name or represent what happened within the insane person. But it was a key transition in philanthropic and in clinical thinking. The old-style philanthropist might have said: "I pity the insane person because I put myself in his place, but he cannot be aware that I pity him any more than he can be aware of his own condition." The Pinelian would make an internal identification: "He is to be pitied because he is not without a wrenching awareness of his estrangement from himself" (ibid., p. 265).

The study of madness allowed contemporaries to see a principle, a law at work in everyone; it was valuable for learning about "the constant and general ways of Nature" itself (Moreau de la Sarthe, in year VIII, cited in Goldstein, 1987, p. 240). This, in its different aspects, is what caught the interest of Stendhal, Hegel, and no doubt of other readers. We are divided within and often against ourselves. The movement in which madness was incorporated within us was also inseparable from the movement which simultaneously absorbed other differences— women, "primitive peoples", animals, children, people of colour, the deaf, the blind—indeed from the whole contemporary call to liberty being heard across the "Atlantic world" (Polasky, 2015): Gauchet and Swain's *decrease* in the alterity of the (external) other. Hierarchies and distinctions of rank, within which everyone, in theory, knew his place, were giving way to the notion of shared citizenship, with the uncertainties, anxieties, and responsibilities this entailed. Accompanying this was an *increase* in the sense of an internal otherness, of the stranger, the tormenting superior or the threatening underdog, within. The way was open to a kind of pure subjectivity and internality, "which we apprehend under a name without precedent in history", *subject*, the internal aspect of what we grasp from the outside as the *individual* (Gauchet & Swain, 1999, p. 257).

Gauchet and Swain sum up. Democratic societies are distinguished by their postulation of inalienable rights "that antedate the collective phenomena". They consist of individuals, "primary, free, and self-sufficient social atoms". Correlatively, we are

> the first beings to discover that we are subjugated from within, internally dependent, dispossessed of ourselves by something that comes from nowhere but ourselves. The social emancipation of the individual has as its consequence or fundamental counterpart the revelation of psychic subjection … the infinitesimal fissure that opened up around 1800 at the boundaries of human experience … the presence-absence to self that was originally uncovered in mental alienation has been extended, bringing about

a complete reconfiguration of the subjective space. (Gauchet &
Swain, 1999, pp. 255–256)

* * *

Hegel had registered this reconfiguration as early as 1805. In that
year or shortly after, he had written a passage called "The Spirit of
Self-Estrangement", which appeared in *Phenomenology of Mind* in 1807.
It made use of Diderot's *Le neveu de Rameau*, which had only just come
out in print. For Hegel, the crazy, fractious nephew's ("Lui"'s) position, or rather wilful refusal of position, his mimicry and flouting of
every social role available, was an assertion that for Spirit to accede
to a "higher level of conscious life", it must become aware of its own
self-estrangement—of estrangement, in fact, as endemic to all social
existence, whether people knew it or not. Here, indeed, is the first
explicit elaboration of "alienation" as a philosophical term, one that
was to become a cornerstone of Marxist thought.

Self, Hegel declared, was "strictly speaking the loss of self", of any
particular identity. Only when roused to revolt does self-consciousness
"know its own peculiar torn and shattered condition; and in its knowing
it has *ipso facto* risen above that condition" (Hegel, 1807, p. 548). Louis
Sass comments that the nephew's rebellion, as Hegel reads it, is no
mere eruption of id, but rather in the service of self-creation, or at least
self-preservation. The way forward was for humans to rise, in Sass's
words, to higher and more complex levels of self-consciousness and
self-alienation—including an awareness that everything is estranged
from itself. For Sass the passage points forward to Baudelaire,
Nietzsche, and irony-laden modernism and postmodernism (Sass,
1994, pp. 103–105). It also links, more immediately, with the ethos of
Romanticism which subtly informed Géricault. It resonates with the
idea, voiced by Hegel's friend the poet Hölderlin and echoed, within
their own distinct idiom and discipline, by the French alienists, of a
split which was both the foundation of all philosophical reflection and
constitutive of the human being: *das Eine in sich selber unterschiedne*, in
Hölderlin's translation of Heraclitus, "the one differentiated from itself"
(cited in McGilchrist, 2010, p. 354).

Perhaps this finds literal figuration in the portraits. The child abductor manifests his dual nature as both brooding philosopher, with his
echo of Rembrandt's philosophers, and troubled and troubling abuser.

It may be in the different directions taken by the eyes of the gambler. If her gaze really was bidirectional, as we might read it if the image occurred in a dream, what would she have seen in the mirror? Confirmation perhaps of what the twentieth-century Hegelian Jean Hyppolite was to call "... the impossibility of the self coinciding with itself in reflection ... the basis of subjectivity" (p. 191, cited in Kohon, 2016, p. 149).

CHAPTER SEVEN

The Golden Age of alienism

Medicine as master-discipline

The medical profession was gradually shedding its former, mixed reputation and gathering prestige. Alongside other professions, civil engineering, for example, or painting, it was consolidating its claim to be a profession in its own right, with its own traditions, high standards, and contributions to make to human progress, rather than a trade with mere guild status. A portrait of 1783 by Jacques-Louis David, for example, brimming with gravity and confidence on the parts both of painter and sitter, shows the gynaecologist Alphonse Leroy as an intellectual, a *philosophe*, whose credentials are founded in a marriage of past and present; he leans on a volume of Hippocrates, and is lit by the latest "Quinquet" device, a lamp of unprecedented brightness patented in France in 1780 (the painting is in the Musée Fabre, Montpellier).

Philosophically grounded medicine, which was uniquely placed to explore the mysteries of body–mind relationships, held out the promise of a more comprehensive understanding still: it saw itself as a new master discipline, a future "omnibus science of man", with vast potential in contemporary minds. Only medicine, wrote Esquirol's pupil Etienne Georget, is able to understand every human function without exception

(1820a, p. 12). It was, in the words of another learned contemporary, "the supreme science of the living man" (Goldstein, 1987, pp. 49–51, 78); no profession, what is more, "requires so comprehensive a mind as medicine", for there are "few departments of either physical or moral science with which [medicine] is not, in a greater or lesser degree, connected" (Almeida, 1991, p. 7 and note 10).

A "belief in the art of healing as the foremost humanistic discipline" extended well beyond France (ibid., p. 3), and this is understandable in the light of contemporary medical achievements. There was Bichât's anatomical chart of life and death; there were

> the surgical insights of the heirs of John Hunter, the zoonomic speculations of Erasmus Darwin, the evolutionary studies of Cuvier and Lamarck, the chemical research of Lavoisier, Davy, and Saussure, the analysis of specific poisons by Orfila, Vauquelin, and Berzelius ... the fraught implications for pathology and subspecial diversity of Alexander von Humboldt's South American journeys, the experiments with induced "suspended animation" during surgery of Hickman, the stethoscope of Laënnec and microscope lenses of Brewster and Wollaston, the revelation of electromagnetic principles by Oersted and Faraday, the linkage of psychology and biology by Cabanis, the study of brain anatomy by Charles Bell, and the attempt to map the geography of the nervous system and the personality by Gall and Spurzheim—all these belong to Romantic medicine and its high concern with the issues of life (ibid., p. 3).

These achievements also

> express a more comprehensive participation in the Romantic movement and its fundamental aspiration to know life and read its meaning with all the radical specificity possible to human thought and discourse—and sight. (ibid., pp. 3–4)

The new value placed on the healing art needs to be understood in the context of the era's broader "commitment to the specifics of empirical, existential truth" (ibid., p. 4). Other historians have made an even clearer link:

> It is probably true that the etiology of European Romanticism is located as much in the medical researches of the eighteenth

century as in the disturbances of the sacred and the profane in the increasingly industrialised society. (G. S. Rousseau, 1970, p. 130, cited in Wright, 2001, p. viii)

Numerous doctrines emerging from medicine found their way into public consciousness, "all of them of the greatest interest to artists" (Wedekind, 2013, p. 18), from Lavater's physiognomy, to Gall's and then Spurzheim's phrenology, to Charles Bell's interest in body–mind relationships. Such interest found expression in the concept of the artist and poet as physician of the soul; Schiller, Coleridge, and Novalis were among poets who had hands-on experience of caring for the sick (Snell, 2012, p. 31). It was the belief voiced by the medical student best known to literary posterity, John Keats, that "… axioms in philosophy are not axioms until they are proved upon our pulses." "Nothing", Keats wrote, echoing the method he had learned at Guy's Hospital, "ever becomes real till it is experienced—Even a Proverb is no proverb to you till your Life has illustrated it." This might have been Géricault's own motto, just as he would have resonated to Wordsworth's resolve that his verse would "deal boldly with substantial things" (Almeida, 1991, p. 4).

For Alexander Crichton, at the end of the eighteenth century, attempting to grasp "the connection of the mind to body … [and the] influence which they mutually exert on each other" was central to understanding "the morbid phenomena of the mind" (1798, pp. iii–iv). In France the key figure behind the excitement generated among the pioneers of alienism, and key to promoting this particular branch of medicine's new claims, was Pinel's friend and patron the *idéologue* Cabanis. Cabanis's emphasis on the importance of human sensibility, as that through which intellectual processes come into being, led him to the concern with mind–body relations that was so intensely to preoccupy Pinel and his successors. His *Rapports du physique et du moral de l'homme* (*On the Relations between the Physical and Moral Aspects of Man*), which Stendhal had found so unreadable, set out the agenda for a "new medicine of psychophysiological reciprocity" (1802; Goldstein, 1987, p. 51).

For Cabanis there were along with *le physique* and *le moral* two categories for the phenomena of life: organic operations that are known to us, and those that are unknown to us. One way in which the unknown manifested itself was in somnambulism and dreams. Cabanis followed Locke in emphasising the importance of human sensibility, but in his *Rapports* he went far further than Locke towards a materialist model of mind. Sensibility being a property of the nervous system, thought is a function of the brain, in exactly the same way as bile is a product of the liver. The brain receives impressions, digests them, and secretes thought; what is more it acts directly on all the other organs. For Cabanis there is no soul; the brain *is* that *moral* or moral aspect which can act on "every part of the living machine". Circumstances can sometimes accidentally lend the cerebral system a "surfeit of power and intensity" and produce insanity (cited in Postel, 1970, pp. 14–15).

Pinel did not, however, take this narrowly mechanistic route. For Pinel and for Esquirol the passions were governed by the epigastrium, the part of the abdomen that extends from the breastbone towards the navel; this made pragmatic, experiential sense, since we are all familiar with the effects of strong feelings on the pits of our stomachs. Quaint as this idea now is, it allowed them "to root madness in the body, while detaching it from the brain" (Gauchet & Swain, 1999, p. 150). It thus sidestepped a view of madness as incurable brain disease, the result of cerebral lesion or irreversible overload, and thus validated the moral treatment, with its direct address to the passions; at the same time it maintained the doctors' activities firmly within the realm of medicine, whose field was the body. In fact neither Pinel nor Esquirol ever gave up performing post-mortems, including on the brain, and nor did Georget (as can be read in the title for his book of 1820), although Esquirol's circumspection grew as the century wore on.

> Thirty years ago I would willingly have written on the pathological cause of madness; I would not attempt such a difficult task today, so great is the uncertainty and contradiction in the results of post-mortems of the insane which have been made to date.

But, he continued, recent researches permit one to hope for clearer and more satisfying results (1838, volume II, p. 26, translated for this edition).

The passions were the way out of Cabanis's psycho-physiological monism and materialism; they work "sympathetically" on the brain by way of the stomach and intestines. In a sense Pinel retraces his steps back to Locke, reinstating the importance of experience; if he evades the problem of the origin of the passions (Postel, 1970, p. 15) it is clear that he sees them as at least in part the products of experience. The moral treatment addressed "moral" causes which might affect the body physically, but this did not mean the insanity was physically caused (Goldstein, 1987, pp. 89–90).

Practitioners of the new branch of medicine which dealt with the aberrations and vicissitudes of the passions and the understanding saw themselves as the most philosophical of the *médecins-philosophes*; for Pinel and the *idéologues* this "special medicine" would occupy a central place in the medical anthropology and philosophy constituting a new science of man. Pinel's "medicine of the imagination" furthered the aim of constituting medicine as the master discipline, within the philosophy of psycho-physiological reciprocity (ibid.).

Esquirol

Esquirol was among the first of his generation to be swept along in this current. One view is that he should be credited for the real birth of modern psychiatry; Pinel, in this account, merely prepared the ground as a philanthropist, and the first great milestone on the road to the new science was Esquirol's later, two-volume *Des Maladies mentales* of 1838. The very titles of the two doctors' books convey the distance travelled: from medico-*philosophical* investigation to *maladie mentale*, mental illness. Esquirol in fact continued along the path laid out by Pinel. For Gauchet and Swain the key publication, after Pinel's *Traité*, is not *Des Maladies mentales* but Esquirol's doctoral thesis. Esquirol presented *Des Passions Considerées comme Causes, Symptômes et Moyens curatifs de l'Aliénation mentale* to the Ecole de Médecine on the 7th Nivôse of year 14 (1805). Where the *Des Maladies mentales* is a collection of lectures given from 1817 onwards, in the context of a larger, more evolved and managed asylum, *Des Passions*, as I have suggested, is the expression of an earlier, formative Romantic moment. There is no evidence that the young Beyle knew it, but reading it we can imagine how it might have spoken to him. It is relatively brief, eighty-six pages long; it is not concerned with developing new diagnostic categories, contenting itself with Pinel's general headings of mania, melancholia, and idiocy. It is nevertheless a key text: in its emphasis on the passions as the most common causes of madness, in the confidence with which it affirms the links between body and mind, and most of all in the unequivocal way in which it now insists on the existence of a healthy part of *all* sufferers: "Ils raisonnent tous plus ou moins"—"They all reason more or less" (Esquirol, 1805, pp. 78–79). *Des Passions* tightens the conceptual circle which Pinel laid out more loosely: the existence of a reasoning part of the mad person calls for the moral approach; successful moral treatment proves the reality of this part. The book communicates the energy and enthusiasm that Esquirol was able to generate in his own students a decade or so later; it also contains the tantalising observation that fathers and mothers pass on their characters and passions to their children, "less through the effects of imitation than through a primitive disposition" (ibid., pp. 27–28).

"… if the passions play such a great role … in mental alienation, how much, up to now, has the idea of enlisting them in treatment been neglected?" (ibid., p. 32). There is continuity, he argues, between the familiar human passions, from the acceptable to the most shameful, and madness—pride, for example (ibid., p. 24) or the impulse to steal (ibid., p. 26).

> All the varieties of alienation have their analogy and, so to speak, their primitive type in the character of each passion. The man who said that fury was a prolonged fit of anger might just as truthfully have said that erotic mania is love carried to excess; religious melancholy is zeal or fear of religion pushed over the limits; melancholy with a tendency towards suicide is a prolonged bout of despair. One might say the same of the other passions, which all more or less resemble a kind of madness ("aliénation"), etc. (ibid., p. 21, translated for this edition)

The passions, as, for Esquirol, common sense would seem to insist, belong to the organic life of the body (ibid., p. 17). Brain, nerves, and vital organs work "in sympathy" with each other, and the

> encephalon, as the seat of intelligence and centre of sensibility, reacts upon the other organs, whose impressions and afflictions it receives; such that, relatively to the present state of our ideas and our moral affections, the vital properties of our organs may be excited, suspended, perverted or even annihilated. (ibid., p. 9, translated for this edition)

The passions make their impact felt "in the epigastric region, where, whether originally or secondarily, they have their home; they manifestly alter the digestion, respiration, circulation and excretions, the organs which form the epigastric centre". For example the sight of a beloved excites the reproductive organs, love acts on breathing and circulation, anger speeds up circulation and pushes the blood towards the head, terror causes convulsive spasms (ibid., pp. 9, 17–18). He is cautious about hypothesising causative links in the opposite direction, from organs to brain: "... one cannot be definite as to whether these abdominal changes are the primary cause of alienation." Nevertheless, "... it is at least certain that they usually co-exist with this illness; while it is rare to come across disorders in the brain."

But how then does it come about that the brain and its functions are so often altered under the influence of the passions?, he asks.

> The vital forces constantly seem to direct themselves onto the organ which enjoys superior activity to that of the other organs, or else onto the weakest organ, as Hippocrates observed. Now individuals stricken with mania are almost all of exquisite sensibility; the brain and nervous system have remarkable energy, and are currently straining themselves. (ibid., p. 19, translated for this edition)

Women, with their "more vivid, animated and erotic passions", their sedentary lives, and imaginations inflamed by novels, the theatre, and "the abuse of music", are extremely susceptible, which is why there are more female than male sufferers (ibid., p. 17). "A passion comes along to trouble the epigastric centre; a reaction is produced on the brain and the nerves, as the most active system"—as for example, following persistent study and concentrated intellectual work, and often preceded by an unusual abundance of ideas and liveliness of imagination (ibid., pp. 19–20, translated for this edition).

Under the direct, acknowledged influence of Pinel and Cabanis, and their view of madness as essentially embodied, Esquirol enlivens his thesis with case vignettes, complete with details of both moral and physical treatments, and generalised physical evocations.

> See that man with the inflamed face, convulsive physiognomy, red, sparkling eyes, trembling body? He is limbering up to some act of vengeance; the sharpest and most humiliating expressions are upon his lips; his voice is rough, hard and threatening; his sentences are short, rapid and broken; it seems the organ of speech is not mobile enough for the expression of all the ideas which are

forming a disorderly crowd in his imagination … (ibid., pp. 21–22, translated for this edition)

In contrast to Pinel's limpid, relatively dry style, Esquirol seems to relish and express a sense of embodiment in the very physicality of the words he uses—the look, sound, and sensation in the mouth when they are spoken—especially when he warms to the topic of the stomach and the rectum: "Crises declare themselves when mucous, viscous, brownish, black matter is vomited up; when yellow, black, very foetid blood-streaked matter flows from the stomach; through haemorrhoids, worms …" ("… par des vomissemens de matières muqueuses, visqueueses, brunâtres, noires; par des flux de ventre de matières jaunes, noires, sanguinolentes très fétides; par les hémorrhoïdes, des vers…" (ibid., p. 18, translated for this edition)).

"… let us", Esquirol writes in his concluding paragraph,

> imitate the superstitious faith of certain southern countries where having a mad person in the family is considered a happy omen, and where every care, and every regard for delicacy and the most refined friendship, is extended to them … (ibid., p. 86, translated for this edition)

Thus, in 1805, he ended on a tender, philanthropic note, a distinctive marker of Romantic sensibility. But Gauchet and Swain sum up the real substance of his achievement, which was an advance on Pinel and a theoretical breakthrough. By decisively locating the root of madness in the passions, and in the body, Esquirol definitively and irreversibly grounded it in the human. Just as madness does not comprehensively abolish the self (Gauchet & Swain, 1999, p. 149), its content and forms also "express elements of a comprehensible humanity with which other human beings can identify … madness resembles humans".

> Esquirol's initial formulation [in *Des Passions*] must be resituated in its own time and understood in its true function … Apart from any question of its truth value, it provided the means for overturning the representation of madness as exteriority, for reintegrating insanity within the space of the human. (ibid., p. 165)

Above all, Esquirol explicitly recognised the limitations of cognition as an agent of change—that presenting the patient with rational arguments was never enough. He could hardly have made the point more persuasively than by citing a patient:

> I hear what you are saying to me very well, a young melancholic told me; I follow your reasoning perfectly, if I could understand you and convince myself, I should no longer be mad, you would have cured me. (Esquirol, 1805, p. 83, translated for this edition)

Here was the shift of anthropological perspective already noted, the dissolution of the idea that "the insane are in some way essentially external to themselves and to humanity" (ibid., p. 166). Alongside this shift was now a sharper clinical understanding: Esquirol more knowingly than Pinel "sought to provoke a reflexive turn within the mad person's self", and thus discovered the "singular power of verbal interaction to get in touch with the healthy part of the insane patient and mobilise it against the influence of madness" (ibid., p. 167). It was not reason and persuasion that would help, the appeal to a Cartesian *cogito*, conceived as abstract and free-floating, as if it were external to the subject and able to turn its attention back onto him; it was, rather, direct engagement with embodied affect.

* * *

Thirty years younger than Pinel and Pussin, Esquirol "personifies the final phase in the evolution of psychiatry in Paris during the Revolution and Empire", seeing insanity as something calling for a national solution based on clear, legal concepts (Weiner, 1993, p. 268). Pussin died in 1811, and Esquirol stepped into his role at the Salpêtrière. "Instead of an untutored, although talented former inmate, the supervisor of the women's asylum would henceforth be a physician with considerable experience in the management of ... patients" (ibid., p. 272). Under Pinel's tutelage, Esquirol became the first specialist in psychiatry, in the sense that after him a new career path opened up; his influence was enormous.

He had also been born in south-western France, in Toulouse, in 1772, the ninth of ten children, of a well-to-do Catholic and royalist family.

His father was a merchant and administrator. He was destined for the Church, but the Revolution, having shut down his seminary, obliged him to return to Toulouse, where he began the study of medicine, continuing in Montpellier and returing to Paris in 1798. Unlike Pinel, he never experienced the humiliations of the *ancien régime*; but his father was bankrupted by the Revolution, and an older brother was tried and executed, in 1799, for his part in leading a royalist uprising in Haute-Garonne (Murat, 2014, pp. 150–151). Hence perhaps, Jacques Postel has suggested, his loyalty towards Louis XVIII and the favour he enjoyed under successive Restoration governments (ibid., p. 254 note 4). With Pinel's professional and possibly financial support, Esquirol had established his own private *maison de santé* a couple of years previously, at 8, rue Buffon, next door to the Jardin des Plantes, and a short walk from the Salpêtrière. It became a sort of laboratory for trying out methods to be used with citizen-patients of the future: isolation from family and friends, awe of the director, firm redirection of the psychosomatic *machine* towards health (Esquirol, 1805, p. 70; Weiner, 1993, pp. 268–269).

Esquirol was, in the words of one contemporary, "a man of exquisite tact" (Lane, 1979, p. 263). An excellent account of his journey to a new kind of professional and political status—his adaptation of the role of *patron* inherited from his merchant father—is given in Goldstein's *Console and Classify* (see in particular Goldstein, 1987, pp. 128 et seq.). Under the Empire in 1810 and 1814, and under the Restoration in 1817, Esquirol funded himself to tour the country in order to gather information about provision for the insane outside Paris, which he found to be generally appalling. He published a memoir, which he submitted to the minister of the interior, and a detailed account in the *Dictionnaire des sciences médicales*; on the basis of these he proposed a national programme of reform that was to recapitulate and consolidate developments already set in train by Pinel in Paris. It established the pattern for care of the insane for the next 150 years: the special hospital as the optimal setting for treatment, headed by doctors with specialist training and absolute authority. All these developments were to be enshrined in the law of 1838 of which he was the chief architect two years before his death; the *loi Esquirol* was not substantially revised until 2011. He was appointed doctor in charge of the Salpêtrière in 1820; he had, as we have seen, been delivering formal lectures there from 1817. Under his direction the existence of a "Salpêtrière School", with its claim to a privileged understanding of insanity, entered public consciousness.

Esquirol was a liberal of the conservative, philanthropic kind. He was on the list of subscribers to a fund-raising drive, launched by the newspaper the *Mercure de France*, for the survivors of the *Méduse* (along with the future king Louis-Philippe, the actor Talma, Benjamin Constant, General Lafayette, and Delacroix (Athanassoglou-Kallmyer, 2010, pp. 123–128)). By 1822, when the Restoration appointed him inspector general of medical faculties, his quasi-governmental role was secure. In 1825 he became director of Charenton, which, purged of the licentiousness with which it had become associated in the days of Coulmier and de Sade, was to be the model asylum he had discussed with Pinel and Pussin in the early 1800s (Weiner, 1993, pp. 274–275).

The Salpêtrière School

In the early years of the Restoration, once the initial political and social convulsions had started to subside, new attempts were made to establish public assistance for the insane; similar initiatives under the Empire had come to little. In 1819, François Guizot, historian, future minister of education and prime minister under Louis-Philippe, was appointed director general of the administration for *départements* and communes. Guizot was a dynamic representative of bourgeois liberalism, a staunch defender of the Charter which put a break on the powers of restored royalty. As part of an ambitious programme of prison, asylum, hospital, and hospice reform, Guizot proposed more comprehensive assistance for the insane, with doctors, under Esquirol's leadership, in the front line. The initative was short-lived; but it was an important boost for the "special medicine" and the morale of its practitioners and students (Castel, 1976, pp. 210–215).

Esquirol, married but childless, seems to have liked nothing better than regularly to gather a dozen or so of his students around his Sunday dinner table (Goldstein, 1987, p. 140). In the late teens and early 1820s his pupils, "special doctors" with their common training in the asylums, typically saw themselves, and seem to have been seen, as a corps apart. They were sarcastically characterised by an opponent around 1830 as "these analysts with their privileged insights into the human intellect". In 1871, Charles Lasègue, another pupil of Esquirol's, wrote glowingly of "that distant time when the Salpêtrière School was flourishing" and of the close-knit circle of students around Esquirol.

> The [alienists'] service was open to all, with no formalities, with no imposed doctrine, each studied according to his bent, and brought to bear his personal observations which were debated and discussed, mulled over together with the master's indulgent participation. Thus we lived in friendly activity of the mind which none of us has ever forgotten. (Castel, 1976, pp. 107, translated for this edition)

Lasègue's tone recalls that of the arch-Romantic Théophile Gautier in his *Histoire du romantisme* of 1872; Gautier was reminiscing about his youth as part of Victor Hugo's circle in 1830:

> We had the honour to belong in the ranks of those youthful cohorts which were fighting for the ideal, for poetry and the liberty of art, with an enthusiasm, a bravery and devotion no longer known today. (Gautier, 1874, pp. 1–2, cited in Snell, 1982, p. 15)

The Salpêtrière School in the early 1820s was in certain respects the medico-philosophical equivalent of the studio of a Guérin or Vernet, without the militaristic overtones (but still all-male). It would nevertheless have offered a sympathetic environment for an artistic collaborator like Géricault; we might imagine too that Géricault quickened Esquirol's paternal feelings. But perhaps the connection lies even deeper. For artists, wrote Gilles Deleuze,

> are astonishing diagnosticians or symptomatologists. There is always a great deal of art involved in the grouping of symptoms, in the organisation of a *table* [*tableau*] where a particular symptom is dissociated from another, juxtaposed to a third, and forms the new figure of a disorder or illness. Clinicians who are able to renew a symptomatological picture produce a work of art; conversely, artists are clinicians, not with respect to their own case, nor even with respect to a case in general; rather, they are clinicians of civilization. (Deleuze, 1990, p. 237, cited in Smith, 1998, p. xvii)

* * *

A turning point in the wider political world came in February 1820, with the assassination, outside the Opéra, of the duc de Berry. The event tipped the political balance decisively to the right. The liberal government under Decazes fell, and Guizot resigned shortly afterwards. Power was now in the hands of the Catholic "Ultras", who, suspicious of disaffected and undisciplined youth, attempted to "re-Catholicise" the education system in earnest (Spitzer, 1987, p. 47 etc.). New repression of liberals suspected of any kind of radicalism also ensued. "The philanthropic current and the alienist movement [were] simultaneously affected, a sign both of their solidarity and of the way in which their activities were seen politically" (Castel, 1976, p. 213). If the Salpêtrière alienists were suspected of dangerous liberalism it was not without reason: among Esquirol's students was Georget's exact contemporary Ulysse Trélat (1795–1879), committed republican, Carbanaro, and freemason, who was to fight on the barricades in 1830 and was briefly minister of public works under the Republic of 1848.

The commission on insanity convened by Guizot lost its powers, and further steps towards state provision for the insane had to wait another ten years. On 22 November 1822 the Faculty of Medicine (which included, of particular interest to Géricault, the Ecole pratique de dissection) was closed following a student riot (one of many across the university in response to the government's "reforms"). Phrenology was purged. Eleven professors were dismissed, including the elderly Pinel himself, who despite his prestige lost the post of professor of medical pathology that he had held for the previous twenty-seven years; even his mild republicanism was now suspect. Esquirol, less politically tainted, had to put his reforming ambitions on hold, and left the Salpêtrière for Charenton, while still frequenting the liberal-philanthropic Société de de la Morale Chrétienne.

Such was the medical and political ambience in which, it seems overwhelmingly likely, Géricault made the portraits.

CHAPTER EIGHT

Géricault and the alienists

Medical friends

Géricault had numerous contacts with the medical profession during his work on the *Raft*, notably with the ship's surgeon Henri Savigny with whom he spent much time in 1818–19, learning from his and Alexandre Corréard's accounts of insanity, delirium, and hallucination on board. He made friends with doctors and students at the hôpital Beaujon where he procured corpses for his studies for the picture. He had also painted the head of a robber who had died at Bicêtre (Clément, 1868, p. 51, catalogue no. 105). He may have met Etienne Georget through these contacts, if he and Georget were not already friends since childhood (Michel, Chenique, & Laveissière, 1991, p. 286), or had not met through their mutual friend Brunet. Perhaps they met through Dr Laurent-Thomas Biett (1780–1840), who in 1819 took possession of a major oil painting, *Le Haquet*, dated 1818 by Clément (ibid., p. 50, catalogue no. 96; Miller, 1940–41, p. 158), showing two magnificent draught horses with a wagon, under an imposing arch. Biett was a pioneering skin specialist who worked and taught at the Hôpital Saint-Louis, where Corréard had also been cared for; it is possible that Biett attended Géricault during his illness and depression in late autumn 1819 (Eitner, 1991, pp. 56–57).

Might he have consulted Biett, who gave his name to a particular syphilitic skin symptom, for a suspected venereal condition? Biett was to attend him on his deathbed.

Other medical friends included Guillaume Dupuytren, surgeon and professor of anatomy at the Ecole de Médecine, and the phrenologist Pierre-Marie-Alexandre Dumoutier; might Géricault also have met the young Jacques-François-André Maréchal, also a member of the Société anatomique de Paris (Delmas, 2011) and the future owner, according to Lachèze, of the missing portraits? He certainly knew an alienist called Victor Lebas, a native of Saint-Lô, whom he met around 1820. He made a fresh and vivid crayon and watercolour portrait of Lebas (now in the Musée municipal, Saint-Lô) (Athanassoglou-Kallmyer, 2010, p. 203). It shows a handsome, smartly dressed young man with a firm penetrating gaze; a follower of Pinel, Lebas submitted a sixteen-page doctoral presentation in the same year, 1820, as Georget, on melancholy, *Observation de mélancolie, et quelques propositions sur cette maladie*. It is of surprising modernity, and worth lingering on. Among its propositions is that melancholy is not an innate, "natural" disposition. It is "a moral product" (Lebas, 1820, p. 11). The text opens with the detailed case history of "Paul", and it might almost have been written by Laing and Esterson. Respect for confidentiality is offered in a footnote: the patient "has himself given me the most detailed information on his case, and … has reviewed and approved the work in which I have striven to give an exact idea of him" (ibid., p. 5 note 1). There is a brief physical description: brown hair, clear complexion with good colour, very developed musculature. The author is most interested, though, in his patient's childhood.

> Various causes imprint on his nascent faculties a sort of continual oscillation. If, on the one hand, his maid's tales of wizards freeze him with terror, on the other his mother entertains him with cheerful and graceful fictions in which he takes indescribable pleasure …
> (ibid., p. 1, translated for this edition)

Paul's parents, writes Lebas, were melancholic, and extreme in everything, alternately indulgent and severe, blindly tender or fierce in their discipline. Melancholy, Lebas concludes, is contagious, in the sense that children contract the whole way of being of their parents: in this he was following in Esquirol's footsteps. These parents let the boy get drunk at meals and allow him to lie in bed in the mornings; he masturbates freely and is interested in "certain parts" of little girls of his age; he avoids the company of other children, and is shy and precociously intelligent. He is sent to a strict secondary school, feels he is weak, and becomes sad, defiant, and moody; he feels persecuted and imagines he is being mocked (Lebas, 1820, pp. 5–12, translated for this edition). Lebas's portrait of a troubled adolescent is a nuanced model of proto-psychodynamic understanding.

Géricault and Georget

Lebas and Georget may well have been fellow students. Etienne Georget, born in 1795, was three years younger than Géricault, and belonged to the third generation of alienists; the generational relation of the three doctors, Pinel, Esquirol, and Georget, was paralleled by that between David, Gros, and Géricault (Miller, 1940–41, p. 156). In 1822 Georget was a lively and significant contributor to the Salpêtrière School. His treatise *De la folie*, published in 1820 when he was twenty-five, has been described as the second great classic of French psychiatric literature, after Pinel's *Traité* (Postel, 1972, back cover). He was perhaps especially close to his teacher: he lived in Esquirol's house right up to his early death in 1828 (Eitner, 1982, p. 244).

Painter and doctor had much in common temperamentally. They shared ambition, sensitivity, a passionate commitment to work, and an engagement with suffering (ibid., p. 245). Each also held liberal, materialist, and thus, by definition in the early 1820s, risky views. Like, in some respects, his almost exact contemporary Keats, Georget would have learnt,

> from his lectures and his reading, to question the existence of God and the Soul, to trust knowledge gained only from experience and to believe that human bodies were simply material objects which underwent continual change. (Wright, 2001, p. viii)

Each, the painter of the *Raft* and the author of *De la folie*, would have seen himself as in the forefront of developments within his field. Each was intensely involved with questions about the relationships between *le physique* and *le moral*. They shared an enjoyment of physical strength and prowess. For Georget being a healthy physical specimen was even professionally important. "The doctor exercises … a very great power over the alienated, simply as the man he is ("en sa qualité d'homme") … it is best if he well set up ("plutôt bien que mal") and that above all he does not have any physical defects that are too pronounced and might lend themeslves to mockery" (Georget, 1820a, p. 287, translated for this edition).

Georget was the son of a miller and corn merchant from Indre-et-Loire (Goldstein, 1987, p. 386); if his early education was poor, he shared Géricault's precocity, winning the first Esquirol prize at the Ecole de Médecine for a student paper. He was explicit about his larger philosophical debts: to Condillac and sensationalism, and to Helvétius, with his conviction that education could change the national character (Georget, 1820a, p. 30). His work was "marked by the same qualities of originality, energy and delicacy" as Géricault's; he worked with similar "lavish, headlong, unsparing energy", with periods of *relâche*—he liked to unwind by playing dominos in a nearby café. The year after *De la folie* he published a *Traité de la Physiologie du système nerveux*, which was written in two months, a "tour de force which surprised the profession"; he became an associate member of the Académie de la Médecine in 1823, published frequently in medical journals and contributed entries on encephalitis, epilepsy, madness, hysteria, suicide, and "liberté morale"—on medico-legal problems and homicidal maniacs—for the *Nouveau Dictionnaire de la Médecine* (Miller, 1940–41, p. 157, and see Dezeimeris, 1834). Following Pinel's example he liked to spend most of his time among his patients. The doctor, he wrote,

> must not content himself with seeing patients only once in the morning; he must be continually in their midst, studying the motives behind their actions, the variations in their characters, keeping them up to scratch, seeing if they are holding to the promises they have made to eat, to be quiet, to work, etc. (Georget, 1820a, p. 287, translated for this edition)

He made active efforts to improve moral treatment at the Salpêtrière, for example encouraging therapeutic groups (Postel, 2014), and, as we shall see, to establish it on even firmer theoretical foundations.

In his thinking he manifested a fierce independence of mind, a "liberté d'esprit presque sauvage": "simple and unpretentious in manner, he defended his … convictions with assurance and was outspoken and impersonal in his criticism of ideas and practices which he considered a hindrance to the advance of psychiatry ..." Tact and discretion could give way to the "directness of a typical *frondeur*", and, according to his obituarist Raige-Delorme, he was revolted by injustice and baseness: "... then he did not stint the violence nor the extent of his blows." Having too much of a mind of his own may have closed career doors: "The hypocritical opinions of the time had to push away a man who had ruffled them on more than one occasion," wrote the clearly partisan, liberal Raige-Delorme. Above all Georget insisted, at least in the early 1820s when Géricault would have known him, on avoiding metaphysical explanations, which opened him to the charge of materialism and atheism.

> A powerful enemy of those metaphysical subtleties which have for so long hampered the advance of the sciences of observation, he forcefully rejects those hidden causes, those substantive principles, distinct from the organism, which so many physiologists have misused in their explanations of the phenomena of organised beings ... he sagaciously pursues and seizes the rapports of vital phenomena with the organic conditions to which they may correspond, the only kinds of knowledge to which it is permitted a physiologist to attain. (Raige-Delorme, 1828, translated for this edition, cited in Miller, 1940–41, p. 157)

In 1820, Georget had opposed the vitalists, a body of medical theorists far more acceptable to the regime, in their refusal to invoke "organization (i.e., physiology) as the sole cause of the operations of living beings" (Goldstein, 1987, p. 253). Within his own physiological orientation he was among the first to take seriously Franz Joseph Gall's anti-mystical, anti-theological science of phrenology, the archetypal variety of physiology; phrenology was indeed a symbol of liberal opposition under the Restoration. He attended Gall's private courses before 1820. In 1820 he had shown the first symptoms of TB; a serious attack followed in 1824, and he died in 1828 with a sense, like Géricault's, of the shortcomings of his work and of disappointment at having had to abandon new projects (Miller, 1940–41, pp. 156–157).

What kinds of conversation might Géricault and Georget have had? How might his thinking have resonated with Géricault's? The introduction to *De la folie* might give us a sense. It is written in an elastic, conversational style. Medicine, Georget insists from its start, is a positive science of observation, one of the natural sciences (1820a, p. 2). Be guided by nature; respect mystery and the limits of your understanding, describe rather than try to explain things on merely hypothetical grounds. Some nervous phenomena are extraordinary and incomprehensible—so much so that it has been thought they must be attributable to "a principle independent of the organisation" (ibid., p. 8). But following the analytic method of the natural sciences, we must proceed from the simplest to the most complex organisms, from polyp to man, rather than (ibid., p. 10) leaving it to the theologians and metaphysicians with their preconceived ideas (ibid., p. 11), who do not observe and "take nature as their guide". It is not good enough to describe something you don't understand as "nervous" (ibid., pp. 34–35). Better to say "unknown" than "nervous" (ibid., p. 42). Don't rush to theorise. Hypotheses will come plentifully and quickly "enough to satisfy an imagination more greedy for the marvellous than friendly to the truth" (ibid., pp. 48–49). "We wish to abstain from putting forward any opinion which is not grounded in the facts" (ibid., pp. 38–39).

> … determine the nature of a function before seeking out its disturbances, advance nothing at random, admit your ignorance, rather than risk losing yourself in hypothetical observations, these are the rules that must constantly guide the pathologist. (ibid., p. 43, translated for this edition)

(As indeed the painter.) "Await and respond to the accident of the moment, such must be the conduct of the enlightened physician" (ibid., p. 63).

Georget's ideas on art, and on the mind as something active and dynamic, would have been congenial to Géricault: painting, music, and calculation are, he wrote, always a "bringing together of ideas and judgements" (ibid., p. 29). Following Gall, Georget believed there are fundamental dispositions, "penchans" (sic), common to us all: self-love and procreation; social and religious dispositions; the urge to calculate, paint, make music, remember, associate ideas (ibid., p. 30). We are in other words creatively driven.

Georget did not in fact deny soul; he saw it, however, as inseparable from the body. He felt that if soul is immaterial it can't be changed. But since it is united with the body, it can only exercise its faculties through the intermediary of the organs. In insanity, "The principle is intact, only its agents are ill." This is how one must see "sicknesses of the soul"; thus there was no conflict with received ideas about the immaterial and immortal body (ibid., p. 52, the above all translated for this edition). For Georget as for Géricault, and as Gregor Wedekind has put it, the essence of humanity lies in our shared "creaturely reality" (2013, pp. 176–181).

Géricault as patient?

"Art", wrote Walter Benjamin,

> posits man's physical and spiritual existence, but in none of its works is it concerned with his response. No poem is intended for the reader, no picture for the beholder, no symphony for the listener. (Benjamin, 1973, p. 69)

There is no reason to suppose that Géricault did not simply paint the portraits for himself, in furtherance of his own project of artistic, critical enquiry. Circumstances suggest, however, that other factors were in play too. It also seems possible that he made them as a kind of therapy for himself, encouraged and perhaps attended by Georget, following his breakdown in the autumn of 1819 (Eitner, 1972, pp. 201–202, 242). Did doctors suggest that painting the portraits, away from the boisterous atmosphere of the rue des Martyrs, might be restorative? If he had not been attended to at home in 1819, he may have stayed in Esquirol's private clinic on the rue Buffon, by the zoo. A letter to Mme Vernet, undated but possibly from 1818, seems to support this possibility: he wrote that he could draw or paint for her "elephants, lions, bears, dromedaries, camels" (Michel, Chenique, & Laveissière, 1991, p. 286). Given the history of madness in his family, he would have had reason to be concerned about his own stability.

The idea of remedial activity in the care of the insane was close to Georget's heart; he recommended, as part of treatment, "occupations analogous to a person's station in life" (1820b, pp. 144–145). It would have been consistent with the therapeutic philosophy and practice within which Georget was educated for him to have encouraged Géricault to paint, whether or not Géricault were an inpatient. Within this theory, the painter might have given the pictures to his doctor in gratitude after his recovery.

Perhaps, as Miller suggested, the portraits may also have been part of a therapeutic programme for the other patients (Miller, 1940–41, p. 160). For Esquirol portrait-taking could be a therapeutic event in itself, part of the armoury of the moral treatment, in which insights about the patient's state could be gleaned from her response to having her portrait done (Kromm, 2002, pp. 223–224). Something about the relative scale and formality of the portraits and the fact that they are oil paintings rather than portrait drawings might seem to support this possibility.

Géricault must, like any portrait painter, have established a rapport with his sitters. For John Berger, his "very brushmarks indicate he knew and thought of them by their names" (Berger, 2016, p. 211). Rapidly as the paintings seem to have been made, he would have spent time with his sitters. If he was a patient himself, his position might have felt ambiguous, as other inmates might have felt theirs to be. He might thus, paradoxically, have felt at home, and his sitters at home with him. For the boundary between sanity and madness was porous: former patients might be used for the daily care of current inmates; Pussin himself had been a patient. As Pussin had commented: "Most of the time one does not seem surrounded by madmen" (Weiner, 1993, pp. 256, 261). In Wedekind's view, Géricault found "something of himself, something that is not only, but also, the painter's alter ego. The boundary between the pathological and the normal has become uncomfortably unclear" (ibid., pp. 176–181).

How were both painter and sitter changed in their encounter, which was sustained at least over the time it took to make the painting? The paintings are a record of that time spent, of the coming into being of a relationship. What did the sitters think when they saw the portraits? What did they give back to them of themselves? Did they remind them of or introduce them to a wider world of culture, history, representation? What did Géricault think? What did they give back to him of himself?

For Georget the most vulnerable temperaments, the most susceptible to going mad, were those

> conspicuous for quirkiness of mind, lack of aptitude for the study
> of the exact sciences, a disorderly taste for the arts of pleasure and
> the products of the imagination, original ideas, unusual conduct …
> (1823, p. 14, translated for this edition)

This might characterise the Romantic artist, like "ce fou de Géricault" himself, "extreme and passionate in everything", as Delacroix described him (Miller, 1940–41, p. 162), although he could hardly have been accused of lacking aptitude for study. In Georget's understanding of 1820, which echoed Esquirol's of 1805, passions are the exaltation or almost the delirium of the natural inclinations, the *penchans* pushed to the extreme, detached from reason; he contrasts domination by the passions with the activity of intelligence, combining, judging, comparing, looking at consequences. Forming a bridge between the two is imagination, which is linked to passion and is "the active exercise of faculties man possesses exclusively", of the *penchans* as manifested in poetry, painting, and music. The poetic imagination, he writes, is the same as the passion for poetry; they are interchangeable (Georget, 1820a, pp. 31–33). His task then, if he had had charge of Géricault's care, would have been to reawaken his imagination and re-channel his disorderly passions into his vocation as an artist.

Outsiders, victims, the cast adrift

How much *did* Géricault, who had so willed himself to experience the deprivations of the *Raft's* survivors, identify consciously or unconsciously with his sitters? Is the thief, for example, a fellow wind-swept outsider? For Donald Meltzer the two distinct classes of artists and the mentally and socially ill both find themselves "at the antipodes of the body of the community". Each is indelibly marked by a failure, or refusal, to adapt and conform, as social life requires, in a way that might still allow the maintenance of a private space "for the passions of intimate relationship with the beauty of the world". The mentally ill are "cut off from intimacy by the severity of their delusional ideas". As for artists, their "… pained perception of the inhumanities daily in force about them, juxtaposed to a vision of the beauty of the world being vandalised by these primitive social processes, forbids them to squander the huge blocks of life-time required for adaptation" (Meltzer & Williams, 1988, pp. 14–15). Such a description certainly has some resonance with what we know about Géricault, whose dandified social armour masked and protected his intense and at times hair-triggered responsiveness both to his own internal life and to the world around him.

An overt identification on Géricault's part with the outsider who suffers as a direct result of his passions exists from this period: an oil sketch possibly painted in 1823, perhaps earlier, called *Mazeppa* [Illustration 12]. Broadly painted in blacks and dark blues, with stark highlights, it shows an athletic, naked male body tied to the back of a powerful horse in an elemental landscape; the horse is in the act of pulling itself out of a river onto the bank. Here is the artist, Athanassoglou-Kallmyer comments, tied like Prometheus to his material condition (2010, pp. 106, 109). The subject is drawn from Byron's *Mazeppa*, of 1819, a narrative poem in twenty stanzas which is based on a legend about a seventeenth-century Ukrainian gentleman who has an affair with a countess, the wife of a much older count. Mazeppa is punished by being tied naked to a wild horse, which is set loose. The poem is mostly a description of their breakneck journey; it is a poem of rage and crazed grief, of atonement and redemption. At one point, near death, Mazeppa revives when the horse swims across a river. This is the moment Géricault depicts, his painting staying close to Canto XV of Byron's text, down to the white specks, spots of dusky green and rising moon.

> With glossy skin, and dripping mane,
> And reeling limbs, and reeking flank,
> The wild steed's sinewy nerves still strain
> Up the repelling bank.
> We gain the top: a boundless plain
> Spreads through the shadow of the night,
> And onward, onward, onward, seems,
> Like precipices in our dreams,
> To stretch beyond the sight;
> And here and there a speck of white,
> Or scatter'd spot of dusky green,
> In masses broke into the light,
> As rose the moon upon my right.

There are inescapable echoes of Géricault's love affair with his aunt (and Byron's own incestuous relationship with his half-sister Augusta Leigh):

> I loved her then—I love her still;
> And such as I am, love indeed
> In fierce extremes—in good and ill.

(Byron, 1819, pp. 351, 361)

Georget seems to have respected and even admired the emotional capacities of his patients (Miller, 1940–41, p. 161). Would it be too modern an idea to wonder if he might have encouraged a therapeutic breakdown in Géricault—that he might have allowed him to go through what would now be called a period of regression, even to embrace it? Might it also have been that Géricault himself found breakdown attractive, a potential liberation? At least one contemporary medical commentator acknowledged this dimension. François-Emmanuel Fodéré (1764–1835), a former pupil of Pinel, in 1817 professor of legal medicine and medical policy at the Strasbourg Faculty of Medicine, drew attention to the carnivalesque, liberating appeal of madness. In the preface to his 1817 treatise on delirium—which Georget was to dismiss as a wittily written novel—Fodéré noted how we all seem to agree that we are creatures of reason, and that this distinguishes us from the beasts, while we simultaneously have a primordial taste for the marvellous and do all we can to bring ourselves closer to madness. "I have tried, in good faith, by studying myself, to undo the knot of this contradiction," he wrote. Madness, in fact, is more in charge in the world than reason.

> ... everywhere, in all periods, among all nations, numerous monuments attest that men have felt there to be something constraining in the permanent state of reason, and something happier, more in conformity with their nature, in the abandon of rules of morality and good behaviour. (Fodéré, 1817, translated for this edition, pp. 3, 5)

Yet we are ashamed of being seen as mad. Why? Because of our dual nature, one aspect linking us to the finite, material universe, to our passions and need to propagate, the other to infinity and "supreme reason". Perfection, wrote Fodéré, anticipating the arguments of an Iain McGilchrist, would lie in an equilibrium between the two, and the increase in madness and crime in the modern world is the result of our having abandoned older traditions which recognised this, in favour of an exclusive faith in reason. For just as the Creator commanded the oceans to stay within the limits he had prescribed for them, so he might have said to human reason, "Here are your limits, beyond them you will float without guide or compass" (ibid., pp. 5–7, translated for this edition).

There was of course an ancient tradition, stemming at least from Plato and ideas of the "divine fury" of the poet (Porter, 2002, p. 66), and long predating Romanticism, that made a positive connection between insanity, creativity, or wisdom, or at least a more agreeable life. Rabelais's Pantagruel advises Panurge to seek advice from "a fool, by which he means a sage" who, writes Rabelais, "departing from himself, rids all his senses of terrene affections, and clears his fancies of those plodding studies which harbour in the minds of thriving men" (Murat, 2014, p. 15). By the mid-eighteenth and early ninetenth centuries madness was becoming attractive. Melancholy can be pleasant, and delusions enjoyable, wrote Diderot in the *Encyclopédie*, citing a man who basked in the illusion that he owned all the ships in the harbour (1762, p. 309). On a less venal note, madness might be a "refuge from unbelief—from Bacon, Newton and Locke", as William Blake claimed the spirit of Cowper had told him. In 1796 Charles Lamb, echoing a character in Goethe's *The Sorrows of Young Werther* and anticipating the sentiments of Gérard de Nerval, recalled to Coleridge the "pure happiness" he had experienced while himself locked up, in a manic state, in an insane asylum: "Dream not Coleridge, of having tasted all the grandeur & wildness of Fancy, till you have gone mad." Madness was gaining "a new ideological charge" as a source of creative energy (Rosen, 1998, pp. 113–114).

At the same time, particularly when manifested as melancholy, madness remained both physically disabling and a soul-death, as the nonconformist divine Richard Baxter, writing from experience, put it in the late seventeenth century: it unfitted the Spirits to serve "the Imagination, Understanding, Memory and Affections; so that by their Distemper the *thinking Faculty* is Diseased ..." (Ingram, 1998, p. 43). For Coleridge and others, some 100 years later, descent into madness was the very opposite of stimulus to creativity. It meant sheer paralysis of the will, "blank idealess Feeling", as Coleridge wrote in 1803 (cited in Ingram, 1998, p. 221).

Perhaps there are elements of both kinds of response in the impetus behind the portraits. They do not directly reflect the carnivalesque aspects of madness as, for example, some of Goya's depictions do. It is however part of their background. The *Raft* certainly carried an echo of the Creator's warning as phrased by Fodéré: "Here are your limits, beyond them you will float without guide or compass." The very existence of the paintings was a contribution to the Romantic critique of pure reason.

The portraits as diagnostic and teaching aids

Géricault may or may not have been a patient himself, although there is plenty to suggest that he was. Another much discussed and perfectly compatible possibility is that his skills as a painter were enlisted for professional purposes, in the context of the Pinelian emphasis on observation and of the Salpêtrière School's lively spirit of investigation. The Enlightenment's drive to classify made itself felt in art too; Géricault was aware of the hugely influential, widely translated ideas of the Swiss philosopher J. C. Lavater (1741–1801), who revived the ancient "science" of physiognomy. Lavater postulated the "congruity" of the human organism: all of the forms, gestures, postures, mannerisms, and expressions of the body and especially the face were of symptomatic significance. His *Physiognomische Fragmente zur Beförderung der Menschenkenntnis und Menschenliebe* was published 1775–1778; it relied on copious illustrations. All post-Enlightenment painters and connoisseurs of the portrait owe a debt to Lavater; what indeed might have been the impact of his ideas on ordinary human relations? They certainly made themselves felt in attitudes to insanity and in the field of alienism.

> If … I were to set down what ought to be represented as the prevailing character and physiognomy of a madman, I should say that, his body should be strong and muscular, rigid and free from fat; his skin bound; his features sharp; his eye sunk; his colour a dark brownish yellow, tinctured with sallowness, without one spot of enlivening carnation; his hair sooty, black, stiff and bushy; or perhaps he might be represented as of a pale sickly yellow, with wiry red hair; yet in this I do not proceed upon the authority of the poet, for such I have seen …

So wrote the anatomist, surgeon, and Christian philosopher Charles Bell in 1806, in his *Essays on the Anatomy of Expression in Painting* (p. 153).

There was an immediate precedent for Géricault's artistic involvement in the asylum. His friend Horace Vernet exhibited a painting based on a visit to the Salpêtrière, a sentimental *Folle par amour*, at the Salon of 1819 [Illustration 13]. Vernet's work had been "facilitated by M. Esquirol", according to a letter of 1835 from Géricault's doctor Laurent-Thomas Biett to Pinel's son Scipion, asking permission for Vernet once again to visit the hospital, in order carefully to observe— "sous le rapport d'art"—insane patients. "I thought, Monsieur and dear colleague, that you who have viewed mental alienation from such a philosophical point of view would take some interest in the studies of another kind which M. Vernet is proposing" (Michel, Chenique, & Laveissière, 1991, pp. 323–324). Vernet's painting had been bought by the duc d'Orléans, the future king Louis-Philippe, but it is no longer traceable. His "folle" is another victim of the wars; she is shown holding the battered military collar of her lover in one hand while indicating with the other the location of his mortal wound, just above her coquettishly exposed right breast (Kromm, 2002, p. 242). She belongs in a lineage of other eroticised portrayals of mad women, on one side Fuseli's *Mad Kate*, for example, of 1806–07, and on the other a jilted *Folle* of 1899, her wedding dress in disarray, by one Pierre-Georges Jeanniot (Musée Petiet, Limoux). Where Vernet and various successors aimed to titillate, Géricault clearly had other concerns in mind.

The idea of painting the portraits of patients in his care would also have been compatible with Esquirol's medical and professional project. There was increasing medical interest in the diagnostic possibilities of physiognomy. Miller cited no less than eight doctoral theses on the subject written in Paris between 1800 and 1822 (Miller, 1940–41, p. 158). Pinel had published engravings of skulls and facial conformations in both editions of the *Traité*; he showed less interest than his successors in facial appearances, although he did quote a passage by Cabanis in which the *idéologue* compared the look of violent maniacs to that of more sanguine temperaments:

> A bolder and more emphatic physiognomy, sparkling eyes, a dry and often yellow face, jet-black hair, sometimes frizzy ("crépu"), a powerful but lean frame ... a thin body with sticking-out bones ... [These men] want to carry all before them by force, violence, impetuousness ... (Cabanis cited in Pinel, 1801, p. 89, translated for this edition)

Does this description fit Géricault's kleptomaniac of some twenty years later? The portraits were certainly consistent in spirit with a major illustrative project of Esquirol's. In *Des Passions* Esquirol was already advocating the usefulness of drawing the physiognomies of his patients, for diagnostic, prognostic, and preventative purposes. Citing Lavater, Crichton, Pinel, and Cabanis on the effects of the passions on the human face, he recommends

> ... drawing the heads of a great number, recording the character of the physiognomy of each during the attack, and comparing these heads with those in which the great masters have applied

themselves in order to paint the passions. By means of this comparison, one would arrive at results as useful as they would be interesting, which would serve not only to cure this illness but also to prevent it. (1805, p. 27, translated for this edition)

In his middle age his view was still that "... study of the physiognomy of the insane is not an object of idle curiosity; such a study helps tease out the character of the ideas and affections which feed the delirium of these patients." He had plans to further this project. "What interesting results might one not obtain from such a study. I have had more than 200 insane inmates drawn with this in view; perhaps I shall publish my observations on this interesting subject one day" (Esquirol, 1838, vol. II, p. 19). A British visitor in 1818 reported Esquirol had a collection of 200 casts of the faces of the insane and 600 skulls (Eitner, 1982, p. 354 note 33). While he never did publish his full collection of images, his entry on madness in the *Dictionnaire des sciences medicales*, volume VIII, of 1819 is illustrated with a number of plates (Boime, 1991, pp. 82 etc.), and *Des Maladies mentales* contains a collection of twenty-seven plates engraved after various artists, notably Georges-François Gabriel (1775-*c*.1850) (Appignanesi, 2008, p. 69), a former "guillotine artist", that is, one who made posthumous portraits of the recently guillotined—as had Géricault himself. Géricault is likely to have seen a folio of Gabriel's drawings "taken from a collection intended for a work on mental illness by Dr E ..." at the Salon of 1814 (Eitner, 1982, p. 244). A bound album of these drawings can be seen in the Bibliothèque Nationale; around 1836 Gabriel also produced a series of pencil portraits of famous criminals (ibid., p. 354 note 35). Esquirol named two other artists who contributed to his 1838 book: M. Desmaisons, "a young medical student" (Esquirol, 1838, vol. I, p. 166), and a M. Roque of Toulouse, "a painter as distinguished by his talents as honoured by his character" (ibid., vol. II, p. 112).

The plates in *Des Maladies mentales*, while showing variations in style and detail, are generally austere line engravings, with simple cross-hatched shadows and modelling, clearly designed to highlight the symptomatic sign, the characteristic bodily and facial contortion, posture or set of the features. They are accompanied by Esquirol's descriptions. Plate XIX, for example, shows M. V., a young man aged seventeen, an "imbecile" seen from the front, with a handsome face, plaintive expression, and full head of dark hair, sitting on a chair and held in by a straitjacket "to which one is often obliged to resort ... to prevent the accidents to which he is exposed by his continual impulsion to hit himself" (ibid., pp. 89–90). G ..., plate XVIII, aged forty-three, entered the Salpêtrière aged nineteen in 1813. The engraving shows a thick-set woman in a smock with a lined face and cropped hair. She too is sitting in a chair and is seen from one side, studying her raised right wrist which she touches with the fingers of her left hand (ibid., pp. 88–89). Aba [Illustration 14], an "idiot" from Bicêtre, aged about thirty, is seated, and seen from the front; he has short hair, downcast eyes, and a turned-down mouth. He wears a full-length overcoat done up to his chin, and large clogs. He might be rubbing his clasped hands. Esquirol writes that he has a "... large head, but flattened at the back ... his physiognomy is vague, uncertain and expressionless ..." (ibid., pp. 93–94, translated for this edition).

Plate VI [Illustration 15] shows L ..., a woman of fifty-seven, in a head and shoulders format identical to that of Géricault's portraits (the only illustration in the book in this format); her dark, fairly unkempt, perhaps grey-streaked hair seems to be done up at the back, and she wears a dress or shawl which is wrapped over her breast in a V, an arrangement very like that of the monomaniac of envy. She is also similar to Géricault's figure in her high forehead, and the slight rightwards and downwards tilt of her head. She looks straight out at us, however, rather than down and to the side. A laundress in her former trade, she had been diagnosed as a "démonomaniaque". She was, Esquirol wrote, "very pious from childhood". Could she be the same person as the woman painted by Géricault? Esquirol noted her

> ... extreme thinness, sunburned, dirty skin, yellow complexion; anxious physiognomy; the whole body is in a sort of continual vacillation and balancing, L ... is always walking, looking to do some harm, to hit, to kill ... she avoids her companions, fears she will hurt them, talks to herself, sees the devil everywhere and often argues with him. (1838, vol. I, p. 246, translated for this edition)

* * *

Athanassoglou-Kallmyer takes the view that unlike his teacher, Georget showed little confidence in physiognomic diagnosis, and that this disqualifies him as Géricault's possible patron or collaborator. She comes to this conclusion on the strength of a passage in *De la folie*, which she translates thus:

> It is difficult to describe the physiognomy of the mentally ill; it is necessary to observe them in order to preserve an image of them. Persons are unrecognisable at times; the features of the face have altered their alignment, their general arrangement is wholly distorted. (Georget, in Athanassoglou-Kallmyer, 2010, p. 195)

There seems no doubt, however, that observation and description, attention to outward appearance and to physical signs that might be clues to inner states, were clinical resources for Georget as they were for Esquirol. Did Géricault possibly make the portraits for a revised edition of *De la folie*, unrealised because of Georget's illness and early death (Miller, 1940–41, p. 158)? In *De la folie* Georget describes the appearance of patients at the onset of periods of excitement. Rather than dismissing physiognomic description, he stresses its difficulties, which result from his patients' facial mobility.

> The capillaries of the face, the eyes, and the skin of the skull, are more or less suffused [with blood] and render the skin and the conjunctiva red, brown, or purplish-blue, depending on the individual's usual colouration. The forehead, the face, and sometimes the whole head, give off more heat than any other part of the body ... The eyes are usually shining ... vivid, animated, sometimes in convulsive movement ... *Describing the physiognomy of the insane is difficult; it is necessary to observe it in order to keep the image of it in one's mind. People are unrecognisable at these moments; the features of the face have changed direction, their ensemble is all mis-shapen.* ("Il est difficile de décrire la physionomie des aliénés; il faut l'observer pour en conserver l'image. Les personnes sont méconnaissables alors; les traits de la face ont changé de direction, leur ensemble est tout déformé.") (My italics.)

He continues:

> Physiognomies are nearly as different as individuals; they vary according to the passions and the various ideas which beset or agitate them, the character of the delirium, the stage of the illness etc..

> Generally, the face of idiots is inane and insignificant; that of mani-
> acs is as disturbed as their spirits, and is sometimes contorted,
> convulsed; with the stupid, the features are downcast and with-
> out expression; the *facies* of melancholics is contracted and bears
> the mark of suffering or of something extremely preoccupying;
> the monomaniac king has a proud and haughty look, the humble
> believer prays with his eyes fixed on the ground; the fearful flees
> looking from side to side etc.. I shall stop at this simple reading, for
> sight alone can give an idea of the rest. (Georget, 1820b, pp. 60–61,
> translated for this edition)

Similarly, 150 years later, Lorenz Eitner brought his art historian's gaze
to bear on Géricault's portraits, noting that the "internal activity" of the
sitters is revealed

> … in slight turns of the postures, much more subtly varied than they
> seem at first sight. There are finely observed differences between
> the alert readinesss of the *Kleptomaniac*, the menacing crouch of the
> *Envious Woman*, and the senile slump of the *Gambler*. (Eitner, 1982,
> p. 246)

He points out that all show only head and shoulders; the focus is on the
face, there are no hands, a minimum of distraction. He observes how
Géricault "took pains to specify his sitters' complexions" and "noted
the difference between the waxy sallowness of the *Gambler's* face, the
flushed cheeks of the *Kleptomaniac*, and the unhealthy, mottled skin of
the *Kidnapper*" (ibid., p. 248). Esquirol, in his chapter on monomania,
"De la monomanie", similarly paid careful, refined attention to nuances
of appearance: "The physiognomy of the monomaniac is animated,
mobile, laughing, the eyes are lively and shining", compared to the
"yellow, pale and … sallow" lypemaniac (melancholic) (1838, vol. I,
p. 332, translated for this edition).

For Georget the insane had more intensity and singleness of feeling
than the normal person: "Each penchant, each passion, can come to
dominate the understanding." Joy, sadness, fear, temper, deceitfulness,
vanity can show themselves "forcefully, violently, persistently" (1823,
p. 18); given Géricault's passionate nature he might, Miller wrote, have
been expected to value these qualities in the patients, especially given
their more-than-normal facial expressiveness, as Georget described it.

> The physiognomy is often very expressive and gives a pretty good indication of the nature of the mental disorder. Joy, contentment, fear, sadness, despair … all these passions have their signs on the physiognomies of the alienated as they do on those of reasonable individuals; only they are a lot more pronounced with the former because the passions which make up the character of the delirium, acting continually and with force, work to leave more profound traces. (1823, p. 19; Miller, 1940–41, pp. 161–162, translated for this edition)

In Miller's account of the portraits, Géricault would have been the ideal choice of painter, with his original ideas of *le beau* which contrasted starkly with, for example, those of his older contemporary Ingres, who abhorred the *Raft* as a wilful celebration of hideousness. "How beautiful you are!", Géricault is alleged to have said to his friend the painter Lebrun, who was suffering from jaundice at the time and looked like a living corpse; his studies of Lebrun were indeed incorporated into the *Raft* (Miller, 1940–41, pp. 159 and 159 note 4; Oprescu, 1927, p. 103).

If diagnostic and teaching aids are what they were, we must also consider the physician's possible role in setting them up. Did the sitters pose themselves, or did Georget, or Esquirol, instruct them and Géricault as to how they were to hold themselves, so that they might, precisely, conform to a preconceived diagnostic, physiognomical idea and "produce already established readings" (Isaak, 1996, pp. 159–160)? How far was the painter himself responsible for their poses? Delacroix recalled "how Géricault used the model, that is to say freely, yet rigorously making him pose" (journal entry of 19 Feb 1847; Delacroix, 1980, p. 133). Or did Géricault arrange the figures, too restless to sustain lengthy poses, in his imagination, or according to his memory of how they could hold themselves from moment to moment? They are consistent in their avoidance of the painter's and the viewer's eye; were the sitters schooled in this? How much is the portraits' apparent naturalism artifice? To what extent is the appeal to "nature", as voiced by both Géricault and Georget, always already subtended by pre-established perceptual and aesthetic codes, and how far is what may be perceived in nature and apparently recorded from it always on the cusp of becoming a new encoding or subtle variant on an old one? There is no avoiding these Gombrichian questions, to which we shall return shortly, in the company of the art historian Jane Kromm; but far from diminishing the paintings, they seem to contribute to the richness of their hermeneutic and emotional possibilities.

If, finally, Georget did have a diagnostic and didactic project in view, it is likely, given what we know about his own temperament and culture, that it would have been on the basis that he could take it for granted that his friend would be approaching his task as an artist; he would be making *paintings*, that is, attempts to embody in paint as much of his lived experience of the embodied person in front of him, with as much authenticity, life, and integrity, as he could summon in himself. The sitters share facial characteristics—the kleptomaniac's reddish nose and bloodshot eye, for example—with other heads painted by Géricault; the 2013–14 Frankfurt and Ghent exhibition allowed a close comparison with portraits made in connection with the *Raft*. A portrait of an African model, Joseph, of 1818–19 (J. Paul Getty Museum, Los Angeles), has similarly bloodshot eyes, and also seems lost in his own thoughts, as do the *Carpenter* (1818–19, Musée des Beaux-Arts, Rouen) and the *Shipwrecked Man* (1818–19, private collection). All, both those made in connection with the *Raft* and the monomaniacs, share the same sophisticated lighting. In fact, exactly contrary to what Athanassoglou-Kallmyer has suggested, it is more likely that it was the very difficulty of describing the plasticity of his patient's faces that led Georget to ask Géricault to paint them. Who would be better equipped than an artist and experienced portraitist to "observe ... and keep the image ... in mind", to see, remember, and remember the moment of seeing? This ability had been the stock-in-trade of the fashionable pastellists of the eighteenth century, who flourished above all in France; the idea that emotional truth might best declare itself to a passing glance was hardly the monopoly of the alienists. "Eugène had not yet learnt to analyse a woman's face by catching a quick or side-on glimpse of it," wrote Balzac of his young hero Eugène de Rastignac, as he sallied forth into society (1830b, p. 148, translated for this edition).

Georget, in this understanding, was relying on Géricault's ability to catch the patients' fugitive expressions in their moments of madness. Whether this was the moment of maximum alienation from themselves, or that at which they most truly and intensely showed themselves, was perhaps a question Georget did not resolve; an aspect of the indeterminacy of the portraits, perhaps it was also one of the open questions warmly debated within the Salpêtrière School. Meanwhile, simply by virtue of their status and apparent truthfulness as serious portraits in oil, the paintings confirmed a key aspect of the Pinelian, medico-philosophical ethic, that the condition of being sane, in abeyance as it might be, was always an inalienable potential of the human being.

Normalising, bourgeoisification

There can be little doubt the portraits were painted within the walls of the asylum, although whether at the Salpêtrière, the rue Buffon, or possibly Bicêtre, is not known. The emphasis on the asylum itself as curative, a machine for socialising, especially after Esquirol's appointment at the Salpêtrière in 1811, reinforced the implication that "cure" meant adaptation and normalisation. But this would not mean reduction to uniformity—on the contrary. Each depiction is the record of a unique individuality, as conveyed in the seemingly inconsequential detail of clothing or gesture, and this kind of attention is particularly echoed in Esquirol's writing. His purely "physiognomic" descriptions are supplemented by other observations, which while they might have been meant to be of future diagnostic use, are also of a kind a novelist or painter might have made. Is this "novelistic" or painterly sense something directly generated by Esquirol's choice of words, or is it that *any* description, verbal or visual, however neutral and sparse, has the potential to evoke a human presence? It is also worth remembering that the wider setting was Paris. "Who can fail to observe that there, as in every other zone of Paris, there is a mode of being which reveals what you are, what you do, where you come from, and what you are after?" wrote Balzac, evoking the masked ball at the Opéra in 1824 (1838/1843, p. 19). Esquirol was acute to what might be read from the physiognomic mask; but he also seems to have been open to what was ineffably social and human behind it.

The intractible seventeen-year-old M. V., for example, has

> a convulsive physiognomy [that] is not without expression, sometimes it is sad and full of pain. The face is lined from habitual grimacing ... He is sweet-tempered, defiant, fearful ... (Esquirol, 1838, vol. II, pp. 89–90)

Another patient, G., is

> obedient but can be very obstinate ... She constantly carries in her right hand some ribbons rolled up to resemble a doll, and to show

her hurt or her contentment she repeatedly and in a lively way carries these ribbons up to her right temple. (ibid., pp. 88–89)

Sometimes Aba, from Bicêtre, plate XXII [Illustration 14],

seems to meditate (it was at a moment like this that he was
drawn) ... sometimes his physiognomy betrays a light smile, a look
of malice, especially when he sees strangers ... he eats slowly and
stops frequently in the posture of a man who is thinking, fearful,
astonished, curious, but this passes quickly ... (ibid., pp. 93–94)

For an instant, in this doctor's description, Aba comes back to life.

As Margaret Miller underlined, Géricault's five canvases were
painted as normal portraits. He represented his sitters "in no specific environment, such as a hospital room, which might betray their
segregatrion from normal society, and in no particular action which
might dramatise their disease and so isolate from the experience of the
average spectator" (1940–41, p. 153). For the art historian Régis Michel
each of the portraits is a plea for an Esquirolian "normalisation of the
mad, who is ill and a victim", to underline that the chained-up nudity
of the old confinement is a thing of the museum, a point Esquirol made
unequivocally, and never more strongly than when he could make a
patrioic comparison. He refers not to the bad old days at the Salpêtrière
or Bicêtre, but reports instead on the case of a naval officer who had
attacked the eminent British alienist John Haslam and been chained at
the neck, waist, and feet for nine years at Newgate prison (1838, vol. II,
p. 200, and plate XXV).

The sitters, citizen-patients, seem cared for. In 1790 the clothing
of inmates of the two great hospitals, renewed every two years, consisted of pants and a jacket for the men at Bicêtre, made of grey home-
spun or linsey-woolsey, and a skirt and a cloak for the women at the
Salpêtrière—or at least, this is what the regulations said (Weiner, 1993,
p. 66). Géricault's sitters wear their own clothes, those of the employed
working class or the lower bourgeoisie, not of some uniform mass of the
abject and dispossessed, and this underlines the invitation to us to view
the wearers as idiosyncratic individuals. There is tension and contradiction: the kleptomaniac's unkempt hair and unshaven beard might be
taken as signs of his asociality (Michel, Chenique, & Laveissière, 1991,
p. 244), but this is in contrast with the white, delicately cross-patterned

cravat, a hint of gentility (might it almost turn up on a character in Jane Austen, a Paris fashion just arrived in Hampshire?).

The art historian Albert Boime further stressed their possible "normalising" purpose; he put forward a view that Géricault's "human documents" may have had a further illustrative and didactic purpose, one also shared by Esquirol, that is, that the original ten paintings were "before" and "after" portraits, the five lost portraits being the "after" ones, showing the sufferers restored to sanity (Boime, 1991, p. 83). *Des Maladies mentales* offers just such pairings: V ..., a servant girl, who was diagnosed as a maniac and left the Salpêtrière in 1815, initially showed her doctor a physiognomy marked by "agitation ... indignation ... rage"; later, she was "calm and poised, with a light hint of melancholy which is so common following an attack of mania", in a remarkable transformation from savagery to demureness (Esquirol, 1838, vol. II, pp. 17–19, plates VIII and IX). Another "femme maniaque", thirty-nine years old, is seen twice in profile; in the first engraving "the features are convulsed and tense, with a sardonic smile ... while the physiognomy of this same woman cured ... expresses sweetness, good will and a kind of gaiety". It is, Esquirol says, hard to believe they are the same person (ibid., p. 19, plates X and XI).

In this account the portraits are documents of the reintroduction of the alien, crazy other into the world of work and normality. Is it appropriate to call the process "bourgeoisification"? Gauchet and Swain are dismissive of "naïve claims about the insidious intention to inculcate the 'bourgeois' work ethic", not to mention "moralising platitudes about complicity with triumphant industrialism"; their interest was in fundamental changes in sensibility which made possible the very idea of reintegrating the insane into the social framework (Gauchet & Swain, 1999, p. 106), and in "the irony of this logic of integration", which could only operate through segregation, thus "giving a foothold to tendencies and beliefs that that kept inmates in a world apart" (Seigel, 1999, p. xvii). All that is known about Géricault's own oppositional and liberal instincts also makes it hard to imagine him involving himself in a project of reintegration that was as adaptive as Boime suggests; there is nothing, indeed, in his work to suggest the Restoration vision of tamed, domesticated femininity that is evident in Esquirol's contrasts.

The portraits come out of a different kind of impulse. There is no doubt, however, that by the time Géricault painted them the idea of the norm was becoming established in public consciousness, and it is against this background that they generate their tensions. They invite—and would have invited at the time—the kinds of question that, for Ian Bostridge, are prompted by the wanderer in Schubert's *Winterreise*: "Do we identify with him, or seek to separate ourselves from him? Is he sympathetic or repellent? Insightful or embarrassing? Weird or normal?" (2015, p. 364).

Professional identity

In Boime's account, Géricault was implicated in a professionalising agenda, in particular as taken forward by Georget: he commissioned the portraits in order to bolster his professional status. The process by which the attempt was being made to induct the inmates of the asylum back into full citizenship was of a piece with the establishment of the alienist's own professional identity. This was underway in specfic respects: patriotic, in relation to the good order of the state, and in relation to other professions. Géricault's portraits might be seen, in their own indirect way, as contributions to the public and the professional self-image of the doctor-alienist. In 1805, the year of Austerlitz and Trafalgar, when he was writing *Des Passions*, Esquirol might not have been expected to have much good to say about England, which he could not even bring himself to name: it was merely "une nation rivale et jalouse" which, he wrote, falsely claimed to have discovered the moral treatment (1805, p. 9). Delicate Anglo-French relations persisted into the Restoration: which nation, post-Waterloo, was the true arbitrator of civilisation? This rivalry played itself out in medicine among other arenas, in, for example, "the Bell-Magendie affair". François Magendie was among Géricault's doctor acquaintances (he gave him a drawing for *The Race of Riderless Horses*), and a groundbreaking figure in the field of physiology and neurology. His experiments in the early 1820s led to the discovery of differentiated sensory and motor nerves in the spinal cord, and this brought him into conflict with Charles Bell, who believed that the sources of perception and sensation were to be found in different parts of the brain and nervous system. We have seen the patriotic use Esquirol made of the visual contrast between the treatment of patients in the French versus the English asylum (the chained-up naval officer; Esquirol, 1838, vol. II, p. 200, and plate XXV). Charles Bell's drawings in his 1806 book did nothing to soften the contrast between antiquated English barbarism and French scientific and humanitarian innovation: a furious, muscle-bound, teeth-grinding maniac writhes half-naked in his chains on the floor [Illustration 16], where Géricault's figures evince an undemonstrative suffering that is contained within the clothes of ordinary citizens and ordinary portrait conventions (Athanassoglou-Kallmyer, 2010, pp. 152, 199–202; Bell, 1806, p. 53). Appeal to national prestige was a powerful aid to professional self-confidence, and the portraits, had they been seen by a wider contemporary public, might certainly have contributed to this.

"Happy coincidence": the disciplinary dimension of the moral treatment

"Happy coincidence, in which the application of rigorous measures unites the patient's interests with the general good", commented the marquis de Barthélemy on the 1838 insanity law (cited in Castel, 1976, p. 204, translated for this edition). Underlying the alienist's sense of professional identity, and partly masked by it, was the real power at the doctor's disposal, and the kinds of force he drew upon in order to exercise it. "It was between the walls of internment", wrote Foucault, "that Pinel and nineteenth-century psychiatry discovered the mad; it is here, we should not forget, that they left them, not without having claimed the glory of redeeming them" (cited in Hazan, 2010, p. 155). How far is this claim justified? How far do the illustrations in *Des Maladies mentales*, and Géricault's portraits, also introduce us to the violence subtending the asylum and the moral treatment?

In 1794 Pinel had delivered a paper which many consider to be the founding document of French psychiatry, his "Observations on Mania at the Service of the Natural History of Mankind" ("Observations sur la manie pour servir l'histoire naturelle de l'homme"); it was perhaps the earliest statement of the essentials of the alienist's position. Madness was an affliction of human sensitivity caused by the tribulations of living; it was never totally overwhelming, and was treatable by means of the moral treatment, which should be gentle, benign, non-repressive and non-violent, except in emergencies. This treatment did, however, embrace another key technique, which was applicable in general and not just in extreme circumstances: intimidation, through a firm and imposing tone of voice or other show of force, for example the presence of several attendants together. Here Pinel was unequivocal.

> One of the major principles of the psychological management of
> the insane is to break their will in a suitably timed manner, [to tame
> them] without causing wounds or imposing hard labour. Rather,
> a formidable show of terror should convince them that they are
> not free to pursue their impetuous willfulness and that their only
> choice is to submit. (cited in Murat, 2014, p. 45)

This apparent contradiction, gentleness and dialogue on the one hand,
and "a formidable show of terror" on the other, catches the ambivalence
at the birth of psychiatry. Murat notes the date, late 1794: the Terror
had only ended in July, with the fall of Robespierre. The emergency
revolutionary council to which, for all his wariness of revolutionary
extremism, Pinel symbolically belonged, was committed to saving the
republic of reason "in its fight against insanity—the insanity of both
tyrants and lunatics". It is a contradiction that, Murat argues, permeates
the whole history of mental therapy, "trapped between the demon of
domination and the ambition of communication with the mad, leading
to a failure we are familiar with" (ibid., p. 46).

Pinel was also explicit about the parallels between moral treatment
and the superiority of the medical master-discipline, and the art of
politics:

> The principle of moral philosophy which learns not to destroy
> human passions but to oppose them one to another, is equally
> applicable in medicine and in politics, and this is by no means the
> only example of contact between the art of governing men and of
> curing them of their infirmities; the difference, if there is one, even
> gives medicine the advantage, which takes the most elevated point
> of view, considers man in himself, and independently of our social
> institutions, and often sees no other remedy than not going against
> the tendencies of nature, or counter-balancing them with more
> powerful affections. (1801, pp. 237–238, translated for this edition)

Esquirol, in 1818, was also clear that powerful counterbalancing measures were generally required: therapy with maniacs needed to involve
not so much reasoning and argument, which he called a pipe dream,
as dominating and capturing the attention (pp. 30, 464). The technique
elides all too easily with the other, not-so-hidden agenda of the asylum,
as a place of correction. Laure Murat puts it bluntly: "Asylum or political

prison?" (2014, p. 71). The asylum was indeed ambiguous in nature; the public hospital during the Napoleonic and post-Napoleonic eras also lent itself to use as one convenient jail among others.

> Administrative detention and medical confinement, whether they succeeded one another or overlapped, were part of the same continuum, made possible by the legal vacuum in which mental illness found itself in the period between the abolition of *lettres de cachet* and the legislation passed in 1838. (ibid., p. 76)

In effect, the old *lettres de cachet* system subsisted in all but name under the Empire and during the Bourbon Restoration and early years of the July Monarchy. The portraits breathe historical violence.

Monomania: alienism and the law

In a lecture at the Salpêtrière in 1819 Esquirol introduced his new and powerful diagnostic category: monomania. It was the logical development and outcome of the notion of partial insanity. If a keystone of the moral treatment, and therefore of the alienist's professional identity, was that the unaffected part of the sufferer was available for the alienist's interventions, and the understanding and passions of the patient her- or himself were to be mobilised in the cure, then monomania was the perfect illness for the treatment, and the monomaniac the ideal patient. It was to remain the dominant diagnostic category in French psychiatry for over three decades.

Pinel had developed his views in the *Traité* with the help of *historiettes* (the king sending out dispatches, the religious fanatic, the clockmaker). He used the case study particularly to illustrate his concept of a *manie sans délire* in which rational thinking and intermittent furore coexisted (Kromm, 2002, p. 216). In *Des Passions*, and in his first articles in the early 1800s (in the *Journal Général de Médecine, de Chirurgie, et de Pharmacie*) Esquirol followed Pinel enthusiastically in arguing for "the efficacy of frank discussion, sympathetic support and gaining the patient's confidence" and presenting these claims within a detailed case-history format in which he gives accounts of changes in facial expression, physical movements, and conversation (Kromm, 2002, p. 219). Later, however, he sought to revise Pinel's nosology, in articles of 1814 on "Démonomanie", of 1818 on "Manie", and of 1819, in which he introduced the new category of monomania. His new diagnostic scheme was based on distinguishing exclusively between different types of mania; the older category of melancholia, which had traditionally taken precedence, was replaced with "lypemania". Full mania was the theoretical benchmark against which variants could be defined; it was "l'image de chaos", a "condition of complete incomprehensibility" (ibid.) for the observer, outside the limits of rational understanding (much as this contradicts his earlier statement, of 1805, that *all* his patients reasoned, more or less; the contradiction seems to have come out of theoretical or rhetorical necessity). In full mania, the whole understanding was disrupted, whereas in monomania "the understanding is healthy, sometimes, even, more active, more lucid" (Esquirol, 1838, vol. I, p. 334). Esquirol argued that if full-blown mania were total, then *manie sans délire* would be a contradiction in terms. Monomania was also different from melancholia (now lypemania): if it involved a similar fixity of ideas and obsession with a single object, it was not depressive like melancholia. Thus Esquirol circumscribed his new category. Unreason, investing only a part of the sufferer, consisted in certain *idées fixes*, an exclusive focus on one idea, passion, or desire, to steal, for example, or to abduct; for Esquirol, Don Quixote was the perfect monomaniac (Murat, 2014, p. 117). Each monomania could be named after its particular fixation, another diagnostic innovation: there might be monomanias of wounded pride or frustrated ambition or monomaniacs who thought they were kings or inventors. Because the patient's apparent reasonableness might deceive the nonexpert eye into seeing sanity where madness lay, training and practice in reading the visible, physiognomic signs were mandatory; the possibility that the portraits served an instructional and diagnostic purpose once more comes back into focus.

Monomania was a counter in what sociologists call a boundary dispute (Goldstein, 1987, pp. 166 etc.). It enabled the new profession to argue for a further expansion of its remit into territory formerly exclusive to the legal profession: the signs of insanity might be visible to the expert eye outside the walls of the asylum. The great debate over monomania and culpability came to a head in 1825: "The figure of the conscious but alienated criminal brought to the social scene for the first time the core of the psychiatric discovery … namely, the drastic reduction of the individual's moral autonomy and conscious power" (Gauchet & Swain, 1999, p. 161). This figure was not, to judge by the virulence of some contemporary reactions, an easy one to tolerate.

The doctor chiefly responsible in the 1820s for the alienist's successful incursion into the domain of criminality and the law was Esquirol's protégé Georget. In staking alienism's place in the courts, Georget extended its remit, while at the same time seeking to underline its humanity. In 1825 and 1826 he published two influential pamphlets, which changed the tenor of the discussion of insanity and the law (Goldstein, 1987, p. 165). In 1826, in a criminal trial that, as Foucault also noted, marks a turning point in medico-legal discourse, Georget testified in defence of a child murderer, Henriette Cornier. Cornier, he argued, was mad, suffering from a "monomanie homicide", and must therefore be confined to an asylum, on both medical and humanitarian grounds; non-experts would have a miscarriage of justice on their hands if they were deceived by her apparent reasonableness and sent her to the guillotine (Appignanesi, 2008, pp. 72–78). Reactions from a hostile royalist and conservative press are revealing, not least of the persistence of ancient fears of the mad and their animality: "… patients of this type probably make no exceptions, and when the appetite comes to them, they are ready to eat their own physician, could they find him in the vicinity of their teeth" (from an article of 1825 cited in Athanassoglou-Kallmyer, 2010, p. 205).

Each of the monomaniacs in Géricault's portraits might in his or her own way have presented threats to the public good, to the family, property, or public morals and order. At least two would have fallen foul of the law (convicted child abductors, for example, faced long prison sentences with hard labour), and this, for Boime, lent weight to the argument that they were commissioned in furtherance of Georget's bureaucratic and professional ambitions: these carefully observed likenesses were done for a specific purpose corresponding to the "deepest aspirations" of the patron, Georget (Boime, 1991, p. 79). While they might indeed have had their use for didactic and training purposes, the paintings were, above all, assertions of the professional status of their commissioner: in this account Georget commissioned the portraits as an illustrative "test case" for his own special clinical expertise, within the wider context of the project to legitimate the nascent psychiatric profession as a whole, especially in relation to the legal profession (ibid., pp. 79, 88 etc.).

In the final analysis, however, the relationship between alienists and lawyers over the monomania diagnosis was not only conflictual. It was also complementary and dialectical: "special medicine" found its niche because it met a political and social need for order in post-Revolutionary society; few jobs, indeed, were as politicised as psychiatric posts

(Murat, 2014, p. 7). It resolved the problem of what to do with those who were not criminals but who were not quite fit to be full citizens. They were reduced to the status of minors, placed in "une rélation de tutelle" (Castel, 1976, pp. 182 etc.). Things were not, furthermore, as simple as they might appear in an account which knowingly concludes that Géricault was enlisted to underpin and legitimise the new profession and its key diagnostic category.

Monomania and revolution

In a perceptive and clarifying exposition, which is a development of Sander Gilman's of 1982 (pp. 76–90), the art historian Jane Kromm has drawn attention to an important contrast, between what Esquirol and his later illustrators like Ambrose Tardieu did, and what Géricault and his precursor Georges-François-Marie Gabriel did *not* do: they did not focus the same degree of attention on the supposed specific visual signs of derangement (grimaces, glances, décolletage, disorderly hair). If some of these are present in the portraits (and in the earlier drawings by Gabriel), they take their places as elements in the more rounded and holistic picture of an individual, who is not a mere symptom-carrier. One other thing that Géricault did—at least if we accept the titling of the portraits—and that, in *Des Maladies mentales*, Esquirol surprisingly did not do, was to depict Esquirol's prize category, monomania. Why? Because, Kromm argues, of its association with revolution.

"Monomania" was both conceptually watertight and highly flexible; as the Restoration swung to the right, Esquirol's diagnostic emphasis was increasingly on its asocial or socially dangerous aspects. All his early articles were illustrated by Georges-François-Marie Gabriel; it is Gabriel's 1814 *démonomaniaque* [Illustration 15] who bears some resemblance to Géricault's *Monomane de l'envie*. As Kromm comments, the subject's features and expression are portrayed in a "seemingly artless fashion that downplays their consistency with the representational tradition of the passions" (as outlined, if negatively, by Bell)—awareness of the observer, contracting brows, close attention to facial musculature and wrinkling (Kromm, 2002, p. 222). The illustrations are, as Kromm goes on to characterise them, "a complicated interweaving of the alienist's precepts and the artist's perceptions"; only cases of lower-class or pauper women—Esquirol's "didactic preference set"?—were chosen for illustration (ibid., p. 223).

Esquirol claimed his correlations of facial appearance with specific disorder were based on careful, individual observation. Yet we have suggested that his verbal descriptions can seem, almost in spite of him, to yield a sort of novelistic surplus. Taken in conjunction with Gabriel's and, later, Tardieu's illustrations, they turn up a limited, repetitive, sometimes contradictory, even stereotypical list of purely *visible* characteristics: hollow eyes (both lypemania and mania), fixed state (mania), suspicious look and contracted dry, wrinkled skin (lypemania, mania, demonomania), mobile features or fixed and compressed features (mania); Kromm notes that a binary configuration of facial and/or eye movement versus stasis is in play across the whole of the diagnostic range. Tension around watchful wariness or shifty eye contact and their interactive implications "sets the visual ground for Esquirol's moral therapeutic goal of winning the patient's confidence" (ibid., p. 224).

While Gabriel's portraits follow these guidelines and work within the play of these tensions—fixed/roaming stares; mobile/impassive faces—they are also remarkable for their reticence [Illustration 17], and for the aliveness of the visual tensions they set up, which links them to a sense of the "eyewitness" urgency of revolutionary portraiture. Gabriel had in fact drawn key players in the Revolution, Hébert, Brissot, Couthon, from the Convention floor, and from the street and the foot of the guillotine (ibid., p. 213). His exhibition of some of his drawings of asylum patients at the Salon of 1814 worked to help establish "the subject's claim for fine art status, and made the new genre of case history portraiture known beyond the medical community" (ibid., p. 224).

For his 1838 book Esquirol did not use Gabriel or his drawings, but employed the engraver and printseller Ambroise Tardieu (1788–1841). In the 1820s Tardieu had edited a work on wax effigies for medical instruction; perhaps the choice of a more mechanical form of reproduction reflected Esquirol's need for professional and creative control. This choice might also be understood in the context of another territorial debate or boundary dispute, that between alienists and artists themselves, with their very long-established claims to visual expertise. Gabriel, on the other hand, was associated with the Revolution; his portraits of famous Jacobins were still popular in Paris printshops. After 1820 such an association was dangerous, leading as we have seen, to the dismissal of alienists suspected of liberal sympathies or of harbouring liberals.

Most strikingly, out of the twenty-seven illustrations in *Des Maladies mentales*, not one represents a monomaniac, not even in the substantial section in volume II exclusively devoted to Esquirol's showpiece diagnosis. None had graced the article of 1819 either (ibid., pp. 228–230). Mad men are in a minority among the illustrated figures, and this downplaying of masculine instances of madness stems, Kromm argues, from the absence of depictions of monomania, a condition in which "male occupations and concerns had predominated" (ibid., pp. 232–233).

Kromm registers further shifts in the illustrations. Those by Tardieu are full-length studies incorporating elements of the asylum setting; they introduce us to something of its reality. Bodily presence and gesture take precedence over physiognomy, permitting the resumption of an older practice showing sufferers to be physically provocative and dangerous [Illustration 18]. An illusion of objectivity was also achieved: what seemed to be provided was dispassionate observation of the patients in their real, present environment. This combination "incorporated previous iconographies but made them seem the invention of a modern psychiatric mentality" (ibid., p. 231). Esquirol "created a 'display culture' for mental disorder in which both past sources and artistic production were purposely obscured" (ibid., p. 202).

Géricault's portraits, in contrast, take Gabriel's informality and tentativeness to a new level, with the addition of colour and inclusion of a larger torso area, allowing increased opportunity for detail and nuance. There are no profiles, in contrast to Gabriel's studies of roughly the same time; but both artists bring to bear "frank appraisal and the socially unpretentious qualities associated with revolutionary era portraiture" (ibid., p. 234). At the same time, and in important respects, the portraits can still be linked to Esquirol's project. Both Géricault and Gabriel are preoccupied with gaze and look, and with the fixity of regard emphasised by Esquirol for most disorders; in Géricault's portraits thick applications of paint "… render the inmates' foreheads, focusing attention around the eye area, but with a softer, more plastic and less linear effect" than that obtainable in drawn or engraved physiognomic illustrations (ibid., p. 235). They have the same three-quarters format originally favoured by Gabriel, and they develop the most interesting aspect of Gabriel's work, the "exploitation of pictorial tensions through subtle shifts in direction and balance".

> There are subtle, counterbalancing shifts in the positioning of the
> head with regard to the torso, and both of these with regard to the

oblique gaze. Such tactical instability focused around the face and on the obliqueness of the gazes has long been acknowledged as Géricault's contribution to making visible a psychology defined in terms of mental state as opposed to one configured as behavior or activity. (ibid., p. 236)

These shifts of balance, tension and torsion are also things Gabriel would have found in Géricault's Salon exhibits in 1812 and 1814; the portraits are like Gabriel's illustrations for Esquirol's article on demonomania of 1814, and those he exhibited at the Salon that year. The sideways glances convey distance or aloofness; raised or contracted brows and furrowed foreheads add to a sense of interiority and preoccupation; downturned mouths and pursed lips suggest further resistance to communicativeness. The women's reddened eyes and sagging features reveal more accumulated unhappiness. All these features, for Kromm, connect the images to the cardinal points of Esquirol's "physiognomical atlas for disorder" (ibid.).

All the figures portrayed by Géricault seem tense or uneasy, and all appear to be dressed in their own clothes. The women's dress is relatively careless and dishevelled compared to the men's, which identifies them as Salpêtrière inmates, where the men, who seem to Kromm better dressed, might be clients at Esquirol's *maison de santé* (ibid., pp. 236–237). Certainly the direction of the light would seem to suggest different locations. Kromm notes the hints of brick or masonry behind the gambler, but the sense of a distinct institutional setting is otherwise avoided (ibid., pp. 234–236). She gives the portraits the earlier date of 1819/20, when Géricault was painting only a small number of portraits in a new, more naturalistic manner.

Esquirol made numerous references to the Revolution and revolutions in general as major precipitating causes of madness, and this was echoed in other contemporary medical writing, that of Jean-Pierre Falret, for example, a member of Esquirol's circle of students (*Observations et propositions médico-chirugicales*, 1819), or J.-B. Bonfils (*De la folie*), or Georget himself, who referred to people who "lost their heads (the double-meaning no doubt intentional) at each of the principal events ... from 1789 to the present day" (Georget, 1820a, p. 14; Kromm, 2002, pp. 239–240). Monomania was for Esquirol the principal disease of the post-Revolution, and this is one reason Kromm links the portraits to him and to Gabriel. We have seen that they focus on the antisocial, criminal elements in monomania. Four of the five have traits of

> the excessive and grandiose kind ... linked to ... the "monomanias of ambition" that were caused by the revolution's failed promises. Gambling, theft and military pretensions were part of this drive for aggrandizement and accumulation, while envy was considered a particular problem for women and connected to the revolution-ary moment when satisfying covetousness was upgraded to an egalitarian activity. (Kromm, 2002, pp. 239–240)

But the royalist liberal Esquirol had to downplay the connection from the early 1820s; madness needed to be de-politicised for professional, political reasons. His position was dependent on his profound suspi-cion of revolutionary radicalism, and public hostility to it. Links to "... artists of a liberal persuasion, like Gabriel and Géricault, threatened to compromise the status Esquirol sought for the visual articulation of his case histories" (ibid., p. 49) and for his profession as a whole. Mania was central to his delineation of political upheaval; by no means brand new, it was also a trope with a future (violent opposition to the *status quo* is "beyond comprehension ... the image of chaos"; the terrorist is, by definiton, a maniac). Among the illustrations of women in *Des Maladies mentales* only one, that of the famous revolutionary Théroigne de Méricourt, is in any way political; her story as told by Esquirol is an exemplary *historiette*. For Kromm, Esquirol's counter-revolutionary politics and his ambitions meant that he and his successors—maybe, eventually, even including Georget, whose interest in criminality might have brought him into conflict with the state—were highly sen-sitive to political disadavantage. "... pictorial works connected to the liberal legacy of the revolution were regarded with suspicion" (ibid., p. 241). An earlier drawing by Gabriel of Louis XVI's former gardener at Versailles, a patient in Esquirol's clinic, is a reminder of his royalist connections.

Monomania was also a gift for caricaturists: Géricault's friend Char-let satirised military manias in 1823, and by the early 1830s monomania was a popular catch-all word. A cartoon by Daumier from *La Caricature* of 21 May 1832, "Le Charenton Ministérial", the ministerial madhouse, shows "différentes monomanies des aliénés politiques" among Louis-Philippe's ministers; there was even a play called *Le Monomane* staged in 1835 (Murat, 2014, pp. 108–109). All this also threatened to compromise the status of Esquirol's category.

As we have seen, much of Géricault's art had also been about social injustice and those on the margins of society, and he was widely identified as a radical, by for example a right-wing journal which claimed his journeys to England were part of a project to portray the world's leading radicals. This, "along with the controversial political status of mania and monomania in assessments of the revolution, helps to explain why his and Gabriel's portraits went so quickly out of circulation, and why Esquirol's treatise, when finally published, omitted all depictions of monomania" (Kromm, 2002, p. 241). It may explain why Lachèze rolled his Géricaults up.

Political/theoretical/aesthetic positions

If monomania itself had become firmly associated with liberalism by the later 1820s, it was thanks in large part to Georget's activity in the courts. In making portraits of monomaniacs with criminal tendencies and no redeeming hints or insignia suggestive of their souls, it would seem that Géricault was firmly aligning himself to Georget and the liberal opposition. Yet Kromm is far from convinced that the portraits had anything to do with Georget. They were not in the inventory drawn up after his death; she too argues that in any case Georget was hostile to physiognomic diagnosis and therefore not interested in the appearance of his patients. But Kromm misunderstands Georget, basing herself on a partial reading of his writings. Opposing "the Pinel–Esquirol position in which diagnosis is grounded in externals of description and appearance" to "the underlying, organic causes that Georget favored", she sees him exclusively as the precursor of an organicist psychiatry, in which madness would be the province of brain-science, and physiognomy and appearance therefore irrelevant (ibid., pp. 237–238).

Georget certainly opposed Pinel and Esquirol in giving the epigastrium as much power to cause madness as they seemed to. It is astonishing, he wrote in 1820, how little account has been taken of the influence of the brain's functions on the other organs. He argued cogently for a primary role for the brain. It is true, he said, that all parts of the body, made of the same materials, communicate in a general consensus, and there is reciprocity; but it is the brain that has empire over the whole of life and acts on the other organs. However, he wrote, it is important not to confuse *cause* with *seat*; for example, the womb is neither cause nor seat of hysteria. The seat is the brain, and the cause—this is critical—is reversal in fortune or love, for both sexes. The state of the emotions can have damaging effects on the organs (men of letters for example are habitually constipated—had he been talking to Coleridge, who suffered horribly in this respect?—and are only able to exercise their wits after washing out the rectum); strong emotions can cause palpitations or even death (Georget, 1820a, pp. 17, 37–39, 42–46, 59, 61, 62). He was also dismissive of approaches to understanding insanity, as adopted by some followers of Pinel and Esquirol, like Fodéré, which were merely descriptive and "read like novels" (ibid., p. 84). Kromm is correct to note his comments on how superfluous and useless whole volumes on "the expression, the intellectual *physiognomy* of the mad" were; but she slips in that this applied both to treatment and to understanding, when Georget's comment was explicitly addressed to *treatment* only: "On pourrait faire des volumes entiers sur l'expression, la *physionomie* intellectuelle des fous; mais ce serait sans aucun but d'utilité pour le traitement" ("One could write whole volumes on the expression and intellectual *physiognomy* of the mad, but this would be of no useful purpose for treatment"). A few lines above, however, he had also noted how important it might be to note variations in the colouring and temperatures of the scalp and face ("La peau du crâne, de la face, offre des variations importantes à noter, dans sa *coloration*, sa *température*, etc.") as *symptom*s (ibid., p. 86; Kromm, 2002, p. 238).

Kromm is not alone among art historians in misreading Georget in this way. For Eitner and for Michel et al. it seemed to make more sense to see the portraits as prompted by Esquirol's view of things rather than Georget's. Georget, they point out, espoused a radical materialism that distanced him from the broad humanism of his great teacher; Georget described insanity in neurological terms, as the result of damage to the nervous system (Eitner, 1972, p. 244); thinking and feeling man in his entirety could be reduced to a single organ, the brain (Michel, Chenique, & Laveissière, 1991, p. 244). In this (mis)understanding Georget was simply a strict follower of the arch-materialist Cabanis. A reading of *De la folie* might in fact suggest that even in 1820 Georget, whose critique of metaphysical explanations did not stretch to out-and-out denial of the existence of the soul, was not quite as radical a materialist as art historians have portrayed him to be. In his defence of materialism and refutation of proofs of the existence of soul in *De la folie*, he does not so much directly deny soul as object to physicians who have recourse to it as a convenient explanation for want of any other, in the same way that appeals to unseen "vital properties" or "lesions of the nerves" were easy options which might foreclose on further investigation, when an admission of ignorance would be more honest (Georget, 1820a, pp. 19, 25–26, 51).

In fact *De la folie,* and much of Georget's other work, contains the seeds *both* of organicist psychiatry *and* of a phenomenological, even arguably a psychoanalytic approach to treatment. By the mid-1820s tensions between the Salpêtrière School and purely physical medicine were becoming overt. The problem for the alienists was not new: can medicine legitimately claim expertise in an area that may not require physical intervention? What happens to the "special medicine"'s claims if madness has no physical basis? (Castel, 1976, pp. 112 etc.; Scull, 2015, p. 211). Georget's position was an exemplary indicator of growing tensions between the special medicine and the larger medical establishment (Castel, 1976, pp. 113 etc.). It was also a response to it, and reveals a further "complicated interweaving" of alienist's and painter's concerns and perceptions.

In *De la folie* Georget stated his theoretical position succinctly: "Madness is an affliction of the brain; it is idiopathic, the nature of the organic alteration is unknown to us" ("La folie est une affection du cerveau; elle est idiopathique, la nature de l'altération organique nous est inconnue") (Georget, 1820b, p. 30). Georget was at pains to insist that madness was an "idiopathic" affliction of the brain, that is, a primary one, a condition in its own right (it is interesting that he used the word "affection" rather than "maladie", illness), not occasioned by another, although, as he went on, what change might have taken place in the brain was unknown. "Idiopathic" can also be used to mean a state or experience peculiar to the individual.

While he opposed Pinel's account of how the passions work on the brain, and Esquirol's "epigastric" theory in *Des Passions*, he in fact found a way of sidestepping both the mechanistic traps of Cabanis's thought, and Pinel's and then Esquirol's attempts to evade this trap by postulating that the cause of madness is the passions which, mediated by the viscera, work "sympathetically" (i.e., through a kind of resonance) on the brain: madness was, on the contrary "une *affection cérébrale idiopathique*" (ibid., p. 29, his italics). There was simply no need to postulate the sympathetic action of the passions on the brain through such an intermediary. The passions work *directly* on the brain, the organ of understanding, because this is their source; the brain is the cause both of the passions and of madness. The passions are stimulated by life events and circumstances, by "causes morales", as well as by "causes physi-ologiques" and "pathologiques" (ibid., pp. 67–83). Georget gives "the cerebral" a less restrictive sense than we would tend to lend it today, to imply not just "organogenetic"; thus he avoided the dilemma organoge-netic versus psychogenetic, since "cerebral" embraced physical *and* men-tal (moral), physiological *and* psychological. It was this, as Jacques Postel has emphasised, that located Georget's psychiatry both as an incontro-vertible branch of medicine, and as a distinct medical sub-discipline in its own right; the latter distinction was facilitated by the emergence, in the early 1820s, of neuropsychiatry as a delineated field, thanks largely to the work of Georget's contemporary Antoine Laurent Jessé Bayle, who discovered the physical, syphilitic basis of general paresis of the insane in 1822—the field, that is, of "symptomatic", purely organic brain illness (Postel, 2007, pp. 233–234). If there was a madness that was symptomatic of an identifiable organic illness, then madness that had no such basis, that had its own seat and causes and was symptomatic of nothing but itself, could exist all the more clearly as a category of its own.

Georget's position was thus far from being "biological" in a simplis-tic sense; it was far from a view of the causes of madness as purely and exclusively physiological or neurological (Postel, 1972, p. 16), therefore only responsive to physical and pharmacological interventions. On the contrary: his conviction was that physical or "indirect" treatments were generally ineffective and almost by definition damaging, and that the only sound treatment, because the only "traitement cérébral direct", was the moral treatment.

> Direct cerebral, or moral and intellectual, treatment ... is entirely physiological: there is no physical agent able to act on the brain as a means of curing madness; in any case anything that could reach this organ in such a way would always be the cause of graver dis-turbances than those one wished to destroy ... ("Il est entièrement physiologique: aucun agent physique ne peut exercer son action sur le cerveau, comme moyen curatif de la folie; et d'ailleurs, tout ce qui pourrait atteindre cet organe de cette manière, causerait toujours des dérangemens plus graves que ceux qu'on voudrait détruire ..."). (Georget, 1820b, p. 130, translated for this edition)

Treatment must aim to work on the patient's feelings and ideas. If Georget differed from Esquirol in maintaining in 1820 (ibid., pp. 121 et seq.)

that it is important for the physician to know the causes of madness in order to know how to proceed, he had no hesitation in agreeing with him that treatment required "managing the passions", by means of a creative variety of interventions. "Moral treatment" was the only valid therapeutic approach because it was the only kind of treatment to have a direct action on the brain; it could be used in groups as well as individually tailored (ibid., p. 130; Postel, 1970, p. 16). Esquirolian isolation and "éducation medicale" are indicated. Postel summarises: "La 'physiologie' célébrale se confond avec la psychologie"—brain physiology merges with psychology (ibid., pp. 16–17). It was on these grounds that Georget supported and sought to extend the moral treatment: reaching the brain required a conversation.

Was the position he took up merely indicative of the ambivalence inherent in the situation in which he and other young alienists found themslves in the 1820s? Was he, as Boime has claimed, merely "flip-flopping"? (1991, p. 87). Georget's position was I believe a measured and coherent resolution consistent with his philosophic/scientific principles, and it was, furthermore, at the cutting edge: superseding the Pinel/Esquirol "viscera" theory, it looked forward, arguably, to twenty-first-century views of the brain and the reciprocal or dialectical interactions of experience and physiology. Georget's insistence on madness as a condition of the brain has confused some later commentators, who ignored what his account also did: it kept the window of "moral medicine" open, at least for a few more years.

The portraits, arguably, reflect this resolution. Géricault's figures are palpably embodied, mobile, and distracted, and their states are "idiopathiques", particular to each one of them individually; for madness, for the alienists, might even be a more emphatic translation of personality (Seigel, 1999, p. ix).The portraits are not essays in pure psychology, depictions of generic, isolatable, fixed emotional states as Charles Bell might have produced, their visual rhetoric of staring eyes and so on notwithstanding. Nor do they show figures dumbly subject to purely organic deficit. They have minds; like Lieutenant Dieudonné, they are thinking. Their originality can be grasped in a parallel way art historically.

Margaret Miller, in her pioneering paper of 1940–41, points to an important distinction, between "mimical" expression, in which a passing emotion is signalled in movements of the facial muscles, and "physiognomic" animation, "which is permanently present in the traces left by passions which have become permanent" (p. 162). Mimical expressions had been famously catalogued in the seventeenth century by Charles Lebrun (1619–1690), in his *Conférence sur l'expression générale et particulière*, published in 1698. Géricault owned a copy; it was a standard reference for artists (Lebrun, painter, administrator, and chancellor of the Royal Academy of Painting and Sculpture under Louis XIV, drew heavily on Descartes's theory of the passions, which, caused by the actions of the body and the "animal spirits", act on the soul which must attempt to master them. It is a theory that, ironically, threatens the supremacy of the thinking subject). Catalogues and tabulations of the "mimical" facial expression of emotions, such as Lavater's or Bell's, focused on supposedly universal expressions of feeling; in Lebrun's terminology they were known as *têtes d'expression*. For Miller, the portraits are not *têtes d'expression* in this tradition, although as she points out Géricault had made this kind of study in the past; they are, instead, truly physiognomic in their facial expression. She cites Georget on his patients, as we have already heard:

> The physiognomy is often very expressive and gives a pretty good indication of the nature of the mental disorder. Joy, contentment, fear, sadness, despair ... all these passions have their signs on the physiognomies of the alienated as with reasonable individuals; they are just much more marked with the former because the passions which form and give the delirium its character, acting continuously and strongly, must leave deeper traces. (Georget, 1823, p. 19, cited in Miller, 1940–41, p. 162)

For the sitters' faces, Miller wrote,

> ... are not attentive, active, but unrested, preoccupied and, with the exception of the *Monomane d'envie*, passive. They are receptacles of feelings, not mirrors of responses. The impression they give is not one of intense singleness, but of an accumulation of past feelings too strong or too habitual to be effaced by sleep or distractions. (Miller, 1940–41, p. 161–162, translated for this edition)

This is a perceptive and persuasive account. It is complemented in the work of a more recent commentator, Gregor Wedekind, who turns to Lebrun's other portrait category, the *tête d'étude*, a kind of study for possible use in larger compositions. Which kind are the portraits, Wedekind asks, *têtes d'étude* or *têtes d'expression*? Both types picture bust-length figures and an anonymous face in isolation. But where the *tête d'expression* understands the face primarily as a conveyor of emotion, the *tête d'étude* represents a specific set of features, and thus comes closer to a true portrait. Its difference from the true portrait is that the artist has posed the sitter for his own benefit (Wedekind, 2013, pp. 109–110), rather than being subject to the commissioning sitter's more or less explicit requirements as to how he or she should be portrayed, although Géricault's sitters were probably not in such a commanding position.

Clearly the portraits are closer to *têtes d'étude* than they are to *têtes d'expression*. Géricault's work, as we have seen, was linked to a number of doctrines emerging from the medical sciences and from the works of Lavater, Gall, Spurzheim, or Bell, but he was interested "neither in the normative systematics of Le Brun nor in emphasising physiognomic structures Lavater would have found interesting"; his *têtes d'étude* transcend such traditions. Even the head of a white horse painted in 1814–15, seen frontally, gazing directly at the viewer, has the quality of a portrait; his portrait studies, from his head of a carabinier painted in 1814–15 to the portraits related to the *Raft* (the head of an African, the carpenter), all have an earnest physical presence, and stand as more than just studies: they are works of art in their own right. All, like the five monomaniacs, are characterised "by a profoundly meditative, unfocused gaze directed inward as well as toward the outside world" (Wedekind, 2013, pp. 118, 123).

Géricault, in the words of another modern commentator,

> … approached the subject with acute sensitivity and, under Georget's direction at the Salpêtrière, created works of art in fulfilment of his commission. [He] interpreted insanity not in terms of behaviour, nor in terms of a disease category that transcends the individual, but as a state of mind which, though disordered and clinically classifiable, emphasised rather than obliterated individuality. The patients were painted as if sitting for portraits, the genre most appropriate to the study of human personality. (Browne, 1985, p. 156)

As Miller remarked, he brought to bear "not a touch of perverse relish in the sensationalism of his subject". Georget was similarly at pains to demolish popular and sensationalist misconceptions of the mad as "continually agitated, violent, furious, or in a sombre and taciturn state of melancholy", brooding on evil projects. One is agreeably surprised, wrote Georget, to meet with individuals in whom the *sentiment du moi*—we might translate this as a sense of me-ness, the sense of being a sentient, cognisant subject, of what D. W. Winnicott was to call "going on being" (e.g., Winnicott, 1992, p. 303)—retains its extent and vigour; they "often observe with their peers all the regard, all the politeness, all the proprieties of society" (Georget, 1823, p. 31; Miller, 1940–41, pp. 162–163). For the deranged, wrote Hegel, "are still ethical beings" (1830, p. 127). Géricault registers this inalienable me-ness, and in this the portraits can be linked with works such as *La Maraîchère* (*The Market Woman*) of 1795, formerly attributed to David [Illustration 19]. Kromm also singles out this superb painting.

> Here the oblique glance, the pictorial shifts and counter-shifts, the wariness and unapologetic resistance were devised as a way of frustrating the hierarchical values immured in traditional portrait practice, replacing them with a subtle interplay of more populist significance. Gericault's portaits of the insane push this logic to a more radical conclusion. (2002, p. 241)

The portraits are latecomers within the genre of the Revolutionary portrait, as Milton Brown first defined it in 1938: conceiving of the human being "as a sort of dynamo", it was egalitarian, respectful of the humanity and dignity of the other, and in solidarity with her (Brown, 1938, pp. 89 etc.).

CHAPTER NINE

History painter

•

In line with Georget's clinical thinking, the portraits reflect both *le physique*—passions impact on the brain and body and can invest the person—and *le moral*—the sitters are not deprived of mind, or of sharply differentiated individualities. As such, the portraits are products of the humanising, democratising impetus of the post-Revolutionary period, and contributions to it; they are more than just throwbacks to the 1790s. Géricault was engaged in a larger project, to paint contemporary history, but as a history without heros. He was also in the process of constructing an audience, in the sense that Bakhtin proposed (1981). For Géricault this imagined, hoped-for audience might well have been based on the template of the Vernet circle: an audience that might resonate to shared themes and messages, some more overt, some more subliminal, and that might engage in imaginary dialogue.

In *The Raft of the Medusa* he demonstrated how the conventions and ambitions of neoclassical history painting as understood by the school of David, with its depictions of morally elevating moments of heroism from antiquity, might be enlisted to comment on the present day—on history-in-the-making. Géricault became the painter of the apparently defeated, of the shipwrecked. In making the portraits of the washed-up inhabitants of the Salpêtrière or Bicêtre he was furthering this project. Contemporary history is inscribed in the faces and bodies of his sitters: portraits, like the *Chasseur's*, as bearers of historical weight. His intense concern with the physical was always also a concern with the existential and psychological, with our embodied psycho-somatic and psychosocial beings: "… in Géricault it is time and again the body that proves to be the residue of all human experience and its affective reflection. Not excluding death" (Wedekind, 2013, p. 93). Understanding and transformation could only be arrived at through the flesh. The head of the child abductor, as another modern critic put it, is

> a dramatisation of a face as flesh, as physical matter … Géricault's paintings animate flesh with singular vividness. This painting pays meticulous attention to the fabric of the flesh. You can feel the man's bone structure, imagine the shape of his skull. He is like a forensic reconstruction of a head, yet living. (Jones, 2000)

For Géricault the artist, the philosophical impetus that the new medicine of psychophysical reciprocity offered had to be supplemented with willed identification and with first-hand, physical experience. Such was the extension of Enlightenment which he was developing, like, to a significant extent, the alienists themselves. It took place on the level of an enactment in his own person. He was a Rousseauist who believed, like Rousseau, and perhaps at heart like Georget too, that the greatest expert on melancholy was a melancholic like himself. By these means he attempted to fathom the secrets of our being-in-history. The portraits belong to his effort to come to grips with how history and experience, which are inscribed in the body, and bodies themselves, the *sine qua non* of history and experience, are indissolubly linked. Confined in the asylum the sitters might be; yet perhaps what Géricault was showing, with their expressions poised between despair and defiance, were history's potential agents as well as its victims. The portraits, along with the writings of the early nineteenth-century French alienists, embody an awareness of the present as lived history (Rosen & Zerner, 1979). In the background too were Esquirol's and Georget's own particular views of the relation between madness and history.

Monomania and history of an era

For all its sobriety Esquirol's writing also conveys a sense of wonder, mixed with some fear, at the relativity of forms and categories of madness, of the extent to which politics, social upheaval and ambition, fashion, history, and madness were mutually implicated. Pinel's vignettes too had been moral and political as well as psychological in inspiration ("derangement of the nobility", for example, was almost always incurable because of aristocratic disdain for a regular, working life, the high road to recovery (Murat, 2014, p. 55)). Under the Restoration such thinking led Esquirol to put forward the idea that the alienist might become the government's "moral statistician" (Goldstein, 1987, pp. 158–159), uniquely placed to take accurate soundings of the emotional state of the nation. He also betrayed his sense of what a malleable container monomania was, as a clinical concept. Monomania, he wrote,

> confronts the observer with the most numerous and the most profound subjects for reflection. It includes all the mysterious anomalies of feeling and of human understanding, all the perversions of our instincts and aberrations of our passions … All scientific progress, artistic inventions, and other important innovations have unfailingly become the causes, and influenced the character, of Monomanias. And this is also true of the dominant ideas, the prevailing errors, the general beliefs, right or wrong, that constitute the life of society. (1838, vol. II, p. 167, cited in Eitner, 1982, p. 243)

Murat sums up Esquirol's rather complicated view of the relationship betwen madness and political and social upheaval: "Latent madness emerges as a function of the vagaries of history." In 1805 his view was this: "By bringing all the passions into play, by giving greater flight to feigned passions and exaggerating hateful passions … political agitation increases the number of madmen," as was evident during the English revolution and the recent turmoil in France. By 1824 he had refined this view: the increase made itself felt over time and with delayed effect. During periods of turmoil madness is subsumed in the heat of the moment, only to erupt all the more forcefully once peace has returned. An additional reason for the increase in madness during the Restoration lay in a general lowering of morals and standards of behaviour since the Revolution, the decline of religion, and the "cold egotism" of a society in which, across the social classes, "each lived for himself". For madness was in the last analysis "a disease of civilization", rooted in the state of contemporary morals even more than politics (Esquirol, 1838, vol. I, pp. 42–43, 200; Murat, 2014, pp. 159–160).

Esquirol claimed he could write a history of the whole revolutionary period without the help of any documents other than the human documents collected at Charenton and the Salpêtrière; in one of his lectures at the Ecole de Médecine he illustrated the history of France from the fall of the Bastille to the Restoration by means of the case history of a single patient (Eitner, 1982, pp. 243, 354 note 32; Miller, 1940–41, p. 163 note 4). He noted a thirteen-year-old boy patient, for example, a reader of Goethe's *Werther*, responsible for a rash of suicides when it was first published in the 1770s, who entered the hospital proclaiming "I bequeath my heart to Rousseau, my body to the earth" (Esquirol, 1838, vol. I, p. 289). Among Esquirol's patients at Charenton, and not as far as I know mentioned in any of the literature on Géricault, was a woman who in 1817 had sailed with her husband for Senegal, and suffered "all the horrors of the shipwreck of the *Medusa*", "naufrage si malheureuesement fameux" (ibid., vol. II, p. 22). Esquirol was among eminent subscribers to the survivors' relief fund; the shipwreck of course owed its continuing position in public consciousness above all to Géricault's painting.

Arguably the most poignant vindication of Esquirol's earlier historical theories was Théroigne de Méricourt, insane since the fall of Robespierre in 1794, in the care first of Pinel then of Esquirol until her death in 1817 (Appignanesi, 2008, pp. 67–71; Roudinesco, 1989). Revolutionary upheaval, the destruction of traditional hierarchies, new social and professional mobility (ibid., p. 66), all contributed to a loss of bearings which, coupled with unbridled ambition, could end in madness or crime. Pinel's *manie ambitieuse*, and, later certain of Esquirol's monomanias, stood for a "socially propelled malaise of the soul", in Lisa Appignanesi's phrase (ibid., p. 56). Such was the malaise that was to be portrayed by Stendhal in *Scarlet and Black*, in the person of the darkly ambitious, glory-hungry Julien Sorel, and by Balzac (who placed great weight on physiognomic description as a way of establishing character), in the miserly *père* Goriot for example. The characters are driven and consumed by their dominant passions.

Georget held views similar to Esquirol's on the relation of madness to historical events. Madness was a particularly modern phenomenon,

> ... due to the development and activity of the human faculties, which have, over roughly the last half century, reached the middle and lower ranks of society, due to the various and powerful interests

which have occupied men of all ranks, events and discoveries of all kinds, which have caught public attention, the shock of vehement passions which have profoundly shaken certain states ... in a word, this illness is born and multiplies in circumstances which vividly excite the attention, activate the mind, and bring all the passions of man into play. (1823, pp. 7–8)

In Miller's summary, Georget considered madness not as "an indication of social or racial decadence", the prevailing medical view later in the century, "but the cruel exaction of the most energetic and progressive human activities" (1940–41, pp. 60–61).

Géricault himself, in his labours on the *Raft*, had been engaged in the most energetic and, as he undoubtedly saw it, the most progressive of human activities. The diagnoses of his sitters, based with the exception of the monomaniac of envy on their actual, concrete activities, link them to specifically modern experience. Each has topical and local resonance, which, had the portraits been publicly shown, would not have been lost on contemporaries. It indeed seems possible that all five portraits were intended, like the London lithographs, as direct social and political commentary. The woman driven mad by the lottery is a case in point. According to a London correspondent in 1826, 25,388,800 francs were paid into the Paris lottery (one of France's five) between 1816 and 1820, that is, about a million sterling per annum (in 1826 values).

> The worst of the French lotteries is, that the lowest class can play them, and as low a sum as five pence can be put in, which may gain, in half an hour, fifteen hundred pounds. This makes all the poor people buy in the lottery, and servants rob their masters. On the eve of drawing the Paris lottery, crowds are seen around the doors of the different offices, which are nearly all kept by women, to whom the government allows the privilege as a livelihood; and it is not uncommon to hear an old hag cry out "Who will buy my dream? I dreamt of three numbers." ("Pry", 1826, pp. 397–398)

Moral objections to the lottery, aimed at the protection of the working poor, began to gain weight as the economic situation improved in the 1820s (it had been a very significant contributor to state revenue; it was finally suppressed under the July Monarchy in 1836, not to be reinvented until 1933 (Willmann, 1999, p. 11)). Géricault's painting was the graphic portrayal of the human consequences of an exploitative, state-sanctioned system.

The child abductor makes more oblique reference to another, increasingly discussed social evil. He would not have been short of victims. The rapid expansion of the urban population, and the relative success of vaccination (another triumph of medicine), led to an increase in the number of children living on the streets. The character of little Gavroche in Victor Hugo's *Les Misérables*, which was published in 1862 but set in the years after 1815, is their literary archetype (Chevalier, 1958, pp. 120–128). Gavroche was possibly inspired too by the boy brandishing pistols in Delacroix's *Liberty Leading the People* of 1830 [Illustration 20]. It was a problem that could not be ignored, especially given this child population's availability for recuitment into criminality and prostitution. A speaker in the Chambre des Députés in 1821, deploring the corruption of morals which he saw as responsible for the situation, went so far as to propose that abandoned children might be used to populate the colonies, Madagascar, or Senegal, for example (ibid., p. 126 note 1). Géricault does not demonise the child abductor, who seems equally to invite the viewer's imaginative sympathy. Might he, like the suspect in a famous case in Lyon in 1820, want to claim that he had stolen a child in order to replace one of his own that had been taken from him? (Une Société d'avocats, 1827/1828, I, p. 297). But in portraying him at all Géricault would also have been reminding potential viewers of the existence of street children and their vulnerability to sexual exploiters, and echoing Esquirol's views on the "the perversions of our instincts and aberrations of our passions", in modern civilisation, as generators of insanity. The child abductor's presence in the group of portraits might suggest that the abuser of children was as common a figure in the Paris of the early 1820s as the gambler, the thief, or the *demi-solde*.

The Paris from which Géricault's sitters came was, in the words of the great historian Richard Cobb,

> as much a hotchpotch of considerable affluence and extreme poverty, often separated only by a couple of storeys, as was the clothing of those who crossed one another on the staircase (which was a point of observation much favoured by petty thieves, some of them dressed in sober black, with pointed shoes further to emphasise their respectability ...), sweated together in August, shivered together in January, lived, procreated, and died, in close and uncomfortable

proximity, in which nothing could be concealed, everything would be overheard; but in which, too, nothing and nobody was *indifferent*. (Cobb, 1978, p. 86)

Cobb was writing about the Paris of the end of the 1790s and turn of the century; conditions in the old parts of the city would however hardly have altered much—except perhaps to have become more densely populated—by the time Géricault made the portraits. It was

> a world of neighbourliness, of watchfulness, of enforced "living together", which, however crude and brutal, noisy and filthy, quarrelsome and envious, was not devoid of compassion, tenderness, kindliness, and disinterestedness. (ibid., p. 102)

The portraits are imbued with this spirit, and it certainly extends to the *Monomane du vol*, who of all the sitters perhaps evokes, and would have evoked in contemporary viewers, the greatest associative richness. It was his face, John Berger noted, that looked out from posters at the time of the 1991 Géricault retrospective in Paris (Berger, 2015, p. 209), and that featured on phone cards of that pre-mobile phone era as well as on the cover of the exhibition catalogue. In his sober black, and with his respectable, fashionable cravat (undermined as the overall effect might have been by his coiffure), he could be just the kind of petty thief—pickpocket, opportunist beggar?—described by Cobb; the memoirs of Vidocq, former criminal turned chief of police, corroborate that this dress style, complete with light shoes (pumps, or buckskin), was indeed the most suitable for the *métier* (ibid., p. 86). But perhaps the *Monomane du vol* got his later nickname, *le fou assassin*, from his link with another, darker figure from the urban underworld. He may be an early incarnation of the *apache*, a type of gangster unique to Paris, distinguished for impeccable shoes and a reputation for ruthless violence. In the 1850s and 1860s Baudelaire invented "the poetry of apachedom" by elevating him as a hero of modern life; in Walter Benjamin's commentary, the *apache*

> abjures virtue and laws; he terminates the *contrat social* for ever. Thus he believes that a world separates him from the bourgeois and fails to recognize in him the features of an accomplice ... (1983, p. 79)

Géricault makes no hero out of his *fou assassin*; if he catches the complicity registered by Benjamin, it is with none of Baudelaire's insinuation and slyness. Where Baudelaire, some thirty years later, approached his reader as an "hypocrite lecteur", a hypocritical reader (1857, I, p. 11), Géricault addresses the viewer candidly, as someone who can be trusted to face facts: murderer-thief and bourgeois simply share a common space, and this is something that precedes the social contract, terminated or not, and transcends the question of his outsider, let alone his heroic status. Géricault's painting of course has an another, underlying twist, which is made explicit by Baudelaire in a line from the key poem "Le vin de l'assassin" in *Les Fleurs du mal*: "We are all more or less mad!" ("Nous sommes tous plus ou moins fous!" (ibid., p. 107)). This would however be a mere commonplace, and the portrait would have no emotional purchase, were it not for the friction provided by the specific cultural and social context, the recognition of the topical and familiar.

Figures of the people

There might, for contemporary viewers from the "respectable" classes, have been another layer of association too. Envy is like a battered but by no means crushed version of the 1795 market woman [Illustration 19]. The child abductor might also be a philosopher of the people, albeit prey to the gravest misgivings. The thief could be imagined resurfacing, in 1830, alongside Liberty on Delacroix's barricade [Illustration 20]. Is there a family resemblance between him and the top-hatted figure on her right, the young bourgeois formerly identified with Delacroix himself, with his white collars awry?

Contemporary and later nineteenth-century views of the Revolutionary crowd surely echo the polarised emotional reactions of Géricault's own generation. Edmund Burke, in his *Reflections on the Revolution in France* of 1790, wrote of "ferocious men ... and women lost to shame", "ruffians and assassins, reeking with ... blood"; "the unutterable abominations of the furies of hell in the abused shapes of the vilest of women". These are the harridans and *sans-culottes* (in reality market women, *petits bourgeois*, small traders, artisans, the unemployed) of Gillray's caricatures. Three French revolutions later (1830, 1848, and 1871), Burke was almost outdone by Hippolyte Taine, disillusioned liberal and spokesman for three-quarters of a century's bourgeois dread of the mob: the insurgents of 1789 and 1792 were "the dregs of society ... the lowest plebs ... bandits ... Vagabonds, in rags, semi-naked ... most armed like savages, with terrifying physiognomies ... hired killers and subversives from evil places, accustomed to blood ..." (Taine, 1876, vol. I, pp. 18, 53–54, and see 130, 272; cited in Rudé, 1959, p. 3, translated for this edition). It has been common ever since to characterise the participants as "brigands", or "scum", "rabble" ("canaille"; the near-synonym "racaille" was directed by Interior Minister Nicolas Sarkozy in 2005 at the Paris rioters of that autumn; in July 2015 David Cameron, marginally more genteel, described the refugees camped in Calais as a "swarm").

In contrast, for historians with Republican sympathies, at the head of whom stands Jules Michelet (*La Révolution française*, 1847–1853), the crowd was the embodiment of popular and civic virtues, that is, as long as it behaved in a way that was congruent with bourgeois aspirations. It was a generic *peuple*, among whom the women who marched on Versailles were, for Michelet, "that in the people which is most *of* the people ("Ce qu'il y a dans le peuple du plus peuple") ... most instinctive, most inspired". Alphonse Aulard (*Histoire politique de la Révolution française*, 1905) similarly conceived of the crowd that stormed the Bastille as homogenous: "Paris se leva, tout entier" ("The whole of Paris rose up").

Thomas Carlyle (*The French Revolution*, 1869), on balance sympathetic to the "Nether Sansculottic World", seems to have felt that the social forces unleashed were so terrifyingly powerful that they could only be evoked in mythic terms: the "enraged national Tiger", "the World-Chimera, bearing fire", "Victorious Anarchy". The Revolution was the "Death-Bird of a World". Carlyle even warned his readers not to attempt a closer analysis, for it would be impossible to gauge and reduce "this immeasurable Thing" to a "dead-logic formula". The 1789 Revolution was nothing less than a "World-Bedlam" (all the above cited in Rudé, 1959, pp. 1–4).

For all their differences, each of these historians treated the crowd as a disembodied abstraction. None of them, unlike Géricault in 1822–23, was able to imagine real, flesh and blood people, caricatures neither of good nor of evil. They also belonged to the class the bourgeois Géricault might have been expected most to have feared. Yet if painting them might have been a way of mastering his fear, the portraits hardly convey a sense that the painter was seeking to master his sitters by framing them as denizens of a Carlylian "World-Bedlam".

The atmosphere of the Salpêtrière itself and its neighbourhood in the 12th arrondissement, the faubourg Saint-Marceau (also known around 1800 as the faubourg Saint-Marcel), would have been redolent of madness-inducing misery and violence. The eighteenth-century chronicler Sébastien Mercier characterised the inhabitants of Saint-Marceau as "a people who lack any relationship with Parisians". It was "the most wretched and dangerous" of places (Hazan, 2010, pp. 153, 160), "smelly and filthy, a place of tanneries". Richard Cobb was careful not to exaggerate the militancy of its inhabitatants, whom he described as "a largely apolitical working population" with only "a small body of organised militants" participating in the September massacres (1978, p. 91). Its *sansculotte* population does nevertheless seem to have been in the forefront of all the great demonstrations, the *journées*, of the early 1790s.

In 1818, the Wall of the Farmers-General which had passed right in front of the Salpêtrière was re-situated; the deserted spaces created behind the new wall became the setting for Hugo's *Les Misérables*, and, later in the century, where the railway tracks of the Gare Saint Lazare now are, the shanty town known as the Cité Doré, the capital of ragpickers, explored by Baudelaire (ibid., pp. 155–156). Nearby was the Clamart cemetery, where executed criminals and paupers who had died in the Hôtel-Dieu were taken; Mercier reported in the eighteenth century that young surgeons would steal fresh corpses on which to practise. Closed in the early nineteenth century, the cemetery became the site of the anatomy theatre for the hospitals, known as the Clamart, and Géricault was certainly familiar with it. No doubt also of special interest to him, the largest horse market in Paris stood opposite the Salpêtrière's gates, specialising in carthorses and "former luxury horses reduced to lower tasks" (ibid., p. 157). (A huge painting by Rosa Bonheur, *The Horse Fair* of 1852–55 in the Metropolitan Museum, New York, with the dome of the Salpêtrière in the background, is a homage to Géricault, with echoes of his *Race of the Riderless Horses in Rome*. An Impasse du Marché-aux-Chevaux still exists; at the end of it is the Association Nationale de Tir de la Police, the National Association of Police Marksmanship.)

* * *

Following the duc de Berry's assassination in February 1820, the public mood was apprehensive: criminals and politically motivated assassins were suspected around every corner (Boime, 1991; Mansel,

2003, pp. 165–198). De Berry's widow had been two months pregnant when he died, and the birth of his son in September—the "miracle child"—was a factor in the royalist reaction which was now taking hold, transforming millions of French citizens from passive observers to ardent royalists (Skuy, 2003, back cover). Public opinion was becoming more rather than less polarised at the likely time of the portraits' making.The young Delacroix made an engraving of de Berry's assassin, Louis-Pierre Louvel, a journeyman saddler who worked in the royal stables at Versailles (ibid., p. 8). As France moved even further to the right in the days following Louvel's execution on 7 June 1820, the crowds, principally from the faubourgs Saint-Marceau and Saint-Antoine, occupied the boulevards shouting, among other things, "Vive Napoléon! Vive la liberté! Vivent nos frères de Manchester!"—the last alluding to the Peterloo Massacre of 1819, in which cavalry had charged into a large crowd of anti-poverty, pro-democracy demonstrators, killing some eighteen people (Mansel, 2003, p. 177). The Christian conservative René Chateaubriand described Louvel as "a small man, with a sly dirty face like thousands whom one sees on the streets of Paris" (ibid., p. 168). The monomaniac of theft, or *fou assassin*, would fit the description nicely. In fact he bears a tantalising resemblance to the tousle-haired Louvel as depicted in a contemporary engraving (reproduced in Skuy, 2003, p. 9).

The portrait of the military commander registers a related contemporary anxiety. He was a *demi-solde*. "… there was … a fear that that the *demi-soldes*, the thousands of ex-Imperial soldiers supposedly in permanent mourning for their Emperor (especially after his death in 1821), were just waiting to join any anti-Bourbon conspiracy." Although this has been shown to be legend,

> … both liberals and royalists believed it to be true. Royalists were of the opinion that … the *demi-soldes* represented the most serious security risk to the Second Restoration. Conspiracy-minded liberals were also seduced by the *demi-soldes* legend, and they concentrated their recruitment on them through the Restoration. (Skuy, 2003, p. 55)

At least ten conspiracies have been identified between 1815 and 1823, among the most notable the so-called 20 August plot of 1820 (ibid., pp. 56–59). A "conspiracy mentality", exacerbated by the duc de Berry's assassination, was imprinted across France's political landscape in the new decade (ibid., p. 59).

A further measure of the topicality and originality of the portraits can be found in a consideration of changing contemporary attitudes to crime and criminality. In his classic study, the historian Louis Chevalier noted the contrast between earlier accounts of crime and criminals in Paris and those that began to appear in the last years of the Restoration—in Hugo and Balzac for example. Descriptive *tableaux* of Paris published under the Empire and early Restoration, following in the footsteps of Sébastien Mercier, dwelt on themes of criminality merely as curiosities, satisfying a taste for the picturesque; crime was "one Parisian spectacle among other spectacles", likely to be incarnated in the figure of some illustrious highwayman or murderer. The assassin Louvel may be a sort of transitional figure in this respect. Between 1817 and 1827 the population of the city increased massively, by some 175,000 to around 890,500; by the later 1820s crime was becoming "everyday, anonymous, impersonal, obscure", no longer confined to insalubrious quarters but present everywhere, a "social criminality, indefinable and ungraspable, growing with the town and infiltrating it like a sort of unhealthy fog or a humidity which would stick to the walls" (Chevalier, 1958, pp. 47–48, translated for this edition). Géricault's portraits, determinedly unpicturesque and everyday, of anonymous, marginal, and suspect figures, are among the earliest and most uncompromising visual statements of this shift in perception. He stood not outside their world, presenting them as spectacle, but, while he was painting them at least, right among them.

Romantic solidarity

"The empire of Liberty is at last extended to them: it breaks their chains; genius is no longer condemned to obscurity" (cited in Brown, 1938, p. 63). So ran the introduction to the catalogue of the Salon that opened at the Louvre, "by order of the Assemblée Nationale", in 1791, the year of Géricault's birth, and of Cabanis's report on the plight of the madwomen in the Salpêtrière. The patriotic writer was referring to artists not to the insane, but the parallels are noteworthy. The idea of freedom became, in Milton Brown's words, a subtle and powerful factor in the artist's consciousness, and during the Revolutionary years to make "genre" paintings dealing with common people became a social virtue. The artist now "thought of himself and other people as free individuals" (ibid., pp. 52–53, 59), and this attitude resonates in Géricault's work from the *Chasseur* onwards. Géricault inherited the energy of Revolutionary art.

Yet in 1820, for all his liberal sentiments, he responded to the duc de Berry's assassination with a drawing of the dying libertine in the pose of a dead Christ (Athanassoglou-Kallmyer, 2010, pp. 114–115): opportunistically, perhaps, in the hope of riding the wave of popular royalist sentiment and making some money; perhaps even out of loyalty, for the duke, as *colonel général des chasseurs et lanciers* and head of the army, had been part of the entourage accompanying the fleeing king in 1815 (Skuy, 2003, pp. 4–5); but perhaps too in a spirit of disenchantment and resignation. He would not have been alone in feeling this, and perhaps all the more so by 1822 when political repression was seeming to triumph. There was a sense that a heroic era, with its promises of transformation, had ended (this sense runs through Stendhal's mature writing). Napoleon died in 1821; the early 1820s were a dead season for liberal hopes, with no clear perspective on a future, only more of the oppressive same. It was, as Ian Bostridge has put it, "a frozen peace" (2015, p. 75), and the political resonances of the season in Schubert's *Winterreise*, first performed in 1828, are perhaps echoed in the winter setting, evident from the heavy clothes, of the portraits. Schubert's friend the playwright Eduard Bauernfeld could have been describing the situation across much of Europe, not just in Metternich's Vienna, when he wrote of it as "purely negative: the fear of spiritual things, the negation of spirit, absolute statis, waterlogged, stultified" (Bauernfeld, 1873, p. 149, cited and translated in Bostridge, 2015, p. 75).

The sources of the malaise felt by many young people were summed up by the poet Alfred de Musset in 1836.

> The scourge of the present age stems from two causes ... People who lived through 1793 and 1814 bear two wounds in their hearts: everything that was is no longer; everything that will be is not yet. Look no further for the secret of our ills. (Murat, 2014, p. 114)

Another young poet, Percy Bysshe Shelley, had offered a similar but more searching analysis in 1818, calling, for example, on the idea that human attitudes may arise "unconsciously". His comments, in the preface to "The Revolt of Islam", contrast with Musset's in that they are a call-to-arms:

> ... on the first reverses of hope in the progress of French liberty, the sanguine eagerness for good overleapt the solution of these

questions, and for a time extinguished itself in the unexpectedness of their result. Thus many of the most ardent and tender-hearted of the worshippers of public good have been morally ruined by what a partial glimpse of the events they deplored appeared to show as the melancholy desolation of all their cherished hopes. Hence gloom and misanthropy have become the characteristics of the age in which we live, the solace of a disappointment that unconsciously finds relief only in the wilful exaggeration of its own despair ... (Shelley, 2012, p. 221)

Like many of his generation across Europe, Géricault seems to have been torn between these two positions, on the one hand gloom, misanthropy, and despair (not, in his case, wilfully exaggerated), and on the other a Shelley-like fighting stance. He and Shelley were not alone in this either. Quite independently of each other such figures as Pushkin, Beethoven, and Byron shared a similar concern for the relief of individual and collective suffering and a determined hope that art might help bring it about. Pushkin started work on his play *Boris Gudunov*, his subversive, satirical exploration of autocracy, in 1823–24. Beethoven's Ninth Symphony, with its famous choral setting of Schiller's "Ode to Joy", was first performed in 1824. In the same year Byron died supporting the Greeks in their war of independence against the Ottoman Empire, and the young Delacroix exhibited his *Massacre at Chios* at the Salon. These artists "internalised and sublimated revolution in an age of political repression and transformed it into what we call Romanticism". Each chose to deal with themes of despair and oppression just as "... Alexander I, Metternich, and Charles X were doing their best to make despair and oppression as endemic as possible ... The theme was airborne across the Continent" (Sachs, 2010, pp. 94–95, 104).

The use of madness as satire and critique and the idea that in itself it constituted a general indictment of the world around it were hardly new.

Here they have a building to put madmen in; you will at once conclude that it is the largest in the town, but no, the remedy is completely inadequate for the disease. Presumably the French, who are much criticized by their neighbours, put a few madmen inside a building so as to give the impression that the ones outside are sane wrote Montesquieu earlier in the eighteenth century (1721, p. 117). The mad also lent themselves without difficulty as archetypical victims of oppression, for across Europe enforced incarceration was still a common-enough reality, as Goya's sketchbooks, for example, attest. In contemporary literature, it was enlisted to highlight injustice, particularly towards women; in Mary Wollstonecraft's *Maria: or, The Wrongs of Woman* of 1798 the heroine is confined to a private madhouse by an unscrupulous male relative (Wollstonecraft, 1798). Metaphors of madness itself as "civil war" and "shipwreck of the soul" were commonplace (Porter, 2002, pp. 15, 36). The madness inherent to the scene of the *Raft* would not have been lost on contemporaries—Carlyle would surely have regarded it as yet another manifestation of "World-Bedlam"— along with other resonances: its echo of the medieval *Narrenschiff*, the ship of fools, its strange sense of homoerotic abandon, its visual play with extreme tensions between discipline and dissolution—a thematic tension later so well explored in the film *Mazeppa*, and experienced at first-hand by Géricault himself in his emotional swings.

The portraits, in this account, were acts of protest and solidarity, products of shared Romantic-artistic and Romantic-medical concern with feeling and suffering. "Would you recognise it, without the title, as a study of madness—of paedophilia?" asked *The Guardian's* critic in 2000 about the child abductor. "It is an examination of suffering ... Géricault's child-kidnapper is as desolate and bereft as those survivors [on the *Raft*]" (Jones, 2000). They were profound acts of identification on another level too. If Géricault himself was not quite reduced to the status of a legal minor, like the monomaniacs, or like Baudelaire a generation later, he found himself in his last year washed up, ill, his fortune gone. The sitters are the displaced and dispossessed to whom, under a future regime, Baudelaire was to refer in the poem "Le Cygne", "The Swan", in *Les Fleurs du Mal*: sailors abandoned on an island, prisoners, the defeated ("matelots oubliés dans une île ... captifs ... vaincus" (1857, vol. I, p. 87)). The portraits underline the peculiar and ambiguous status of the sitters, neither quite criminals, enemies of the state, nor full participants in it. Their potential agency, as the citizens they still theoretically were, was in suspense. As such they symbolised the powerlessness and voicelessness, the sense of internal exile, shared by thousands across Europe. At the same time, as "therapeutic subjects", they resonate to the contemporary impetus towards universal emancipation across the Atlantic world.

It is to a sense of potency constrained and suspended that the absence of hands in the portraits speaks. One of the last works Géricault made, on his deathbed, is a drawing of his own hand, his primary, physical means of engaging with the world. It casts an ambiguous shadow, which could be taken for another, black-skinned hand on which his own rests. It is hard not to be reminded of the almost contemporary, chilling, farewell evocation of his hand which Keats, who also knew he was dying, offered to Fanny Brawne: "This living hand, now warm and capable/Of earnest grasping ..." (Keats, 2001, p. 461). For all Géricault's despair, this hand, like the medical ethics of a Georget and the portraits themselves, is also an expression of defiance and connectedness.

CHAPTER TEN

Surplus and the limits of interpretation

Perhaps no one among his near contemporaries manifested the energy of Géricault's figures more powerfully and consistently than Honoré de Balzac—born in 1799—in his own characters. Among Balzac's earliest published writings, from the late 1820s, are fictions centring on the question of madness: *Adieu* (1830a), *Le colonel Chabert* (1832a), *Louis Lambert* (1832b). Despite his defence of throne and altar, "... you never find in him the least contempt for ordinary people," wrote Eric Hazan (Hazan, 2010, p. 154). For Baudelaire, Balzac's characters were "weapons loaded with will right up to the end of the barrel", ready to go off at any moment; in their intense vitality, they were "more fircely alive, more active and cunning in combat, more patient in misery, more gluttonous in their pleasures, more angelic in devotion than the comedy of the real world shows us"—except, Baudelaire might have added, the world inside the asylum; each, down to the humblest, has genius (1859, vol. II, p. 120, and see Calasso, 2012, p. 163). In *Adieu* Balzac, drawing on contemporary medical models, depicted different types of *aliénation*: the "idiot" Geneviève, the demented Stéphanie, driven mad by the trauma of the crossing of the Berezina during the retreat from Moscow in 1812, and the "monomaniac" former soldier Philippe, who is also a victim of his experiences in Russia. Philippe's *idée fixe*, in a nice ironic twist, is nothing more antisocial than a wish for the cure of Stéphanie (Balzac, 1830b). The *Comédie humaine* (the title Balzac gave his great series of novels on nineteenth-century life) is full of figures destroyed by the force of their own thoughts, ambitions, and passions. His thinking was also informed by contemporary ideas on the links between mind and body, as is evident in the vividness of his physiological and physiognomic descriptions and their power to evoke character.

Géricault's sitters, like Balzac's Colonel Chabert, who was presumed dead and was therefore a kind of non-person on his return to France, are in a highly ambiguous position, a legal no-man's-land; Chabert, significantly, finds a home of sorts in the faubourg Saint-Marceau and ends his days at Bicêtre. This might point us towards the question on which Géricault seems, with increasing urgency and like Balzac a few years later, to have been working: what, in the direst of circumstances, the usual frameworks which support life having disappeared, are the minimal conditions for aliveness? Where are the gaps within which life and libido subsist and break through? It was Géricault's personal elaboration and extension of the late Enlightenment question, posed in literarature, philosophy, and medicine: what is it to be human? What drives us? The promise of an answer seemed, in the late eighteenth and early nineteenth centuries, to lie in a study of extremes—the predicament of the *enfant sauvage*, for example, or the shipwrecked—and in the strange manifestations of the invisible: in dreams, trance, somnabulism, madness. The answer for Géricault emerged with the greatest force from his practice *as a painter*. It could be sensed in the inherent life of the painting itself, and we can sense it too, in what this experience can liberate in us.

Reason–unreason

Esquirol himself sometimes regarded madness as a reversion to a primordial, amoral state.

> In an asylum social bonds are severed … one acts free of social conventions … one curses, denounces, indulges in the most stupid excesses, rapes, the son curses his father, the mother slaughters her children … one steals, one kills … (cited in Athanassoglou-Kallmyer, 2010, p. 204)

For Athanassoglou-Kallmyer, in Foucauldian mode, "Madness was the catalyst that revealed humanity's inmost nature, its darkest truth, the ultimate aim of Géricault's quest." The paintings were portraiture's

> ... ironic inversion. Challenged here is portraiture's very identity as a genre associated with rational social order, self-aggrandisement and the establishment of an authoritative social presence. Géricault's featured individuals, sprung from the dark underbelly of a society ruled by crime and madness, pose as the negation of sanctioned social and moral hierarchies, as emissaries of an upside-down world in which established values have been reversed or even annulled, in which madmen now occupy the wall of fame for the edification of their sane audiences.

And more: the unstable quality of the *Monomane de l'envie* "exposes the uncertain boundaries that separate reason from insanity, and denounces the apparent calm of its companion pieces as a mere semblance of reason, as a temporary and fragile reprieve within the vast and mysterious realms of unreason" (ibid., pp. 204–205).

In 1963 Jacques Derrida delivered an important lecture in response to Foucault's *Histoire de la folie*. How, he asked, is it possible to write, as Foucault claimed he was writing, "the archaeology of a silence", except by using logos? How is it possible, in other words, to write a history of madness itself, before its capture by reason, without employing the same rational concepts as those which supposedly effected its exclusion? (Derrida, 1978, pp. 31–62). "In what invariable but never revealed sense", adds Laure Murat, glossing Derrida's question, "could Foucault speak of 'madness'?" (2014, p. 14).

Gauchet and Swain wrote of something "for which we do not yet have a true concept, but only a strong intuitive apprehension, the subject of madness, which both presupposes the philosophers' indivisible I and radically challenges it" (1999, pp. 257–258). Another answer to Derrida's question—and one that avoids the mystifications of an "inmost nature" or "darkest truth"—might be sought in the idea of an unknowable, ungraspable surplus, something close perhaps to what Lacan meant by "the Real". The Lacanian Real is all that lies beyond and defies symbolisation. If the portraits connect us to irrepressible, untameable id, they also radically unsettle, by offering us the apprehension of a negation, something impossible to figure.

The uncanny

The art historian Stefan Germer, in an unfinished paper of 1999, took up this sense in terms of the uncanny: the uncanniness, for example, of Géricault's paintings of horses, children, and severed limbs. Germer found in them a surplus of signification, a "quality which does not allow itself to become frozen in representation". In this they echo disturbing feelings of loss of control, linked to their specific historical circumstances: the unprecedented erasure of former boundaries as widely experienced by contemporaries in the years following the Revolution (Germer, 1999, p. 159).

Not the least unsettling question concerned the very unity and integrity of body and soul, *physique* and *moral*, and a focal point for such concerns was the action of the guillotine. If a conscious head did survive, it could only think one thing: "I think, but I do not exist any more." The reassurance provided by the Cartesian *cogito* was negated; instead of "I think therefore I am" was the "the 'non-thing' of experiencing one's own death" (Arasse, 1988, p. 21, cited in Germer, 1999, p. 161). Germer does not go into this, but it seems highly likely Géricault would have discussed these matters with Georget. Georget was certain conscious life stops immediately when the brain loses communication with the rest of the body (Georget, 1820a, p. 37). However, he also seems to have followed Cabanis in the idea that the body contains independent centres of the life principle.

> The nervous apparatus, independent in lower animals, is not so in those [humans] deprived of [a brain]. How useful it would be for physiology and pathology to determine the conditions for this dependence, at what point it can cease in man without the internal life suffering!

In this way we should know "the source of a crowd of phenomena, of illnesses, up to now not understandable in their nature and seat" (ibid., pp. 17–18, translated for this edition).

Géricault's paintings of severed heads are, for Germer, "an ambivalent mixture of destructive and sexual emotions" (1999, p. 163). Some, like those in the Nationalmuseum in Stockholm [Illustration 11], may register the states of emotion from the different phases of execution by guillotine, in parallel with the different phases of sex; in their deeply disturbing ambiguity they deprive the viewer of power, reassurance, and ego-satisfaction. The composition with severed limbs in the Musée Fabre, Montpellier, similarly permits the viewer "neither voyeuristic interest nor narcissistic identification"; we are denied both "sovereign access" and "prideful self-mirroring". The viewer is given an uncanny oedipal "moment in psycho-sexual development" to experience, a primal scene "in a form displaced onto history". In other words, instead of a piling up of muscled bodies as in the *Raft*, Géricault has discovered a way of generating bodies other than by narcissistic projection: figures need no longer be "enlarged vehicles of the self" but can also be "manifestations of the alien, the having-become-alien or the experienced-as-alien". They break out of "armoured bodily limits" (ibid., pp. 164–165). The limbs leave room for the viewer's associations; they do not determine them in advance, but license switching between different readings: on the one hand we seem to be looking at an intimately lit, homely still life, on the other we are confronted by uncanny liveliness and sexuality, in severed muscles, bone, and supposedly dead flesh. Géricault, writes Germer with economy and understatement, increasingly aimed to keep open "feelings of indecisiveness" (ibid., p. 166).

As for Géricault's horses, what frightens about them "is not the instinctual being, but rather the suspicion that they possess a consciousness similar (if not superior) to that of humans, so that they will elude control—not out of dumbly stubborn obstinacy, but out of calculation". Germer traces the depiction of animals from Buffon and Enlightenment naturalism—description in terms of characteristic profiles, situated in humanised landscapes, and seen in relation to man—through to George Stubbs's anatomical, physiological studies. These show death, but do not qualify as uncanny: Stubbs's *écorché* horse, observes Germer, trots bravely on. The transformation into uncanniness occurs when the animal becomes "a kind of machine functioning according to its own laws" (ibid., p. 168).

These acute observations allows us to make a link with Pinel's postulation of madness as an illness functioning according to its own laws, the madman as like a stone carried along by gravity and its own weight, and alienism, therefore, as a branch of the natural sciences. The monomaniac as painted by Géricault becomes, like the horse, a signifier in her own right, in a "viewer-dismissing picture" that insists on its subject's and its own autonomy. Earlier in his career, Géricault had achieved this by taking iconographical and compositional *topoi* to extremes of dissolution, as for example in the *Wounded Cuirassier*, which is a sort of tensile deconstruction of David's famous equestrian portrait of Napoleon crossing the Alps, in the Louvre. Later, he employed what Germer, in a difficult but accurate formulation, called a "dramatizing absolutization of empirical observations": that is, an absolute refusal, as supremely evident in the portraits of monomaniacs, to allow the subject to be a symbol or a substitute for anything else. In this, they attract the wishes and fears and strengthen the involvement of the viewer, who is invited to lend meaning, to bring a full range of associations (as we have been doing) to what appears to have become senseless. The viewer is thus turned "from one expecting elevation into one caught in the act of desiring ... an experience undergone in the moment of viewing" (ibid., p. 169). Participation is mandatory (ibid., pp. 170–174), disappointment is guaranteed, and worse, exposure is threatened. The paintings can be persecuting.

Something similar takes place in Géricault's depictions of children. Louise Vernet's gaze in the extraordinary portrait of 1817–18 in the Louvre "reverses power relations" between picture and viewer. The viewer is attracted merely to be captured, to be seized "desiring Louise". Once this is really taken on, we must ask what then becomes of us, of our identifications, our claims to be viewers outside the labyrinths of desire, when we look at the child abductor? What happens in front of the portrait of Louise Vernet is for Germer more than a "turning of the gaze", that which, for Lacan, was painting's characteristic achievement: it is rather a "disarming of the phallic gaze" (ibid., pp. 178–179). Louise's power resides in the fact that she seems to ignore the boundaries between child and adult that are constituted by knowledge of sex and by repression; it is as if she is caught in the moment of apprehending the other's, Laplanchian, "enigmatic message". She "drops out of the societally established familial, natural order" and confounds it. Like, we might add, the monomaniacs, she is "simultaneously naïve and aware". In a dialectic of Enlightenment, "Géricault works out the irrational consequences of progressive rationalisation," in theories of madness as in education and theories of childhood. For "To know more about something in no way means to take the horror away" (ibid., pp. 180–181).

Unlike Louise, however, and other children painted by Géricault, the monomaniacs do not meet our gaze. Their uncanny, viewer-disabling power also comes from their sheer embodiment, their communication of *Dasein*, the sense of a life within—like the third arm which Germer feels to exist beneath the cloak in Gericault's portrait of the young Alfred Dedreux, or like the life-centres which Cabanis posited all around the body, which no longer even need to be seen. They too escape and frustrate our gaze. For projects of total visibility and control have, Gauchet and Swain remind us, failed repeatedly, "falling very far short of the kind of individual and social transformations for which their agendas have called". The panoptical eye, so central to Foucault's postulation of an all-powerful, clinical/disciplinary gaze, is ultimately

> ... unable to recognise the subjects it seeks to oversee for what they are. In the human world, we never see less than when we try to see all. What has frustrated attempts to revolutionize individual and social existence has not been insufficient effort, but "the indomitable inventiveness" human persons bear within them. (Seigel, 1999, p. xv)

Géricault's monomaniacs are portraits of this indomitable inventiveness, and of the "aberrant singularity that waits only to express itself in each subject" (Gauchet & Swain, 1999, p. 72)—"aberrant", perhaps, because it can also contain a drive towards its own negation.

Eruptions of the invisible

From the witch-hunts at the start of the modern age—responses to intolerable eruptions of the invisible from the outside—Gauchet and Swain see a development that stretches through to mesmerism in the late eighteenth century. Mesmerism marks a crucial turning point, "the moment at which the force of the outside comes back into the human orbit". It correlates with the specific way in which madness was imputed to the subject during the same period, as an essentially internal event in which one could be successively present and absent to oneself and know the "wrenching gap" of active presence to oneself preserved "at the core of the absence experienced". In this "suspension of the reflective property", as Gauchet and Swain put it, also lay the conditions for "an extrasubjective lucidity or veracity" (1999, p. 273).

Their analysis resonates with the contemporary fascination with the guillotine, and with hallucination, drug- or otherwise induced, somnambulism and trance-like states, as evident in late eighteenth-century images such as Fuseli's *Lady Macbeth Sleepwalking* (1783, Louvre), through to Byron, Polidori, and Shelley's experiments with somnambulism, and beyond. Out of these, in Mary Shelley's *Frankenstein*, emerged the most famous living-dead creature of all, possessed and animated by a libidinal-destructive life force over which neither he nor his creator had control. In 1847, Verdi wrote the "The Great Sleepwalking Scene" for his *Macbeth*, which, the composer said, was the most important in the whole opera. He wanted the soprano playing Lady Macbeth to capture the physical mannerisms of the sleepwalker, immobile face, lips hardly moving: all the visible signs of the active presence of the invisible.

These were phenomena of the shadows and the night, and the *chiaroscuro* of the portraits is perhaps the most powerful of their visual metaphors. Half-light and transitional states are tropes of late eighteenth-century and Romantic literature and painting, from Gray's *Elegy* and Young's *Night Thoughts* to Keats's *Ode to Autumn*, Shelley's *Ode to the West Wind*, and Goya's paintings and prints from the mid-1790s onwards. Such states have, in Iain McGilchrist's analysis, affinities with (right-brain) "complexity, transience, emotional weight, dream states, the implicit and the unconscious, rather than clarity, simplicity, fixity, detachment, the explicit and full consciousness". *Chiaroscuro* in painting evokes space and depth, which in turn draws us into "a felt relationship" rather than encouraging detached observation, while, at the same time, providing evidence of our separation; we enter "a state of awareness of separation and loss—the primal condition of the Romantics" (McGilchrist, 2010, pp. 361–362). We are introduced to nameless longing, to mystery and the unsayable. Romanticism, with its love of the fragment, the sketch, the unfinished, the merely suggestive, is thus, for McGilchrist, an induction into "the world as delivered by the right hemisphere". It involves us as co-creators of the work and the world, with responsibilities for it and for ourselves and each other in it. In the process of attempting to complete in imagination the fragmentary or half-hidden, one becomes the part-creator of what one perceives. Only part, however; for as Wordsworth wrote, we "half-create" and "half-perceive" the world. If it were otherwise, and the object were either wholly given or wholly created by us, "there would be no betweenness, nothing to be shared" (ibid., p. 369), or, perhaps, feared.

That we take part in a changing world, and that the world evokes faculties, dimensions, and characteristics in us, just as we bring aspects of the world into existence, is perhaps the most profound perception of Romanticism. (ibid., p. 360)

Such was Géricault's democratic message, which, however, also includes an acknowledgement of the extent to which we are driven to negate, destroy, reduce to fragments, and cast into darkness in the first place.

SOME CONCLUSIONS

A historical and biographical summary

If Rousseau had sought to establish feelings as reason's natural allies, the sheer force of the popular movement in 1789 and 1790, and especially after 1794, brought about a new recognition of just how powerful in their own right feelings and the irrational could be. Differences now arose as to how they were to be valued. For thinkers of the Enlightenment, and for the triumphant bourgeoisie of the later 1790s, feelings must be understood, worked with, harnessed, contained, and socialised within an expanded vision of sociality, of citizenship, with its new, democratic dimensions and obligations. But there must also be the force of law to keep them within bounds. In Freudian terms, binding of the drives through repression.

Napoleon provided the means for this channelling and enforcing, with a new, all-embracing legal Code, a universal system of measurement, and a highly policed state. In this he was a true child of Enlightenment. But he was also the focal point for another way of valuing feeling and the irrational: he seemed to demonstrate that passion had its own creative/destructive motive force and logic, that it could break old moulds and constrictions in a continuation of the spirit

177

of 1789–1795, literally smashing borders and boundaries. Fused with ideas from Germany on the power of what Schelling christened "the unconscious" (1800, esp. Part III, pp. 47–154), this ethic became Romanticism, with the help, in France, of the former Napoleonic soldier Stendhal (Stendal is a town in Prussia Beyle may have passed through with the Grande Armée, on its way to Moscow), and then Hugo.

Géricault was touched by this current, and he responded with authenticity: powerfully, and ambivalently. The *Chasseur* looks both forwards and backwards. But in the face of renewed repression under the Restoration, especially after 1820, a new attempt to curb and contain the irrational power of the crowd, he came to identify with this current and to analyse it more closely. In the bodies on the *Raft*, partly unconsciously perhaps, he articulates the conflict, its dialectics. All the elements are there: the irrationality of the crowd (alcohol-fuelled murder and cannibalism) followed by the restoration of a degree of order and hierarchy, echoed in the pyramidal ordering of the composition; a sense of abandon and abandonment; a loss of boundaries (the perilous, tilting, sinking edges of the raft); the murderous, venal irrationality behind the event; emotional response across a wide spectrum, from the deepest grief, to despair, to resignation, to renewed hope. The naked bodies, once vehicles for revolutionary optimism, now enact immense, impersonal forces, almost as powerful as the sea itself; if they contain these forces at all they are also tossed to and fro by them. The shipwreck and its terrible aftermath were caused by the failure and breakdown of compassion, of fellow-feeling, community, and communication; the scenes of civil war and cannibalism subsumed within the finished composition are also mutually attacking and devouring parts of the psyche. The tiny sail on the horizon is a tenuous hope for reconnection and reconciliation. The *Raft* works on the spectator's psyche-soma, his physical and emotional experience in its huge material presence. With its future echo of the awful plight of twenty-first-century migrants, it invites a profound meditation on the play of historical forces. It also enshrines a new understanding of the human predicament itself.

This is taken further in the portraits. For Eitner, the internal activity of the monomaniacs was the very opposite of the physical athleticism of Géricault's earlier work (Eitner, 1982, p. 246); but perhaps this view could be refined. If the *Chasseur* showed body and mind anxiously and tenuously united in the conquest of id, and the Roman horse-tamers presented an idealised vision of a dynamic new unity, the *Raft* unveiled a terrible vision of their severance, and of id set terrifyingly free: life- become death-drive. In the portraits Géricault conveyed "the anxiousness of an individual, the wounded soul hidden beneath the smooth facial surface", in a way that invites comparison with Artaud's self-portraits (Fornari, 2013, p. 164). The portraits arrive at a new awakening: *this* is what we are like: not heroic, not amenable, but severed within, engaged in a war between life and death that can now be understood as internal. In Gauchet and Swain's rather abstract language, here is the source of the subject's decentring, the "moment when the fundamental ambiguity of the proximity of man to himself became perceptible experience". In this way the portraits work "a complete reconfiguration of the subjective space" (Gauchet & Swain, 1999, pp. 255–256).

They are undoubtedly too projections of Géricault's private sense of social alienation, "lostness", and marginality. He was perhaps free to paint the monomaniacs as he did because he had nothing to lose (these were not big Salon pieces), so something else could break through. At this point—assuming they were made at the later date proposed for them—he had lost everything, he was ill and possibly suicidal. They are profound acts of engagement; unconsciously he was free to engage. Contrast this state with the tremendous rational decision-making involved in the *Raft*, in tandem with a consciously planned programme of physical and emotional identification. It is not that the portraits are pure spontaneity; they are the productions of an artist at the top of his form, who had deeply internalised his craft, and refined the relationships between his hand and eyes, brush and paint. They bear comparison with Keats's Odes. So unlike the Odes in tone and subject matter, they nevertheless announce the painter as—to paraphrase the poet Stanley Plumly—the entity to whom the subject of the painting is happening, his eye "a sentient, capacious yet focusing lens … [which] affects a certain neutrality" but in the end makes "shibboleths of the distinctions between subjective and objective voices" (Plumly, 2008, pp. 176–177). Like the Odes, the portraits "enter the life of the pictured scene" (Hartman, 1975, p. 130).

* * *

We could of course try to give a psychoanalytic account of Géricault's predicament. Was he a man in unconscious search of a father, perhaps like his friend Georget? We have noted the parallel paternal lineages: David–Gros–Géricault; Pinel–Esquirol–Georget. It is hard to avoid seeing an oedipal battle being played out around his aunt; he was also the inheritor of his mother's money, and the psychoanalytic sleuth might speculate that Géricault was able, unconsciously, to claim exclusive possession of her. There are hints of barely sublimated castratory anxieties in his work, for example a drawing of some woodcutters in which an infant—is it a boy or a girl?—sits with his/her back to the viewer astride a plank which is being sawed by two adult men. Another drawing shows an executioner holding the head of a victim he has just dispatched with his axe (Michel, Chenique, & Laveissière, 1991, pp. 92–93). Both drawings were made in Rome after Géricault's flight from his incestuous love affair. Perhaps his identification with the monomaniacs was identification with their abjection, an instance of what André Green called "negative narcissism" (2002), a feature of which might be the sort of self-punishment and global negation—"it's all rubbish"—which works to maintain a secret sense of grandeur and superiority. At times Géricault sounds more straightforwardly ambitious, and at times almost megalomaniacally so. Like Keats, who felt just before his death in 1821 that he had achieved hardly anything, Géricault was reported to have lamented on his deathbed that he had done nothing to give a measure of what he could have done, dismissing the *Raft* as a mere vignette (Michel, Chenique, & Laveissière, 1991, p. 305). Perhaps it is some indirect measure of the depth and breadth of contemporary despair that Shelley's early death, in 1822, and Byron's, in 1824, also belong to these first years of the decade. Schubert's, in 1828, left behind a similar sense of massive potential only partly realised.

Was Géricault just a gilded youth caught up in grandiosity and fantasies of conquest? Contemporaries also experienced him as modest—this was what the Géricault biographer Clément sensed—and lacking in confidence to the point of persecution. In Rome, the sculptor Pradier complimented him on a drawing; at first Géricault thought he was being mocked and challenged the other artist to a duel. When he understood that Pradier was being sincere he is reported to have said, "Is it true then I've got talent?" (ibid., pp. 277–278). He was clearly loved by his friends (the Vernets, the Isabeys, the Dedreux, Charlet …); but he seems always to have felt in doubt, unsure of his ground, living as he did in an in-between historical moment. He was *unhinged* from his family and from inter-generational supports, no doubt partly in consequence of the post-Revolutionary shock to social and familial assurances and certainties. There was no precedent or map for this. He was the type of the artist evoked by Meltzer and Williams, ultimately unable to protect himself against his "pained perception" of the world (Meltzer & Williams, 1988, p. 15), open to the emotional currents, the social unconscious, the "enigmatic signifiers", of his time. The process of painting, we might hypothesise, also enabled him to sublimate or bracket off a certain amount of rage, disappointment, and terror of retribution, so that he was not totally overwhelmed by it (although at times it did all break through and lay him low). In Laplanchean terms, his work represented only a partially successful translation; but it is perhaps because this translation was only a partial success that it remains so eloquent, working on our unconsciouses, allowing so many emotional and historical resonances to make themselves felt, connecting us to the psychopathology of his and of our times.

* * *

Géricault found relief in physical activity and among male friends, and seems more than once to have grasped at a resolution to his conflicts and malaise through suicide. Finally he managed to lose his money (it took two attempts) and destroy his body (after several attempts), and then he made the portraits. His question was Montaigne's, and the Stoics': how should one live? What is it that makes a life meaningful? Géricault's personal sense of displacement, social, political, ideological, lent the question extreme poignancy and urgency for him, and nowhere did it come into sharper focus than in the portraits, images of a degree-zero of existence. In this sense Géricault was among the first moderns.

Whom can one love? With whom identify? One answer, for Géricault, was the transcendent *horse*, untroubled on all these fronts.

> Intelligent, with a sense of humour, she has a mind of her own ...
> But she must be feared as well as loved, for it is clear she can kill
> you with a kick ... she seems loving and eager to give pleasure. Yet
> she will not be mastered ... She does not love people as she does
> other horses ... (Meltzer & Williams, 1988, p. 202)

So wrote Donald Meltzer in a magnificent paragraph. Recognised in this way, she becomes Germer's uncanny horse. The domesticated horse is self-possessed, able to let herself go with immense power and speed, and lives within the tension between libidinal energy and a regimen of training, discipline, and culture (a tension fiercely conveyed in *Mazeppa*—both the painting and the film). It was a tension Géricault came to conclude was not liveable for him. The horse became the vehicle for his death (together with "a knot in his trousers")—as if like Mazeppa he could be carried off towards atonement or redemption.

A psychoanalytic future?

"It would be some time before people understood that there can be no 'snapshot' of madness and that psychiatry, like psychoanalysis, is more a matter of listening than looking" (Quetel, 2013, p. 210). The argument has gone back and forth ever since the early nineteenth century. "Although the patients sometimes spoke, we did not take sufficient account of what they said," wrote Dr Jacques-Joseph Moreau de Tours in 1845 (Murat, 2014, p. 228). (Moreau de Tours was a former intern of Esquirol's at Charenton and a member of the Romantics' Club des Haschischins, along with Hugo, Balzac, and Baudelaire.) But "physiognomy" had far from uttered its last word. In France it found weighty support, in 1852 and 1853, in two volumes of *Etudes cliniques sur les maladies mentales*, by Dr Bénédict-Augustin Morel, a publication steeped in the new theories of degeneration. Photography provided further stimulus to investigations into the appearance of the biologically degraded or otherwise symptomatic asylum-dweller, as evident in the work of Charcot and of such figures as Dr Hugh Welch Diamond, at Springfield Hospital, Illinois, around 1850, or of Henry Hering, who photographed patients at Bethlem in the 1850s (a selection is reproduced in Wedekind & Hollein, 2013, pp. 196–199). Pleas for looking to be tempered with listening and human interaction have needed periodic repetition. The psychiatrist William Alanson White, influential chief of the Government Hospital for the Insane in Washington DC, felt he needed to insist, in 1935, that it was important to try to establish relationships with people in severe, non-communicative distress. "I believe that a tremendous amount of suffering is still the lot of the insane person because he is misunderstood" (White, 1935, p. 72). In contrast, the British psychiatrists Richard Hunter and Ida Macalpine were unequivocal that psychiatry needed to reorientate itself from listening to looking. "Patients are victims of their brain rather than their mind. To reap the rewards of this medical approach … means a reorientation of psychiatry, from listening to looking" (cited in Porter, 2002, pp. 156–157).

It can be salutary to revisit the ideas of the "founding fathers" of medical psychiatry. Perhaps, concluded Esquirol in *Des Passions* in 1805,

> ... it may one day be possible to establish the principles of a moral therapy. But what intelligence, what experience, what sagacity, what tact is required in the application of these principles and then in finding every possible means to back them up! Professor Pinel has felt the difficulty of bringing together all the circumstances favourable to the cure of the alienated. They had almost all been misrecognised or neglected, because it was thought that the insane, lunatics, the mad could never reason. This error has its source in the abandon in which these sufferers had been left, in the lack of care given to untangling the principles determining their illness. They all reason more or less; they only appear delirious to us by virtue of the difficulty we find ourselves in, in knowing the founding idea to which all their thoughts, all their reasonings attach. If it were easy to put oneself in harmony with this mother-idea, no doubt a greater number of alienated people would be cured ... but no effort at all was made to get to know the alienated person's moral and intellectual situation ... (pp. 78–79, translated for this edition)

The idea that there may be a "principle" to be untangled, a "mother-idea" to which thoughts and actions might be traced, if one were able to put oneself in harmony with it; a split subject: here is most of the essential material of psychoanalysis, psychoanlysis in embryo. The passage also contains the seeds of a future critique of the tendency, inherent in all diagnoses, once again to reify the patient rather than seek to understand his or her world, critiques developed in psychoanalysis, and—partly in response to a tendency towards diagnostic reification within psychoanalysis itself—in existentialism, phenomenology, and the anti-psychiatry movement.

Medical misgivings in France in the 1820s as to whether alienism was proper medicine were echoed 100 years later in the 1920s in the debates over the question of lay analysis. We know which side Freud came out on: he stressed the importance of a broad cultural and artistic rather than exclusively scientific or medical education. That he did so may echo the discovery that was first made explicit in 1805 by Esquirol and that is a cornerstone of psychoanalysis: it is feeling rather than cognition alone which, like an artist or poet, the practitioner must address and engage. Rather than merely offering blanket consolation or other formulaic responses, the therapist must learn to gauge the effects of his interventions, at every juncture and with each patient, in a live and unique relationship that he is committed to trying to develop. Esquirol was also alert to the childhood roots of character and disturbance, which might be transmitted from parent to child "through a primitive disposition" (1805, pp. 27–28). All that was missing, and had to wait for Freud and Breuer, was a more evolved theoretical understanding of the fact that feelings and their effects might not always be conscious.

* * *

In 1828 Georget's colleague and obituarist Dr Jacques Raige-Delorme published a testament that Georget was alleged to have written two years before his death. In it, he retracted "philosophical opinions he later believed to be unfounded", with the request that he wished this retraction to have the widest possible publicity. Raige-Delorme quoted Georget as writing that, in his *Physiologie du système nerveux* of 1821, he had openly professed materialism; in the previous year, however, in *De la folie*, he had voiced "the contrary principles or at least ideas in a rapport with generally accepted beliefs" (Raige-Delorme cited pages 48, 51–52, 114). No sooner was the *Physiologie du système nerveux* published than, the testament says,

> … new meditations on a more extraordinary phenomenon, *somnambulism, allowed me no longer to doubt the existence in us and outside us of an intelligent principle, quite different from material existences.* This is, if you wish, the *soul* and *God*. I have in this respect *a profound conviction, founded in facts* which I believe to be incontestable. Perhaps one day I shall have the leisure to write about this subject … Was I convinced of what I was writing in 1821? At least I thought I was. However I recall on more than one occasion being shaken by great uncertainty, and often telling myself that one could only form conjectures, if one referred to the facts, to the judgement of the senses. But soon I came back to that favourite idea that there is no effect without cause, and that what is not matter is nothing. As if man had not twenty times tried in vain to impose limits on the possible. Was I not dominated by the wish to make a noise and aggrandize

myself, in so brutally attacking generally received beliefs of such great importance in the eyes of almost all men? ...

Georget went on to cite words to the same effect recently published by the most Catholic of Romantic writers, the Christian philosopher and Restoration statesman René Châteaubriand. "This declaration", the document concludes, "will only see the light of day when it will no longer be possible to doubt its sincerity and suspect my intentions ... that is after my death ... 1 March 1826" (Raige-Delorme, 1828, pp. 155–156, Georget's or Raige-Delorme's italics, translated for this edition).

Is this fascinating and ambiguous text sincere? Was it merely politic, written to support Esquirol? According to Eitner, who was drawing on Esquirol's biography of Georget in the *Biographie Universelle*, 1856 (Eitner, 1982, pp. 244, 354–355 notes 36 & 37), Georget came to realise that the soul-denying materialism of *De la folie* was, in the climate of Restoration Catholicity, professionally dangerous; however, Esquirol may well have been following his own prudent agenda in insisting that his former pupil, just before his death, renounce his former "openly professed materialism" in his testament of recantation (Goldstein, 1987, pp. 254–256). Esquirol's own philosophical credentials in the early 1820s would not indeed have been very satisfactory to "ultra" conservatives. In the opening lecture of his 1822 course he had complained, like his pupil, that metaphysicians who "disdained familiarity with the material man" thereby "threw themselves into empty theories and obscured their subject matter with abstractions" (cited in Goldstein, 1987, p. 248).

Georget's retraction could be seen to be in line with other contemporary critiques of materialism, that of the physician and educator Edouard Séguin, for example, who wrote that the sensualist philosophy of Locke and Condillac reached only the senses and never penetrated to the mind and soul (Lane, 1979, p. 67). Might it also be read as a premonition of the unconscious? There can be little doubt about the genuineness of Georget's open-mindedness. We might almost see him as a sort of proto-Bion. Attention is essential for the exercise of the intellectual faculties, he wrote in 1820, in order "to put into action, direct, wake up the brain, render it apt for fulfilling its functions; it is the erection in the genital organs, the appetite in the organs of digestion". He invites the reader to consider the nervous system in the same way as the digestive. Why, he asks, have we placed it outside the laws governing the body? (Georget, 1820a, pp. 37, 40).

Was the retraction in fact, contrary to first impressions, a return to a more pragmatic and open-minded position, a retreat from a religiously upheld materialism that failed to account for anomalies by not relying enough on direct observation and experience? In other words, the opposite of the capitulation to Catholic orthodoxy that it might at first seem? Perhaps it was his materialism that now seemed the orthodoxy that could blinker him to facts such as the inexplicable, disruptive, uncanny, "somnambulistic" aspects of some of his patients' actions and ideas. Might his retraction and his acceptance of a mysterious agency be an early "scientific" intimation of an embodied Freudian unconscious?

* * *

Historians have also found in the history of the French alienists the roots of a more adaptive and repressive psychoanalysis. There was a contradiction in the alienists' project between the need to dominate and the wish to communicate, which Laure Murat understood as "the incompatability between a collective ideological program and an individual encounter with the singularity of madness". Murat felt that only psychoanalysis has properly been able to take this incompatibility into account (2014, pp. 43–46). Klaus Dörner left the question open, as to "whether psychiatry [/psychoanalysis] is more of an emancipatory or integrative science i.e. whether it aims more at the liberation of the mentally suffering or the disciplining of bourgeois society". He added that "no psychiatrist has the right to that designation if in his dealings with himself and with those under his care he has not reflected on that question" (1981, p. 291).

Other commentators have been forthright in their hostility. Foucault declared that psychoanalysis was simply "a stranger to the sovereign enterprise of unreason" (Foucault, 1967, pp. 277–278). Castel similarly saw psychoanalysis as a new variation on the old coercive theme, just a subtler *relation de tutelle*, employing the tacit violence of the interpretation (Castel, 1973, 1976). Lisa Appignanesi has noted that the case of the murderess Henriette Cornier, in which Georget decisively intervened in her favour, marks "perhaps the first instance we have in the annals of psychological medicine in which the female patient resists the doctor's diagnosis: Henriette is ... akin to Freud's Dora", for Cornier herself never agreed with Georget that she was mad. The doctors argued that this proved her madness beyond doubt; the liberal Georget, believing he was promoting a more caring and enlightened society, positioned himself as the expert who could see beyond the patient's self-perception, his assessment more neutral, "clinical". Georget's argument led, in Foucault's terms, to a double incarceration: imprisonment within a diagnostic category as well as in an asylum/prison (Appignanesi, 2008, pp. 76–77).

In Gauchet and Swain's account, in pre-modern times we were ontologically different from one another, "thus mutually indispensible"; this was the bedrock of the feudal system. The egalitarian revolution replaced a system of dissimilarity with one of mutual belonging, "forcing beings to discover themselves substantially in one another instead of simply having to recognise and acknowledge one another's existence". The corollary, when faced with a true other, of irrefutable, irreducible difference, was that maintaining general likeness of being could call for "rejection, denial, even elimination" (Gauchet & Swain, 1999, p. 263).

Confinement of the mad in the asylum was, for Gauchet and Swain, directed towards incorporation and integration, but with the paradoxical or ironic result that the frame of the hospital made room for madness to express and assert itself (ibid., p. 268). This opens a question for critical followers of an apparent logic of history such as Foucault or Castel. How much might psychoanalysis, with its own forms of confinement, its "frame", the "time out of time" analyst and patient share, also be a dynamic space for the "singularity of madness" to make itself known? For an unknown something else to emerge?

Gauchet and Swain identified three moments in the development of the idea "of a properly psychological cure for alienation". The Pinelian moment, the discovery of an ineradicable remnant of reason in the insane, allowed the doctor to enter into relation with the patient's disorder through "a refusal to counter the discourse of the insane and an effort to remain at a benevolent distance". It led to "the discovery of a therapeutic space in the element of communication". This was very shortly followed by the second, asylum, moment. The public health impetus provided by the early Revolution was what made reform possible; it also provided the conditions, large hospitals, for realising the Enlightenment classificatory project, observing, grouping, ordering, refining—and surveillance. This was "psychiatry's political moment ... when it is invested and taken over by a pioneering institutional model that came straight out of the revolutionary upheavals of the social world". This "collectivist implementation of the alienist project" was utterly consistent with the moral treatment: no contradicting, no pandering either; it offered, in addition, an "infallible means" to mobilise the patient's surviving, intact subjectivity, through the possibility of drawing him out of solitude. All this, as the failure of the asylum project showed, was pure mirage, for "in reality, there is no way to seize subjects from within so as to bring them outside themselves into the controllable field of a coherent and fusional community".

Hence the third moment, the Freudian reversal. Freud took "the irreducibility of the individual into account", and established the principle that "[I]t is impossible to maintain oneself in a place from which one might penetrate others, play subtly on their inner mainsprings, and seize them in their very depths." There is only one way to proceed, in order to help others question and rid themselves of the chasm separating them from their aberrant element, and that is "to make them experience an absence—the irredeemable, unfathomable absence of some one who could pierce them through and through". The cure of the soul, leaving behind the manifestly political terrain of the asylum as "exemplary embodiment of the social ideal of power", now offered "the subtly polemical image of a gap and a renunciation with respect to the will to power". Does this "power of non-power" nevertheless contain its own "secret political exemplarity", a "politics of psychoanalysis"? The lesson however remains: "no claiming of power, if one is seeking to liberate the possible; no aiming at mastery, if one is seeking authentically to act" (ibid., pp. 96–99).

Pinel made madness available to conceptualisation as "becoming-other-for-oneself from within". Madness became, in its essential alterity, "the constitutive principle of subjectivity" itself. No wonder such figures as Stendhal, Hegel, and Géricault were drawn towards it. It also became the key indicator on the basis of which all other forms of division between visible and invisible could be understood. The powers of the invisible, just as they were disappearing as factors governing the world, finally transferred themselves onto us in the form of the Freudian drives, rendering the "co-presence of the subject and the subject's other" uncannily indissociable (ibid., pp. 264, 269, 272).

At this point the "therapeutic subject" was born, and its coming-into-being was a crucial historical prerequisite for psychoanalysis. For if the sane could no longer insist on total self-transparency, neither could the mad claim a monopoly on opacity and impermeability to relationship and communication.

Analytic positions

The portraits require us to take up multiple emotional and intellectual positions, and different ways of approaching them historically and art-historically invite us to find their counterparts in forms of analytic thinking, attitude, and orientation. As Stefan Germer demonstrated, in exemplary fashion, we can go a long way towards grounding the portraits historically without blunting the challenges they offer. They show us that they, and we, are constitutionally more than the sum of our accounts and explanations of ourselves and each other. Mobile in themselves, they cause us to shift in our moment-to-moment responses to them; they do not allow us to settle down with and "grasp" them. Dwelling with them becomes like listening to jazz: we recognise harmonies, melodies, rhythmic patterns, only to feel them dissolve. Studying them can alert us to the involuntarily dynamic, kaleidoscopic quality of our own mental lives.

It is not possible to fit the paintings into the iconography of the Seven Deadly Sins in any convincing, systematic way—but they do have a lingering, archetypal quality. The child abductor carries an echo of Rembrandt's 1632 philosopher, of which the editors of Jung's *Man and His Symbols* wrote: "The inward-looking old man provides an image of Jung's belief that each of us must explore his own unconscious" (Jung, 1964, p. 103). Recognition that the portraits activate a great deal in us unconsciously is fundamental and mandatory. So of course does each encounter with a living person, especially when this takes place in the focusing frame of the consulting room. For the work of art is like the analytic session as described by Laplanche: he called it a particle accelerator, "a cyclotron of libido" (1987, p. 6).

One view we have explored is that the paintings were made as diagnostic illustrations. Do we therefore locate ourselves as readers of symptoms and signs, casting a rationalising, expert gaze on the person in front of us? Do we look for signs—verbal, behavioural, visual, or even countertransferential, in our own reactions and sense of how we are being transferentially positioned or projectively identified—of pathology: for narcissism, for example, oedipal conflict, borderlinity? How we do this would depend on our theoretical orientation. Lacanians for example would seek to identify a psychic structure, neurotic, psychotic, or perverse; Kleinians would keep in focus the patient's current location on the spectrum paranoid-schizoid–depressive.

The argument over whether the portraits are diagnostic or not has run throughout the book, sometimes more sometimes less explicitly. But might the question "either diagnostic or not" itself be the product of what Iain McGilchrist would see as reductionist, left-brain thinking? The portraits represent an advance on Enlightenment in its cruder forms: they do not so much invite us to read them off, like lessons or satires, as to meet them for what they are, as paintings. At the same time they require us to recognise that their history is part of them. Their subjects after all come to us with no names, only labels. We are obliged to look at them as "as mediated conceptual moments which come to fulfilment only in the development of their social, historical, and human significance" (Adorno & Horkheimer, 1944, pp. 26–27). It is not possible to ignore the fact that the portraits emerged out of a context in which physiognomic diagnosis was taken seriously and in good faith, as part of a search to establish general laws and principles. Wary as some of us might be of medicalising diagnosis today, we have to accept that it exists. Even the patient with no psychiatric history, not referred by a psychiatrist or doctor, might complain to the non-medical analyst that she "has" depression, or Asperger's, or is worried that he is bipolar. Similarly, rejecting a medicalised notion of "mental illness" as a disease like any other obviously does not have to mean excluding physical illness or injury or actual brain damage as possible factors in existential suffering. Géricault's friends at the Salpêtrière School, inspired by Cabanis's *Rapports du physique et du moral*, were fervently debating these matters, and to be reminded of these historical debates might help us hold our theoretical, philosophical, and ethical judgements lightly enough not to disable our thinking.

The figures in the portraits seem to invite both our detachment and our engagement simultaneously. Might finding ourselves deploying an appraising, clinical gaze also be a response to the way the *other* is caught up in some excessive form of rationalisation, of left-brain thinking? The figures in the portraits certainly seem in the grip of the sort of left-brain state McGilchrist (2010) has described: distrustful, wary, and ready to exploit others, to thieve, envy, abduct, get something for nothing, conquer, and control. They can have a dual effect on us. They might activate our own defences and prompt us to stay at a distance;

they also, if we can bear to hear from them, call to us, communicating a state of mind, a degree of "alienation" from (more "right-brain") forms of ordinary emotional and social contact. Our task must then be to sustain a sense of, and confidence in, our own capacity to feel alive and in contact, and thus, as André Green recommended, to stay alive to the deadness in the other (Green, 1986, especially p. 163). The portraits hold us to this.

The paintings insist both on their subjects' destitution and their sheer individuality. Might we adopt a more empathic and "Romantic" frame of mind, which we then ascribe to the painter so that we can thereby see the figures as projections of his own emotional state? This, however, might also keep both the figures and the painter nicely at a distance; it would let us off the hook, and send us spiralling back towards detached appraisal. For it might be to operate a sort of double defence: not our disturbance, but the sitters', and if not theirs, still not ours but the projected disturbance of the painter. But this is not, in the end, a manoeuvre that the paintings will easily allow. They give off little sense that the painter went through any such mediated process as knowingly to see himself in them; no self-conscious pathetic fallacy here. The invitation to identify is more directly with the sitters themselves, and in taking it up, as we cannot avoid doing, and attempting to engage with them empathically, we come up a against a greater challenge: to enter into personal and particular relationship with our own violence, lust, envy, greed, megalomania, internal poverty, and shrunkenness, alongside our fearfulness, watchful wariness, and nameless terror.

Might it, on the other hand, be more satisfying to regard the portraits as statements about the human condition and suffering in general, in this way avoiding the risk of over-identification and maintaining, rather like a Pinel, Esquirol, or Georget, or a well-trained therapist with her patient, a certain thoughtful distance? Or might this in turn merely be a ploy to protect ourselves from an awareness, immanent both in the portraits and in the practice of psychoanalysis, of the hazy boundaries between normality and madness, reason and unreason? But might an awakening to such an awareness in its turn court another danger: that we might be excited and seduced into a sort of idealisation of the crazy and irrational (perhaps like some of the artists and poets of Surrealism) and lose sight of the infant trauma and human distress informing it? It is an excitement to which historical commentators, particularly those dwelling on the transformative years around 1800, can be prone ("Challenged here is portraiture's very identity as a genre associated with rational social order ... emissaries of an upside-down world ..." etc. (Athanassoglou-Kallmyer, 2010, p. 205)).

The paintings also work as reminders of our own place as social beings in historical time. There can be no doubt that they are informed by powerful socio-political subtexts, of some of which the artist would have been well aware, others of which, elements of a contemporary social unsconscious, only come more clearly to light subsequently. Might adopting a more socially and historically context-sensitive perspective with those who come to us for help—in the face of a persuasive analytic tradition that insists on the priority of the unconscious and the internal life of the individual—open up new possibilities of interpretation and meaning? A Bakhtinian sensitivity to the dialogic? In what world, the therapist might ask, interrelational, emotional, social, political, existential, is this person who sits with me, and invites me in (or not)? A keener awareness of ourselves as social beings might also help us think afresh about the dynamics between internal and external in therapeutic work, indeed to question the very validity of such binaries: internal-external, individual-group.

For the portraits, like each of us, are "nodal points", in the sense that the great German sociologist Norbert Elias gave this phrase, in the following powerful passage.

> ... each gesture and act ... is a function and *precipitate of relations*, and can be understood—like the figure of a thread in a net—only from the totality of the network ... ideas, convictions, affects, needs and character traits are produced in the individual through *intercourse with others*, things which make up his *personal "self"* and in which is expressed, for this very reason, the *network of relations* from which he has emerged and into which he passes. And in this way this self, this personal "essence", is formed in a continuous interweaving of needs. It is *the order of this incessant interweaving* without a beginning that *determines the nature and form of the individual human being*. Even the nature and form of his solitude, even what he feels to be his "inner life", is stamped by the history of his *relationships*—by the structure of the *human network* in which, as one of its *nodal points*, he develops and lives as an individual. (1939, p. 13, cited in Lavie, 2011, p. 168)

Each encounter connects us to this network although we are rarely conscious of it, and this of course includes the therapist's encounter with the individual patient, who is also a "precipitate of relations". At what nodal point of multiple intersection is she/are we?

The figures inhabit a world. They are caught up in *re-presentations*, of what, arguably, has been projected into them, what they have been called upon to carry and represent. It might not be too much to suppose that there was once, for each of them in his or her different way, too much other, an overwhelming, abusive, intrusive other, at whose nature, individual, social, cultural, we can only guess. But this would explain why none of them, except possibly the army veteran, seems just at the moment to have room for another living human. In painting them, Géricault gave them back to themselves, as if he were an analyst making a sound, descriptive interpretation, which might help draw the patient back into relationship and into her more social state. The challenge he presents *us* is to allow the figures not merely to be other, in their strangeness, but to be *other than* the transferential objects, either too distant or too close, as which they might at first invite us to see them: receptacles for our own fears, of our own envy or fear of being envied, of stealing or being stolen from.

Art-historical consideration of how Géricault might have actively or intuitively, unconsciously, posed the sitters, in reality or in his mind's eye, invites reflection on the therapist's part in projectively "constructing" the patient. But however posed, they challenge through the sheer life that the painter finds in them, which comes from somewhere else and has its own independent, non-contingent existence. He finds that they are alive *to* something. It is perhaps, in terms of psychoanalytic "object relations" thinking, an "internal object" which must be engaged with, appeased, or satisfied. Perhaps it is a psychic stucture that seems the only one in which life may be possible (Pinel and the early alienists implicitly recognised the form of the sufferer's insanity as a way of allowing a liveable life). Is the viewer more struck by the figures' entrappedness or their aliveness? Géricault makes us register both, or to feel a tension of back and forward movement between the two (like the bi-directional pulls, hope and despair, past and future, which Julian Barnes detected in the *Raft*), and this in the end is what *he* is alive to, both aliveness and deadness, as the analyst must be.

The portraits embrace *all* these possibilities—social, political, philosophical—and are not exhausted by them or made fully transparent by them. The push and pull between these possibilities arouses our attention. They can also contribute to a continuing, necessary, rejuvenating project for psychotherapy. Looking at them can reconnect us to the fundamental Romantic intuition that to observe can be to make present—that, as Goethe said, "perception is itself a thinking", and each new object can open up "a new organ of perception in us" (McGilchrist, 2010, pp. 359–360). Therapy can lie above all in the analyst's and patient's shared perceiving and thinking activity itself, with its own inherent yield of pleasure.

The aesthetic experience

The portraits challenge us to keep the good, creative object alive. Nowhere did Géricault make the challenge more explicit than in the most uncanny of his works, the guillotined heads and severed arms and feet, which present themselves as lovers in bed, or limbs caressing each other. The canvas can serve the function of the analyst, allowing unconscious projections (both painter's and viewer's, in their different ways) to be returned sufficiently mediated as to allow us to take them in both consciously and unconsciously, to respond emotionally and with anxiety, but without being driven to act. Because they disallow our narcissistic gratification and can help us to bear our own disturbance and the anxiety that facing it produces, the portraits point us towards a containing, "therapeutic" capacity in ourselves.

They have their own inherent restorative power. That tilt of the head in counterpoint with the torso and the direction of the gaze, the play of light over forehead, cheek, and shirt collar, the subtle, irregular geometry of eye, line of mouth, shoulder are both pleasures in themselves and transformations of experience—the painter's experience of the sitter and his sense of her or his experience as held in the body, with its characteristic tension or slump, given to us, the specatators of however many years later, in the form of a new experience, the painting.

In a fascinating book Gregorio Kohon (2016) has recently proposed an understanding of the aesthetic experience as *in essence* uncanny, relating this to the uncanniness of our encounter with ourselves as both familiar and unfamiliar. He draws particularly on the work of André Green and the key notion of the negative which, in Green's development of Freud's and of Winnicott's thinking, has a dual function. The negative is on the one hand structuring, and on the other destructive, "no"-saying. Greatly to oversimply, it is the trace of the mother's holding after contact with her body is broken, an imprint of which survives in the form of a "negative hallucination". This becomes the template for all future object relations (Green, 2005, p. 161). It is also the child's "no", a radical refusal of the other which is also an essential basis for a sense of personal identity, the establishment of a self. The portraits are a negative hallucination—how do we fit ourselves into their lost embrace? What sorts of actual facial and postural mirroring do they invite? What "object relations"?—and a "no", a refusal to be other than themselves, prompting us similarly.

But that a sense of identity equates with a fully coherent self is, as Lacan demonstrated in his account of the mirror stage, an illusion: the image of narcissistic plenitude which the figure in the mirror offers is just that, an image, an "other" to the subject who gazes at it. If the mirror stage is the moment of access to a sense of subjecthood, it is also a source of alienation: "Being turns into not-being, the familiar becomes unfamiliar" (Kohon, 2016, p. 149), and all the while primary confusion between me and not-me persists as a psychic function. In the words of Michel de M'Uzan, there is no true boundary between ego and non-ego, only "a vague transitional zone, a *spectrum of identity*" (de M'Uzan, 1976, pp. 28–29). The Freudian uncanny, as met with in the work of art, is "an encounter with the negative, something secret or repressed in the subject, which the artistic or literary object has brought to light or around which it is at least circling, threatening to do so" (Kohon, 2016, p. 150).

> In the aesthetic, we face ghosts, doubles, unsolicited apparitions, *déjà vu*, dangers, anxious anticipations, unsolicited presences … being open—at some level—to experiencing the uncanny is fundamental to our experience of aesthetic pleasure … (ibid., pp. 150–151)

In my exploration of the portraits I have leaned on Stefan Germer's use of the uncanny. For Germer the notion illuminates a kind of viewer-painting relationship specifically evolved by Géricault, one that knowingly invites and denies the viewer's narcissistic involvement and gratification; perhaps it is a particular, historically specific case within the more global understanding Kohon may be proposing (although his examples are mostly, but not exclusively, drawn from sculpture and painting made within the last hundred years). Géricault's is perhaps, like so much else still shaping our world from the late Enlightenment and Romantic period, a foundational case. I should in any event like to supplement Kohon's powerful and evocative account with one drawn from Green's colleague and contemporary Laplanche; this, like Green's, also makes its starting point the mother's body and the psyche-soma.

In the portraits, perhaps in any portraits, or any paintings, but we might wonder about portraits in particular, we are exposed to the enigmatic message of the other. This recapitulates the original (albeit mythical, as if it were a question of a singular) moment of inscription, in which the unconscious message of the caregiver overwhelms the neonate's capacity to "translate" it. In another psychoanalytic idiom, it is exposure to the mother's unbearable beauty (Meltzer & Williams, 1988). This is the moment of primary repression, of the birth of the unconscious. Hence the compelling insistence of the portraits. They echo internally and reactivate a foundational process; they call on us, drive us, to translate—to try to master what we can only very partially hope to master. They come to inhabit our unconscious.

A sense of something profound happening in us—the opening up or tumescence of an organ of perception—can be particularly acute in front of these particular portraits precisely because of the way they withhold from us and hold us in suspense. They are supremely in the place of the analyst, generating free associations, unconscious links. They are also, fundamentally, the face of the other.

Ethics and the face

The portraits announce the possibility of a radically suspended relation to the other, assessed not in terms of worth, as unit of labour for example, worth investing in (for in these terms the figures would be merely worthless pieces of human flotsam), but in which what is suspended is final judgement of any kind. With this can come an experience of interconnectedness, and of shared vulnerability, especially when we come up against the question of what we are to do with each other when, as in an analysis, ordinary, polite social relations are suspended. There are different ways of finding words for this experience and its implications; I should like to offer a little album of quotations, approaches to the enigma and ineffable draw of the other's face, that with which the portraits can so compellingly put us in touch.

For the art historian Gregor Wedekind the portraits

> ... picture people in their mental helplessness as debased creatures to whom the dignity of all humanity is accorded not inspite of but because of their affliction. In this Géricault stands firmly in the tradition of Christian anthropology, which employs the incarnation and self-sacrificial death of Jesus Christ as a model for its image of Man. Yet the religious aspect is shattered; what remains is simply adherence to the notion that man's dignity resides in his predestined mortality. Such a message can only be communicated by way of an emotional pact with the viewer, one established by a close-up view that involves him. Only in this way can the strange and incommensurable be truly experienced as something corresponding to one's own, familar reality ... such realism, which is far more than clinical observation or documentary factuality ... was rooted in the recognition of the fate of the individual in his or her historical and social context.

Géricault's close-up delineation of individuality aimed to capture what we all share, "the tragic reality of life" (Wedekind, 2013, p. 186). The feeling of common participation this induces is profound. Géricault's heads, lost in their own thoughts and solitary in their frames, paradoxically invoke the possibility of relationship itself. They are given to us through the most intimately social of Western art forms, the portrait in oils.

In the penetrating words of another critic, Kristin Schrader, writing on Géricault and the painter Marlene Dumas (who made haunting, limpid versions of the portraits),

> The paint layer *becomes* skin, physical, characterised by chance and flaws in the pigment. Equivalent to the loss of control and command of our own faces ... the face as vis-à-vis is also a mirror, shattering the composure of one's own, as do past sins and useless guilt. The inscrutability of the face, which can express the inscrutability of the person, makes Géricault and Dumas seem closely related to each other, and is in the best sense trivial—because it affects everyone. (Schrader, 2013, p. 180)

Géricault's paint layer gives body to the "vague transitional zone", the "risk zone" (de M'Uzan, 1976, pp. 28–29; Kohon, 2016, p. 151) between I and not-I: it is the skin of the face itself.

For the portraits confront us with our own desire. "Man's desire is the Other's desire," wrote Lacan. Slavov Žižek has responded with this:

> … the subject desires only in so far as it experiences the Other itself as desiring, as the site of an unfathomable desire, as if an opaque desire is emanating from him or her. Not only does the other address me with an enigmatic desire, it also confronts me with the fact that I myself do not know what I really desire, with the enigma of my own desire. For Lacan, who follows Freud here, this abyssal dimension of another human being—the abyss of the depth of another personality, its utter impenetrability—first found its full expression in Judaism, with its injunction to love your neighbour as yourself. For Freud as well as for Lacan, this injunction is deeply problematic, since it obfuscates the fact that, beneath the neighbour as my mirror-image, the one who resembles me, with whom I can empathise, there always lurks the unfathomable abyss of radical Otherness, of one about whom I finally know nothing. Can I really rely on him? Who is he? … (Žižek, 2006, pp. 42–43)

If, faced with this abyss of Otherness, this impenetrability, we try to force the other into our grasp, we are, for Emmanuel Levinas, doing violence. Perhaps, indeed, we do violence in the very act of giving sustained attention to these portrayed faces. Perhaps those of us who work analytically are right to encourage our patients to lie on the couch, rather than sit with them face-to-face. Access to the face, said Levinas,

> … is straightaway ethical. You turn yourself toward the Other as toward an object when you see a nose, eyes, a forehead, a chin, and you can describe them. The best way of encountering the Other is not even to notice the colour of his eyes! When one observes the colour of the eyes one is not in social relationship with the Other. The relation with the face can surely be dominated by perception, but what is specifically the face cannot be reduced to that.
>
> There is first the very uprightness of the face, its upright exposure, without defence. The skin of the face is that which stays most naked, most destitute. It is the most naked, though with a decent nudity.

It is the most destitute also: there is an essential poverty in the face; the proof of this is that one tries to mask this poverty by putting on poses, by taking on a countenance. The face is exposed, menaced, as if inviting us to an act of violence. At the same time, the face is what forbids us to kill. (Levinas, 1982, pp. 85–86)

The nakedness of his face and the apprehensiveness of its expression place upon us the injunction to do it no violence. Writing on Velázquez, whose work Géricault had copied in the Louvre, the Spanish philosopher and critic José Ortega y Gasset emphasised Velázquez's extraordinary ability, in his portraits, to convey a sense of the fleetingly glimpsed, mobile-featured human face—just what Georget, I believe, tasked Géricault to do. Perhaps, after all, the portraits' ideal viewer would be one who understood that the best way to register their humanity might be to catch them out of the corner of the eye, in passing (like the patient's face glimpsed at the start and end of the session). They "float within a margin of imprecision which is their true presence" (Ortega y Gasset, 1972, p. 100). Géricault's portraits align him with Velázquez, Rembrandt, and Goya; they confront us with the finally ungraspable, uncolonisable nature of the other.

What then is an ethical position with regard to this other? Judith Butler, through her engagement with Foucault, Hegel, and Levinas, could hardly have put matters more cogently:

… the question of ethics emerges precisely at the limits of our schemes of intelligibility, the site where we ask ourselves what it might mean to continue in a dialogue where no common ground can be assumed, where one is, as it were, at the limits of what one knows yet still under the demand to offer and receive acknowledgement: to someone else who is there to be addressed and whose address is there to be received. (2005, pp. 21–22)

Modern madness

Historically and culturally, however, the experience of the face of the other undergoes changes; it has a history. Perhaps it is enough to think of prevailing ways in which the face is represented to grasp this. Géricault was painting human faces in the years just before the invention of photography. We live in an age of unprecedented reproduction of our own and each other's faces. Our images are less likely to be rolled up in a trunk in an attic than to be uploaded on Facebook, which stores them in enormous datacentres at the rate of 350 million photographs a day, a rate which is currently (September 2015) doubling every eighteen months (Harding, 2015, p. 25), and Facebook is only one social medium and repository of faces among others.

One way of trying to articulate this shift is precisely in portraiture's terms, of "likeness" and "unlikeness". For Gauchet and Swain, in the pre-modern culture of master and serf, unlikeness was a principle of social relations, "a bond between human beings based on an intimate estrangement" (Gauchet & Swain, 1999, p. 260). Unfortunates of all sorts—cripples, the mad, the deaf and blind, women—were confined or excluded "within the difference that afflicts them". They could thus become spectacle. This is in contrast to the modern (democratic) world in which, at first, it was the demand for sameness that determined exclusion and produced the citizen-patients of the alienists. Today, however,

> ... the same identificatory aim at work within the social-human space ... commands the end of exclusion [of the asylum] ... there must be no place of the other, no sphere of the outside, no separate universe of difference within society ... an obligatory, unsurpassable [*incontournable*—without appeal] integration from which no one is exempt. (ibid., pp. 268–269)

This, Gauchet and Swain continued, is precisely the gap separating us from Pinel's or Esquirol's patients, whose "... paroxysms, their physical appearance, and their stories ... stem first of all from a social mode of production of the gap between self and self and between self and others that is different from the one with which we have become familiar." Madness has changed, and the fundamental difference is in the way "the singular subject is inscribed within the collective framework". Formerly, madness for others, under the sign of rupture (manic explosion or savage melancholic withdrawal), constituted itself "under the gaze that will be cast upon it, in relation to the presence of a fellow-being inherently recognised as unsurpassable" (*incontournable* here might also translate as "unanswerable" or "not to be gainsaid" (ibid., pp. 276–277; 1980, p. 510)).

The portraits belong, historically, at the intersection of old and new, of what Gauchet and Swain thought of in terms of a shift from madness for others, to madness for self. The portraits enshrine a contradiction and tension between belonging and being recognisable, and not-belonging, being apart, alien. They picture "the divided being that the observer still senses as 'himself' beneath whatever alienates him" (ibid., p. 163).

The madness of our own times no longer signals the dimension of not-belonging and apartness, "visibly or positively a withdrawal in relation to common experience". Instead we have an alienation

> ... entirely incorporated in the sphere of presence to oneself ... in which subjects no longer have to exit from themselves just as society no longer entails exteriority. This world entails a de facto severing of self from others, but a severing that is no longer signified as such. Psychic space absorbs the symbolic outside (ibid., p. 281).

Perhaps, as John Berger suggested, the way Géricault's sitters avoid our eyes is now something familiar and everyday. "How often today can one encounter a not dissimilar glance refusing to focus on the near—in trains, parking lots, bus queues, shopping precincts ..." (Berger, 2016, p. 212). It can be hard for us to look one another in the eye; alienation has become generalised.

* * *

A much loved and widely acclaimed entertainer at the peak of his career, his ordinary-Joe sort of face familiar to millions acros the world, takes his own life, to the shock and dismay of his public and his profession. It is known, of course, that he has been depressed and drug-addicted for years, with manic interludes upon which he has also, it seems, been able to draw in his work, creating a trademark, highly upbeat style of delivery. He has, in the words of the popular press, been "battling with bipolar disorder", and in interviews given in the last few years of his life he frames his difficulties in just these terms: he has been wrestling with an illness, something he must beat. After his death, experts and researchers in the field of mental illness are among the first to be called upon for their views, which they tend to assert with a certain stridency: people suffering from similar symptoms should seek medical help, the only kind which is evidence-based; the entertainer's death is a tragedy, but he and his professional carers were up against a genetic condition, which only continuing, rigorous, and well-funded research will elucidate. Before the unsuspecting viewer, reader, or listener can register the thought: so the genetic explanation is still only a theory? So bipolar disorder is not really a proper disease, like TB or AIDS, with a proper aetiology?—comes the killer line: to suggest anything other than a brain disorder with a genetic basis is, unforgivably, to stigmatise sufferers.

Looked at in another light, in what deep loneliness may this man have found himself? The weight of a contemporary culture, enshrining a "severing that is no longer signified as such" and which, it seems, he himself had fully internalised, is likely to have pushed him and his helpers to attend to his symptoms rather than his experience. His experience and what he might have had to say about it would have been of no interest to the experts; so possibly no one, including the sufferer himself, listened to it. Perhaps no one asked him how he was, what things were like for him. And what a conversation, had it been allowed to develop, it might have been. For this particular entertainer had impersonated, embodied, people traumatised in ways specific to his contemporary culture: by a particular, cynical war, by ruthless competition …

* * *

"We do not know what shape the madness of the absolute individual will take. At least we are learning … to anticipate the difference" (ibid., p. 281). Gauchet and Swain wrote this in 1980. Have their worst predictions been realised; does their analysis still stand? In 1980 the cyber-revolution was barely underway and had not yet infiltrated daily life. We were on the threshold of the atomised world of the ironically named "social media" in which the (perhaps once *incontournable*) face of the other calls less insistently and far less immediately than the portable, electronic self-object.

In France in 1980 it would have still seemed tenable to claim general consensus that the state's role was to ensure homogeneity; anything to do with the "social outside", *les exclus*, the homeless, the mad, was the state's responsibility, as the agency "charged with producing and maintaining the identity of the social body" (ibid., pp. 267–268). Can this still be claimed across much of the world in 2016, under triumphant economic neoliberalism? Is feudal alterity making a comeback?

Ian McGilchrist, in his deeply disturbing analysis of left-brain dominance and contemporary life in the UK, would seem not far off agreeing.
He writes—he could equally have been writing about Restoration France
in Géricault's last years, and the climate internalised by his sitters—of
characteristically left-brain social "identification by categories", "implicit
or explicit resentment or competition", of "paranoia and lack of trust the
pervading stance between individuals and groups" and of "government
towards its people". Even doctors are under suspicion (2010, pp. 431–432).
Brexit might seem to confirm McGilchrist's worst fears.

A Romantic science?

What hope, if any, might psychoanalysis have to offer? What strengths
and resources might it be able to draw upon, from its own deeper historical roots? Psychoanalysis has much in common with an early nineteenth-
century spirit of enquiry. It has roots in the era—Pinel's, Géricault's,
Georget's, Coleridge's, Goethe's—before the modern art/science divide
was definitively established, and the findings of "natural philosophy"
were tested against day-to-day experience, perception, and relationship.
Seen in this light, psychoanalysis at its best is a "Romantic science"—
the phrase was coined by the great Russian neurologist Alexander Luria
in response to Oliver Sacks's *Awakenings* in 1973 (Lamb, 2013; Sacks,
2015, p. 200). Psychoanalysis as Romantic science would be historically
informed and culturally and critically aware; it would be a practice
within which, in Gauchet and Swain's terms, subjectivity might be conceived "as the capacity for self-awareness that survives even the kind of
agonised suspension of wholeness that madness brings" (Seigel, 1999,
p. xvii). It would marry discipline and tact, in its address to the unconscious, with respect for the infinite variety and complexity of humans
and our representations of each other; it would resist the expediency
of reducing the human to mere organism, mechanism, cyber-system,
or collection of signs and symptoms. It would stand as an alternative
to the scenario of left-brain dominance and absolute, internal twenty-
first century madness, aggressively theorised and promoted in terms
of genetics and neurology, terms which often signally lack the sense of
wonder, the awe at human resilience and creativity, that made Sacks's
work so remarkable.

Historically Romanticism was a "rear-guard action against repression", and although it occupied a mere speck of time, its legacy is a

reminder that "spiritual and intellectual liberation requires endless internal warfare against everything in ourselves that narrows us down instead of opening us up and that replaces questing with certitude" (Sachs, 2010, p. 10). To be a "Romantic", in the way in which a Stendhal or a Géricault was a Romantic, meant attempting to tell things as they were, in the face of powerful counter-narratives, while at the same time holding a recognition of oneself as constitutionally caught up in misrecognitions. Romanticism still contains a tremendous charge of potential for the relief of unnecessary suffering. "You are mad or bad if you do not believe us when we tell you that you are mad or bad to trust your own perceptions and memory," wrote Laing and Esterson (1964, p. 118). The Romantic imperative was to do just that, trust one's perceptions and memory, and candidly face the consequences. As the trajectory of Géricault's life amply demonstrates, this involves risks. The portraits and their era nevertheless reaffirm the cardinal importance for us of this act of faith. They can help us maintain a focus on psychoanalysis and psychotherapy as dynamic spaces for new experience: for the exercise of humility in the face of our mysteriousness to ourselves and each other, and for discoveries about our distracted and suppressed capabilities, with transformative possibilities, perhaps, for sociality itself.

REFERENCES

Adorno, T., & Horkheimer, M. (1944). *Dialectic of Enlightenment*. J. Cumming (Trans.). London: Verso, 1989.

Alexander, F. G., & Selesnick, S. T. (1966). *The History of Psychiatry: An Evaluation of Psychiatric Thought and Practice from Prehistoric Times to the Present*. New York: Harper & Row.

Almeida, H. de (1991). *Romantic Medicine and John Keats*. Oxford: Oxford University Press.

Appignanesi, L. (2008). *Mad, Bad and Sad. A History of Women and the Mind Doctors from 1800 to the Present*. London: Virago.

Aragon, L. (1958/9). *La Semaine Sainte. (2 vols.)* Paris: Gallimard.

Arasse, D. (1988). *Die Guillotine. Die Macht der Machine und das Schauspiel der Gerechtigkeit*. Hamburg, Germany: Reinbek.

Arnold, C. (2009). *Bedlam. London and its Mad*. London: Simon & Schuster.

Athanassoglou-Kallmyer, N. (2010). *Théodore Géricault*. London: Phaidon.

Audi, R. (Ed.) (1999). *The Cambridge Dictionary of Philosophy. (Second edition)*. Cambridge: Cambridge University Press.

Azouvi, F. (1980). Présentation. In: P. Pinel (1800), *Traité médico-philosophique sur l'aliénation mentale ou la manie*. Geneva: Editions Slatkine.

Bakhtin, M. (1981). *The Dialogic Imagination. Four Essays*. Austin, TX: University of Texas Press.

Balzac, H. de (1830a). *Adieu*. K. Wormeley (Trans.). Gloucester: Dodo Press, 2006.

Balzac, H. de (1830b). Etude de femme. In: P. Maury (Ed.), *Les trente meilleures nouvelles de la littérature française*. Verviers, Belgium: Marabout, 1986.

Balzac, H. de (1832a). *Le colonel Chabert*. E. Marriage (Trans.). Amazon, Create Space, 2012.

Balzac, H. de (1832b). *Louis Lambert*. C. Bell & J. Waring (Trans.). Amazon, Create Space, 2015.

Balzac, H. de (1837/1843). *Les Illusions perdues*. Paris: Editions Garnier Frères, 1961.

Balzac, H. de (1838/1843). *A Harlot High and Low*. R. Heppenstall (Trans. & Intro.). London: Penguin, 1970.

Barnes, J. (1989). *A History of the World in 10½ Chapters*. London: Jonathan Cape.

Bartabas, & Karmitz, M. (1993). *Mazeppa*. M. Bosé & Bartabas (Perf.). MK2 Productions, CED productions en coproduction avec La SPF Cinéma, La Sept Cinéma et France 3 avec la participation de Canal+ et le soutien de PROCIREP.

Baudelaire, C. (1857). *Les Fleurs du mal*. In: *Oeuvres complètes. 2 vols.* (Texte établi, présenté et annoté par C. Pichois). Paris: Gallimard, Bibliothèque de la Pléiade, 1975–76.

Baudelaire, C. (1859). Théophile Gautier. In: *Oeuvres complètes. 2 vols.* (Texte établi, présenté et annoté par C. Pichois). Paris: Gallimard, Bibliothèque de la Pléiade, 1975–76.

Bauernfeld, E. (1873). *Aus Alt- und Neu-Wien*. Hamburg, Germany: Tredition Classics, 2012.

Beerbohm, M. (2015). *The Prince of Minor Writers. The Selected Essays of Max Beerbohm*. P. Lopate (Ed.). New York: New York Review of Books.

Bell, C. (1806). *Essays on the Anatomy of Expression in Painting*. London: Longman, Hurst, Rees, and Orme. (Republished in 1824 as *Essays on the Anatomy and Philosophy of Expression*.)

Benjamin, W. (1973). *Illuminations*. H. Arendt (Ed. & Intro.), H. Zohn (Trans.). London: Collins/Fontana.

Benjamin, W. (1983). *Charles Baudelaire. A Lyric Poet in the Era of High Capitalism*. H. Zohn (Trans.). London: Verso.

Berger, J. (2016). *Portraits. John Berger on Artists*. T. Overton (Ed.). London: Verso.

Bernard, C. (2015). Polémique autour de la philosophie de la folie. Available at: serpsy.org/histoire/Chantal_polemique.htlm. Downloaded 28 February 2015.

Berthier, P. (2008). In: H. de Balzac (1838/1843), *Splendeurs et misères des courtisanes*. Paris: Livre de Poche, 2008.

Bikker, J., Weber, J. M., Wieseman, M. E., & Hinterding, E. (2014). *Rembrandt. The Late Works.* London: The National Gallery in association with the Rijksmuseum, Amsterdam.

Black, J. (1991). The French Revolution. In: J. W. Yolton, R. Porter, P. Rogers, & B. M. Stafford (1991), *The Blackwell Companion to the Enlightenment.* L. G. Crocker (Intro.). Oxford: Blackwell.

Boime, A. (1991). Portraying monomaniacs to service the alienist's monomania: Géricault and Georget. *Oxford Art Journal, 14*: 1991. Oxford: Oxford University Press.

Bonnefoy, Y. (2006). *Goya, les peintures noires.* Bordeaux, France: William Blake.

Bostridge, I. (2015). *Schubert's Winter Journey. Anatomy of an Obsession.* London: Faber & Faber.

Bosworth, M. (2001). Anatomy of a massacre: gender, power, and punishment in Revolutionary Paris. *Violence Against Women, 7*(10), 2001: 1101–1121.

Brookner, A. (1981). *Jacques-Louis David.* London: Icon.

Brown, M. (1938). *The Painting of the French Revolution.* New York: Critics Group (Kessinger Legacy Reprints), 2010.

Browne, J. (1985). Darwin and the face of madness. In: F. Bynum, R. Porter, & M. Shepherd (1985), *The Anatomy of Madness. Essays in the History of Psychiatry. Volume I, People and Ideas.* London: Tavistock.

Bryson, N. (1983). *Word and Image. French Painting of the Ancien Régime.* Cambridge: Cambridge University Press.

Büchner, G. (1839). Lenz. In: *Complete Plays, Lenz and Other Writings.* J. Reddick (Trans. & Intro.). London: Penguin, 1993.

Burton, R. (1621). *The Anatomy of Melancholy. 5 vols.* T. C. Faulkner, N. K. Kiessling, & R. L. Blair (Eds.). Oxford: Oxford University Press, 1989.

Butler, J. (2005). *Giving an Account of Oneself.* New York: Fordham University Press.

Byron, G. G. (1819). Mazeppa. In: *The Major Works.* J. J. McGann (Ed.). Oxford: Oxford University Press (Oxford World Classics), 2008.

Byron, G. G. (2015). Letter to John Murray, Ravenna, 21 February 1820. *Byron's Letters and Journals. A New Selection.* R. Lansdown (Ed.). Oxford: Oxford University Press.

Cabanis, P.-J. G. (1802). *Rapports du physique et du moral de l'homme. 2 vols.* Boston, MA: Elibron Classics.

Calasso, R. (2012). *La Folie Baudelaire.* London: Allen Lane.

Castel, R. (1973). *Le psychanalysme. L'ordre psychanalytique et le pouvoir.* Paris: Editions Maspero.

Castel, R. (1976). *L'ordre psychiatrique. L'âge d'or de l'aliénisme.* Paris: Les Editions de Minuit.

Chénique, B. (2006). *Géricault. La folie d'un monde.* (Catalogue of exhibition at the Musée des Beaux-Arts, Lyon, 21 April–31 July 2006, with a posthumously published and translated essay by S. Germer, and a contribution by P. Wat.) Paris: Editions Hazan.

Chevalier, L. (1958). *Classes laborieuses et classes dangereuses à Paris pendant la première moitié du XIXe siècle.* Paris: Editions Perrin, 2007.

Clément, C. (1868). *Géricault—Etude biographique et critique avec le catalogue raisonné de son oeuvre.* Paris: Didier, 2012.

Cobb, R. (1978). *Death in Paris. The Records of the Basse-Geôle de la Seine, October 1795—September 1801, Vendémiaire Year IV—Fructidor Year IX.* Oxford: Oxford University Press.

Cooper, D. (1967). Introduction to: M. Foucault, *Madness and Civilization. A History of Insanity in the Age of Reason.* R. Howard (Trans.). London: Tavistock, 1971.

Crichton, A. (1798). *An Inquiry into the Nature and Origin of Mental Derangement. Comprehending a Concise System of the Physiology and Pathology of the Human Mind and a History of the Passions and their Effects.* London: T. Cadell, Junior, and W. Davies, in the Strand.

Crosland, M. (2004). The *Officiers de Santé* of the French Revolution. A case study in the changing language of medicine. *Medical History*, April 1, *48*(2): 229–244. Cambridge: Cambridge University Press (Cambridge Journals).

Daquin, J. (1792). *La Philosophie de la folie.* Paris: Editions Frénesie (Collection Insania), 1987.

Delacroix, E. (1980). *Journal 1822–1863.* H. Damisch (Préface). Paris: Plon.

Deleuze, G. (1990). *The Logic of Sense.* C. V. Boundas (Ed.), & M. Lester with C. Stivale (Trans.). New York: Columbia University Press.

Deleuze, G. (1998). *Essays Critical and Clinical.* D. W. Smith & M. A. Greco (Trans.). London: Verso.

Delmas, V. (2011). Maréchal Jacques-François-André. Available at: http://cths.fr/an/prosopo.php?id=10574. Consulted 16 May 2015.

de M'Uzan, M. (1976). *Death and Identity: Being and the Psycho-Sexual Drama.* A. Weller (Trans.). London: Karnac, 2013.

D'Eramo, M. (2015). After Waterloo. *New Left Review, 94,* July August.

Derrida, J. (1978). Cogito and the history of madness. In: *Writing and Difference.* A. Bass (Trans., Intro., & Additional Notes). Chicago, IL: Chicago University Press.

Dezeimeris, J.-E. (1834). Georget. In: *Dictionnaire historique de la médecine ancienne et moderne.* Paris: Béchet Jeune, & Leroux et Périchon.

Diderot, D. (1762). Mélancolie; Mélancholie réligieuse; and Mélancholie. In: *Encyclopédie ou Dictionnaire raisonné des sciences, des arts et des metiers. Tome dixième.* Neufchastel (Neuchâtel), Switzerland: chez Samuel Faulche.

Diderot, D. (1805). *Rameau's Nephew. D'Alembert's Dream*. L. W. Tancock (Trans.). London: Penguin 1966.

Dörner, K. (1981). *Madmen and the Bourgeoisie. A Social History of Insanity and Psychiatry*. J. Neugroschel & J. Steinberg (Trans.). Oxford: Basil Blackwell.

Du Camp, M. (1882–1883). *Souvenirs Littéraires. Flaubert, Fromentin, Gautier, Musset, Sand*. Paris: Editions Complexe, 2002.

Edridge, L. (2002). Géricault's monomaniacs and an alienist's vision. Unpublished thesis presented for the master's of philosophy in visual arts, at the National Institute of the Arts, Australian National University.

Eitner, L. (1972). *Géricault's "Raft of the Medusa"*. New York: Phaidon.

Eitner, L. (1982). *Géricault. His Life and Work*. London: Orbis.

Eitner, L. (1991). Théodore Géricault, a cart loaded with kegs. In: D. Rosenfeld (Ed.), *European Painting and Sculpture, Ca. 1770—1937, in the Museum of Art, Rhode Island School of Design*. Philadephia, PA: University of Pennsylvania Press.

Elias, N. (1939). *The Society of Individuals*. Oxford: Basil Blackwell, 1991.

Ellenberger, H. (1970). *The Discovery of the Unconscious. The History and Evolution of Dynamic Psychiatry*. New York: Basic Books.

Esquirol, J.-E. D. (1805). *Des Passions Considerées comme Causes, Symptômes et Moyens curatifs de l'Aliénation mentale*. Précedé de *Du traitement de la manie aux passions: la folie et l'union de l'âme et du corps*, par M. Gauchet, & G. Swain, et suivi de Documents pour servir à l'histoire de la naissance de l'asile 1797–1811. Paris: Librairie des Deux-Mondes, 1980.

Esquirol, J.-E. D. (1818). Manie. In: *Dictionnaire des sciences médicales*. Paris: Panckoucke.

Esquirol, J.-E. D. (1838). *Des Maladies mentales considérées sous les rapports médical, hygiénique et médico-légal*. Accompagnées de vingt-sept planches gravées. 2 vols. Brussels: Meline, Cans.

Fodéré, F. E. (1817). *Traité du délire, appliqué à la médecine, à la morale et à la législation*. 2 vols. Paris: Chez Croullebois, Librairie de la Société de Médecine et la Direction générale des Mines.

Fornari, B. (2013). Géricault or the cruelty of the everyday. In: G. Wedekind, & M. Hollein (Eds.), *Géricault. Images of Life and Death*. Frankfurt, Germany: Schirn Kunsthalle.

Foucault, M. (1961). *Histoire de la folie à l'âge classique—Folie et déraison*. Paris: Plon.

Foucault, M. (1967). *Madness and Civilization. A History of Insanity in the Age of Reason*. R. Howard (Trans.), D. Cooper (Intro.). London: Tavistock, 1971.

Foucault, M. (1973). *The Birth of the Clinic. An Archaeology of Medical Perception*. A. M. Sheridan (Trans.). London: Tavistock.

Gauchet, M., & Swain, G. (1980). *La pratique de l'esprit humain. L'institution asilaire et la révolution démocratique*. Paris: Gallimard.

Gauchet, M., & Swain, G. (1999). *Madness and Democracy: The Modern Psychiatric Universe*. C. Porter (Trans.), J. Seigel (Foreword). Princeton, NJ: Princeton University Press.

Gautier, T. (1874). *Histoire du romantisme. Notices romantiques. Les progrès de la poésie française depuis 1830*. Paris: Charpentier.

Georget, E. (1820a). *De la folie. Considérations sur cette maladie: son siège et ses symptômes; la nature et le mode d'action de ses causes; sa marche et ses terminaisons; les différences qui la distinguent du délire aigu; les moyens de traitement qui lui conviennent; suivies de recherches cadavériques*. Paris: Chez Crevot.

Georget, E. (1820b). *De la folie*. (Textes choisis et présentés par J. Postel.). Paris: Privat, 1972.

Georget, E. (1823). De la folie, ou aliénation mentale. In: N. P. Adelon (Ed.), *Dictionnaire De Médecine: Ou, Répertoire Général Des Sciences Médicales Considérées Sous Le Rapport Théorique Et Pratique*. Paris: Béchet jeune.

Germer, S. (1999). Pleasurable fear: Géricault and uncanny trends at the opening of the nineteenth century. *Art History*, 22(2), June: 159–183.

Gilman, S. (1982). *Seeing the Insane. A Visual and Cultural History of our Attitudes towards the Mentally Ill*. Lincoln, NE: University of Nebraska Press.

Goldstein, J. (1987). *Console and Classify: The French Psychiatric Profession in the Nineteenth Century*. Chicago, IL: University of Chicago Press, 2001.

Green, A. (1986). The dead mother. In: *On Private Madness*. London: Karnac, 1997.

Green, A. (1999). *The Work of the Negative*. A. Weller (Trans.). London: Free Association.

Green, A. (2002). A dual conception of narcissism: positive and negative organisations. *Psychoanlyic Quarterly*, 71: 631–649.

Green, A. (2005). *Key Ideas for a Contemporary Psychoanalysis. Misrecogntion and Recognition of the Unconscious*. A. Weller (Trans.). London: Routledge.

Hacking, I. (1990). *The Taming of Chance*. Cambridge: Cambridge University Press.

Harding, L. (2015). How Facebook puts data into cold storage. *The Guardian*, 26 September.

Hardman, J. (1998). *The French Revolution Sourcebook*. London: Bloomsbury Academic.

Hartman, G. (1975). *The Fate of Reading*. Chicago, IL: Chicago University Press.

Hazan, E. (2010). *The Invention of Paris. A History in Footsteps*. D. Fernbach (Trans.). London: Verso.

Hegel, G. W. F. (1807). *Phenomenology of Mind*. J. B. Baillie (Trans.). New York: Harper & Row, 1967.

Hegel, G. W. F. (1830). *Hegel's Philosophy of Mind. Part Three of the Encyclopaedia of the Philosophical Sciences.* W. Wallace & A. V. Miller (Trans.), J. N. Findlay (Foreword). Oxford: Oxford University Press, 2007.

Hunter, R., & Macalpine, I. (1963). *Three Hundred Years of Psychiatry: 1535–1860.* Oxford: Oxford University Press.

Hyppolite, J. (1946). *Genesis and Structure in Hegel's Phenomenology.* S. Cherniak & J. Heckman (Trans.). Evanston, IL: Northwestern University Press, 1974.

Ingram, A. (1998). *Patterns of Madness in the Eighteenth Century. A Reader.* Liverpool, UK: Liverpool University Press.

Isaak, J. A. (1996). *Feminism and Contemporary Art. The Revolutionary Power of Women's Laughter.* London: Routledge.

Jay, M. (2012). *The Influencing Machine. James Tilly Matthews and the Air Loom.* O. Sacks (Foreword). London: Strange Attractor Press.

Jones, J. (2000). Portrait of the week no. 30: Théodore Géricault's man with the "monomania" of child kidnapping. *The Guardian,* 4 November.

Jung, C. G. (1964). *Man and his Symbols.* J. L. Henderson, M.-L. von Franz, A. Jaffé, & J. Jacobi (Eds.). Garden City, NY: Doubleday.

Keats, J. (2001). *The Complete Poems of John Keats.* P. Wright (Intro., Glossary & Notes). Ware, UK: Wordsworth Poetry Library.

Kohon, G. (2016). *Reflections on the Aesthetic Experience. Psychoanalysis and the Uncanny.* London: Routledge.

Kromm, J. (2002). *The Art of Frenzy. Public Madness in the Visual Culture of Europe, 1500–1850.* London: Continuum.

Lacan, J. (1988). *The Seminar of Jacques Lacan, Book II, The Ego in Freud's Theory and in the Technique of Psychoanalysis 1954–55.* S. Tomaselli & J. Forrester (Trans.). New York: W. W. Norton.

Lacan, J. (2007). *Ecrits. The First Complete Edition in English.* B. Fink, in collaboration with H. Fink, & R. Grigg (Trans.). New York: W. W. Norton.

Laing, R. D., & Esterson, A. (1964). *Sanity, Madness and the Family. Families of Schizophrenics.* London: Penguin, 1980.

Lamb, G. (2013). Awakenings: the romantic science of Oliver Sacks. Available at: leakygrammar.net/2013/06/06/awakenings-the-romantic-science-of-oliver-sacks/. Consulted 18 July 2015.

Lane, H. (1979). *The Wild Boy of Aveyron.* London: Granada.

Laplanche, J. (1987). *Problématiques V. Le baquet. Transcendance du transfert.* Paris: Presses Universitaires de France.

Laplanche, J. (1999). *Essays on Otherness.* J. Fletcher (Ed. & Intro.). London: Routledge.

Lavater, J. C. (1775–78). *Physiognomische Fragmente zur Beförderung der Menschenkenntnis und Menschenliebe.* Stuttgart, Germany: Reclam, 1984.

Lavie, J. (2011). The lost roots of the theory of group analysis: "interrelational individuals" or "persons". In: E. Hopper & H. Weinberg (Eds.) *The Social Unconscious in Persons, Groups and Societies. Volume 1: Mainly Theory*. London: Karnac.

Leader, D. (2011). *What is Madness?* London: Hamish Hamilton.

Lebas, V. (1820). *Observation de mélancolie, et quelques propositions sur cette maladie. Thèse présentée et soutenue à la Faculté de Médecine de Paris, le 18 avril 1820, pour obtenir le grade de Docteur en médecine*. Paris: Imprimerie de Didot Jeune.

Levinas, E. (1982). *Ethics and Infinity. Conversations with Philippe Nemo*. R. A. Cohen (Trans.). Pittsburgh, PA: Duquesne University Press, 1985.

Mansel, P. (2003). *Paris between Empires 1814–1852. Monarchy and Revolution*. London: Phoenix.

McGilchrist, I. (2009). *The Master and his Emissary. The Divided Brain and the Making of the Western World*. New Haven, CT: Yale University Press, 2010.

Meltzer, D., & Williams, M. H. (1988). *The Apprehension of Beauty. The Role of Aesthetic Conflict in Development, Art and Violence*. Strath Tay, UK: The Clunie Press.

Michel, R., Chenique, B., & Laveissière, S. (1991). *Géricault*. Catalogue of exhibition, Galéries nationales du Grand Palais, Paris 1991–92. Paris: Editions de la Réunion des musées nationaux.

Miles, J. (2007). *"Medusa". The Shipwreck, the Scandal, the Masterpiece*. London: Jonathan Cape.

Miller, M. (1940–41). Géricault's paintings of the insane. *Journal of the Warburg and Courtauld Institutes*, 4(3/4): 151–163.

Montesquieu, C.-J. de S. (1721). *Persian Letters*. C. J. Betts (Trans. & Intro.). London: Penguin, 1973.

Motion, A. (1998). *Keats*. London: Faber and Faber.

Murat, L. (2001). *La Maison du docteur Blanche. Histoire d'un asile et de ses pensionnaires de Nerval à Maupassant*. Paris: J. C. Lattès.

Murat, L. (2014). *The Man Who Thought He Was Napoleon. Toward a Political History of Madness*. D. Dusinberre (Trans.), D. A. Bell (Foreword). Chicago, IL: Chicago University Press.

Nerval, G. (1855). *Aurélia*. In: *Promenades et souvenirs. Lettres à Jenny. Pandora. Aurélia*. Paris: Garnier Flammarion, 1972.

Oprescu, G. (1927). *Géricault*. Paris: La Renaissance du Livre.

Ortega y Gasset, J. (1972). *Velazquez, Goya and The Dehumanization of Art*. A. Brown (Trans.), P. Troutman (Intro.). London: Studio Vista.

Parsons, M. (2014). *Living Psychoanalysis. From Theory to Experience*. London: Routledge.

Pélicier, Y. (1976). *Histoire de la psychiatrie*. Paris: Presses Universitaires de France.

Pinel, P. (1801). *Traité médico-philosophique sur l'aliénation mentale ou la manie.* Présentation par F. Azouvi. Geneva: Editions Slatkine, 1980.

Pinel, P. (1809). *Traité médico-philosophique sur l'aliénation mentale. Entièrement refondue et très-augmentée.* Paris: J. Ant. Brosson.

Plumly, S. (2008). *Posthumous Keats. A Personal Biography.* New York: W. W. Norton.

Polasky, J. (2015). *Revolutions without Borders: The Call to Liberty in the Atlantic World.* New Haven, CT: Yale University Press.

Porter, R. (2002). *Madness. A Brief History.* Oxford: Oxford University Press.

Postel, J. (1972). Preface. In: E. Georget (1820b), *De la folie.* Paris: Privat.

Postel, J. (2007). *Eléments pour une histoire de la psychiatrie occidentale.* Paris: L'Harmattan.

Postel, J. (2014). Georget, Étienne Jean (1795–1828). In: *Encyclopædia Universalis.* Available at: www.universalis.fr/encyclopedie/etienne-jean-georget/. Consulted 29 November 2014.

Postel, J., & Quetel, C. (2012). *Nouvelle histoire de la psychiatrie.* Paris: Dunod.

"Pry, P." (1826). Travels, letter XI. *The London Literary Gazette, and Journal of the Belles Lettres, Arts, Sciences, &c.,* no. 492, June 24.

Quetel, C. (2013). Géricault and Romantic psychiatry—a dual encounter. In: G. Wedekind & M. Hollein (Eds.), *Géricault. Images of Life and Death.* Frankfurt, Germany: Schirn Kunsthalle.

Quetel, C., & Morel, P. (1979). *Les fous et leurs médecines. De la Renaissance au XXe siècle.* Paris: Hachette.

Raige-Delorme, J. (1828). Notice sur M. Georget. In: *Archives Générales de Médecine, Journal publié par une société de médecins. Composée de membres de l'Académie Royale de Médecine ... 6me année—Tome XVII* (pp. 154–156, 319–329). Paris: Béchet jeune, and Migneret.

Rosen, C. (1998). *Romantic Poets, Critics, and Other Madmen.* Cambridge, MA: Harvard University Press.

Rosen, C., & Zerner, H. (1979). Romanticism: the permanent revolution. In: *Romanticism and Realism. The Mythology of Nineteenth-Century Art.* New York: Viking Press, 1984.

Roudinesco, E. (1989). *Théroigne de Méricourt. Une femme mélancolique sous la Révolution.* Paris: Editions du Seuil.

Rousseau, G. S. (1970). Science and the discovery of imagination. *Eighteenth-Century Studies*, 3: 108–135.

Rousseau, J.-J. (1782). *Rêveries du promeneur solitaire.* Paris: Livre de Poche, 1971.

Rudé, G. (1959). *The Crowd in the French Revolution*. Oxford: Oxford University Press, 1967.

Ruskin, J. (1870). *Lectures on Art. Delivered before the University of Oxford in Hilary Term 1870. Seventh Edition.* London: George Allen, 1894.

Sachs, H. (2010). *The Ninth. Beethoven and the World in 1824*. London: Faber and Faber.

Sacks, O. (2015). *On the Move: A Life*. London: Picador.

Sass, L. A. (1994). *Madness and Modernism. Insanity in the Light of Modern Art, Literature, and Thought*. Cambridge, MA: Harvard University Press.

Schelling, F. W. J. (1800). *System of Transcendental Idealism*. P. L. Heath (Trans.), M. Vater (Intro.). Charlottesville, VA: University Press of Virginia, 1993.

Schrader, K. (2013). The facial and the contradictive. Kinships between Marlene Dumas and Géricault. In: G. Wedekind & M. Hollein (Eds.), *Géricault. Images of Life and Death*. Frankfurt, Germany: Schirn Kunsthalle.

Schwarz, R. (2009). Brecht's relevance: highs and lows. *New Left Review, 57*, May/June.

Scull, A. (2015). *Madness in Civilization. A Cultural History of Insanity from the Bible to Freud, from the Madhouse to Modern Medicine*. London: Thames & Hudson.

Seigel, J. (1999). Foreword. In: M. Gauchet & G. Swain (1999), *Madness and Democracy: The Modern Psychiatric Universe*. C. Porter (Trans.). Princeton, NJ: Princeton University Press.

Sells, C. (1986). New light on Géricault, his travels and his friends. *Apollo, CXXIII*(292): 390–395.

Shelley, P. B. (2012). *Complete Works of Poetry and Prose (1914 Edition), volumes 1–3*. J. M. Beach (Ed. & Intro.). Austin, TX: West by Southwest Press.

Shorter, E. (1997). *A History of Psychiatry. From the Era of the Asylum to the Age of Prozac*. New York: John Wiley.

Siedentop, L. (2014). *Inventing the Individual. The Origins of Western Liberalism*. London: Penguin, 2015.

Skuy, D. (2003). *Assassination, Politics, and Miracles. France and the Royalist Reaction of 1820*. Quebec, Canada: McGill-Queen's University Press.

Smith, A. (1776). *The Wealth of Nations. Books I–III*. A. Skinner (Intro. & Notes). London: Penguin, 1999.

Smith, D. W. (1998). Introduction. In: G. Deleuze, *Essays Critical and Clinical*. D. W. Smith & M. A. Greco (Trans.). London: Verso.

Snell, R. (1982). *Théophile Gautier. A Romantic Critic of the Visual Arts*. Oxford: Oxford University Press.

Snell, R. (2012). *Uncertainties, Mysteries, Doubts. Romanticism and the Analytic Attitude*. London: Routledge.

Spitzer, A. B. (1987). *The French Generation of 1820*. Princeton, NJ: Princeton University Press.

Starobinski, J. (1979). *1789. Les emblèmes de la raison*. Paris: Flammarion.

Stendhal (1817). *Histoire de la peinture en Italie*. Paris: Didot.

Stendhal (1888). *Oeuvres intimes. 2 vols*. V. Litto (Ed.). Paris: Gallimard (Bibliothèque de la Pléiade), 1981.

Stendhal (1973). *Stendhal and the Arts*. D. Wakefield (Ed. & Select.). London: Phaidon.

Stoichita, V. I., & Coderch, A. M. (1999). *Goya. The Last Carnival*. London: Reaktion.

Swain, G. (1977). *Le sujet de la folie. Naissance de la psychiatrie*. Toulouse, France: "Rhadamanthe" Privat.

Symington, N. (1986). *The Analytic Experience. Lectures from the Tavistock*. London: Free Association Books.

Taine, H. (1876). *Les Origines de la France contemporaine. La Révolution. 3 vols*. Paris: Hachette.

Turner, J. (Ed.) (2000). *The Grove Dictionary of Art*. London: St Martin's Press.

Tweedy, R. (2012). *The God of the Left Hemisphere. Blake, Bolte Taylor, and the Myth of Creation*. London: Karnac.

Une Société d'avocats (1827–28). *Causes criminelles célèbres du XIXe siècle. 4 vols*. Paris: H. Langlois Fils.

Ussher, J. (1991). *Women's Madness. Misogyny or Mental Illness?* New York: Harvester Wheatsheaf.

Van Zuylen, M. (2005). *Monomania: The Flight from Everyday Life in Literature and Art*. Ithaca, NY: Cornell University Press.

Wedekind, G. (2007). *Le portrait mis à nu. Théodore Géricault und die Monomanien*. Munich, Germany: Deutscher Kunstverlag.

Wedekind, G. (2013). Counteracting forces of resistance. Théodore Géricault's tragic realism. In: G. Wedekind & M. Hollein (Eds.), *Géricault. Images of Life and Death*. Frankfurt, Germany: Schirn Kunsthalle.

Wedekind, G., & Hollein, M. (Eds.) (2013). *Géricault. Images of Life and Death*. Frankfurt, Germany: Schirn Kunsthalle.

Weiner, D. B. (1993). *The Citizen-Patient in Revolutionary and Imperial Paris*. (The Henry E Sigerist Series in the History of Medicine). Baltimore, MD: Johns Hopkins University Press.

Weiner, D. B. (1999). *Comprendre et soigner: Philippe Pinel (1745–1826), la médecine de l'esprit*. Paris: Fayard.

White, W. A. (1935). *Outlines of Psychiatry. 14th edition*. Washington, DC: Nervous and Mental Disease Publishing.

Willmann, G. (1999). *The History of Lotteries*. Stanford, CA: Department of Economics, Stanford University. Available at: willmann.com/-gerald/history.pdf. Accessed 22 September 2015.

Winnicott, D. W. (1992). *Through Paediatrics to Psychoanalysis. Collected Papers.* London: Karnac and the Institute of Psychoanalysis.

Wittgenstein, L. (1980). *Culture and Value.* G. H. Von Wright (Ed.). Oxford: Blackwell.

Wollstonecraft, M. (1798). *Maria: or, The Wrongs of Woman.* New York: W. W. Norton, 1994.

Woshinsky, B. R. (2010). *Imagining Women's Conventual Spaces in France, 1600–1800: The Cloister Disclosed.* Farnham, UK: Ashgate.

Wright, P. (2001). Introduction. In: *The Complete Poems of John Keats.* Ware, UK: Wordsworth Poetry Library.

Yolton, J. W., Porter, R., Rogers, P., & Stafford, B. M. (1991). *The Blackwell Companion to the Enlightenment.* L. G. Crocker (Intro.). Oxford: Blackwell.

Žižek, S. (2006). *How to Read Lacan.* London: Granta.

INDEX